CR[...]
EASTER[N KENTUCKY]
UNIVERSITY
RICHMOND, KENTUCKY

12462
2 Vol
225

Byzantine
and Roman
Architecture

Volume One

HACKER ART BOOKS, INC. NEW YORK, 1975

BYZANTINE

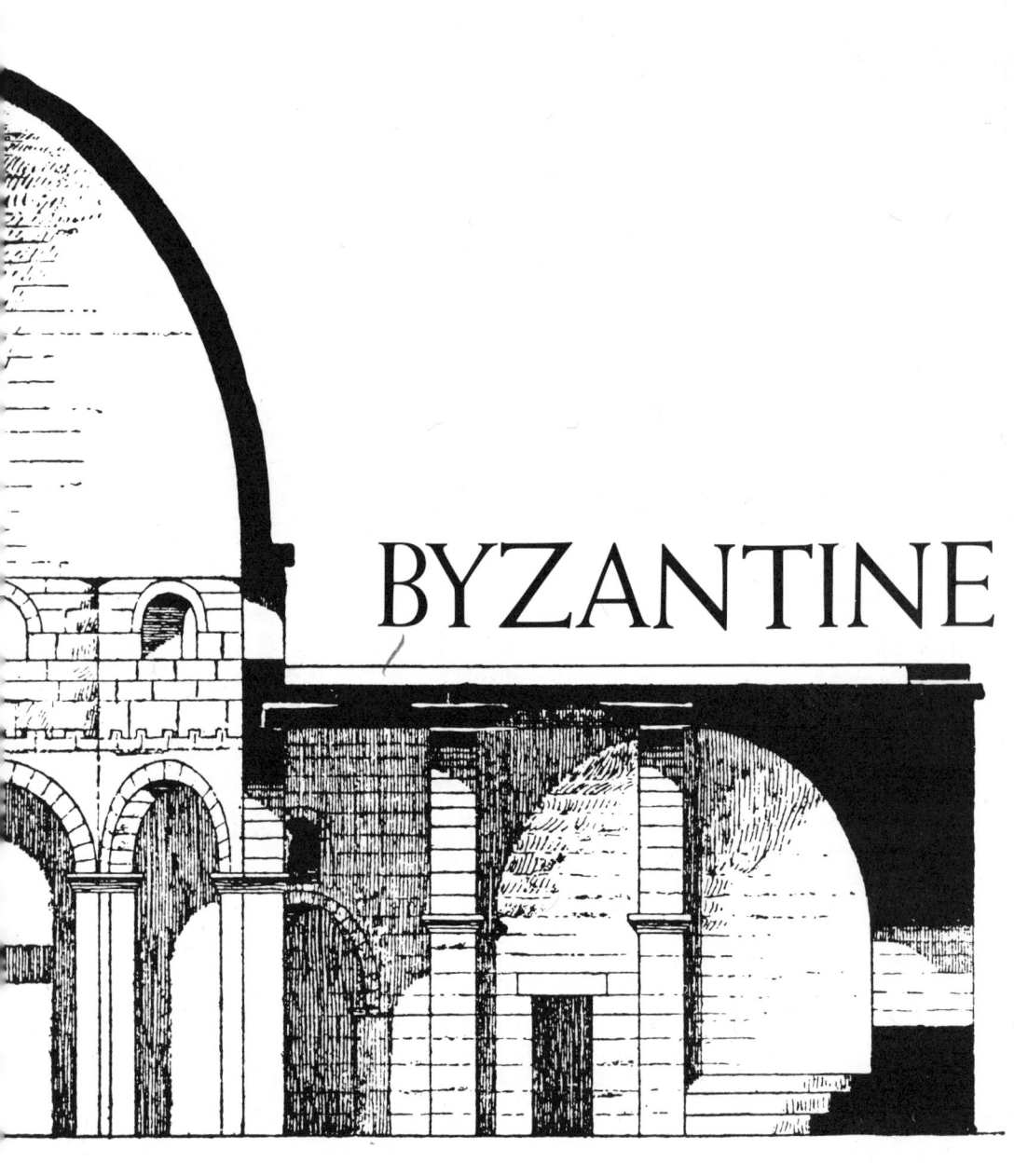

SIR
THOMAS
GRAHAM
JACKSON

AND
ROMANESQUE
ARCHITECTURE

Second Edition

Volume One

First edition published 1913.
Second edition published 1920.
Reprinted from the second edition by permission of
Cambridge University Press.

Reissued 1975 by
Hacker Art Books, Inc.
New York.

Library of Congress Catalogue Card Number 75-143353
ISBN 0-87817-073-1

Printed in the United States of America.

BYZANTINE AND ROMANESQUE ARCHITECTURE

by

Sir THOMAS GRAHAM JACKSON, Bart., R.A.

Hon. D.C.L. Oxford, Hon. LL.D. Cambridge
Hon. Fellow of Wadham College, Oxford
Associé de l'Académie Royale
de Belgique

Nunquam vera species ab utilitate dividitur.
QUINTIL. *Or. Inst.* VIII. 3

SECOND EDITION

Cambridge:
at the University Press
1920

IN MEMORIAM
A. M. J.

First Edition, 1913
Second Edition, 1920

PREFACE TO THE FIRST EDITION

SEVERAL years ago, when I used to take pupils, they came to my house occasionally for an informal talk about our art, illustrated by reference to books and sketches, and for their use I gathered together rough materials for a history of Post-Roman Architecture. It seemed to me that these might be of service to others also if put into a literary form, so far at all events as time permitted me to carry the scheme, which is not likely to go beyond the present volumes.

While thus engaged I was asked to give a course of lectures to the Royal Institution and afterwards to the University of Cambridge, for which I chose the Byzantine and Romanesque period. These lectures, expanded, form the foundation of this book, which will I trust help those who are interested in Architecture, whether professionally or not, to appreciate a chapter in Art which yields to none in importance, and is inferior to none in attractiveness.

The buildings I have chosen for description and illustration are, so far as it was possible, those I have visited and studied myself. In cases where I have not seen a building to which I refer I have generally said so. Information derived at second-hand is only of second-rate importance.

PREFACE

It has not been possible to avoid photography entirely in the illustrations, but I have employed it as little as I could. I am indebted to my son Basil H. Jackson for some drawings which are marked with his initials; the rest of the illustrations which are not otherwise acknowledged are from my own sketches, some of which, being made more than 50 years ago, have an accidental value as showing buildings that have since been altered or renovated.

I am indebted to the Society of Antiquaries for the plan of Silchester (Fig. 113) from *Archaeologia*; to Signor Gaetano Nave, the architect engaged at Ravenna, for much useful information, and many facilities for examining the buildings, and for the plan of S. Vitale (Fig. 37); to my friend Mr Phené Spiers, F.S.A., for the loan of several photographs of S. Mark's and for the plans of that church and S. Front; to Mr Keyser, F.S.A., for Plates CLVIII, CLIX, CLX from his *Norman tympana and lintels*; to the Clarendon Press for the plan of Parenzo (Fig. 38) from my book on Dalmatia; to the Rev. R. M. Serjeantson for permission to copy his plan of S. Peter's, Northampton (Fig. 136); to the Editor of the *Building News* for Plate XLIX ; and to Mr Raffles Davidson for leave to reproduce his beautiful drawing of Tewkesbury (Fig. 135).

Finally my thanks are due to the University Press for the trouble they have taken in producing the book handsomely.

T. G. J.

EAGLE HOUSE, WIMBLEDON.
October, 1912.

PREFACE TO THE SECOND EDITION

IN the seven years that have passed since the first edition of this book was published many things have happened to the buildings and places of which it treats. Constantinople, indeed, still belongs to the Turks, who have once more escaped the ejection which seemed inevitable, and they are likely to remain there so long as the world cannot agree whom to put in their place. But their European territory, like that of the Byzantine Empire when they finally attacked it, extends only a short way beyond the city walls.

Salonica is once more in Christian hands, and the ancient churches are restored to their original rite. Unhappily the finest of them, S. Demetrius with its wealth of sculpture, mosaic, and marble, has perished in the flames. I have been promised particulars of interesting discoveries that the ruin has brought to light,—of a crypt with remains of older buildings below ground decorated with painting or mosaic,—but the promise has not hitherto been redeemed. S. Sophia is once more the Cathedral of the Greek rite, and has been covered with decorative painting, not altogether to its advantage if one may judge from photographs. It does not appear that any other of the old churches have suffered by the fire which swept through the heart of the city and destroyed S. Demetrius.

Ravenna has been bombed, and if it is true that the west end of S. Apollinare Nuovo has been thrown down it is to be feared that some of the earlier and better mosaics of Theodoric's time must have perished. I have no certain information as to this.

The hostile bombs that fell at Venice do not seem to have touched any of the most important buildings, though a good deal of mischief has been done; and we have yet to learn what has happened in Friuli, where it is recorded that Cividale, among other places has fared badly.

Nearer home, the Romanesque buildings of France lay beyond the scene of warfare; and our own have happily escaped.

During this period Professor Van Millingen's excellent book on the churches of Constantinople has appeared, of which I have been glad to make use and I have to thank Messrs Macmillan for leave to reproduce some of the plans it contains. We have unhappily to deplore the death of its accomplished author. I have also been much indebted to M. Antoniades' great work Ἔκφρασις τῆς Ἁγίας Σοφίας which I had not previously seen. I may also mention the work of MM. Ebersolt and Thiers (Paris 1913) on *Les Eglises de Constantinople*, describing and illustrating thirteen of the Byzantine churches in that city.

With regard to Sign. Rivoira's contention that the Pulvino was not a Byzantine invention, but originated in Italy, and probably at Ravenna, I have reconsidered what I wrote, after seeing Buonamici's drawings of the Ursian basilica which he destroyed. They certainly show pulvini with a cross on them over the colonnades, and though the exact date of Ursus is disputed, they would in any case be older than those at Salonica and any that we know of elsewhere in the Eastern Empire. So far as this goes Sign. Rivoira's contention seems justified.

There are a few additional illustrations in this edition, and Plate VI is this time reproduced in colour.

I have to thank the University Press for their care in producing this edition, in spite of many commercial difficulties, the legacy of the late hideous war.

T. G. JACKSON.

EAGLE HOUSE, WIMBLEDON.
Sept. 23, 1920.

CONTENTS OF VOLUME I

CHAP.		PAGE
	Preface to First Edition	v
	Preface to Second Edition	vii
	List of Illustrations	x
	Introduction	xviii
I	Roman architecture	1
II	Decay of Roman architecture. Foundation of Constantinople. The Basilican plan	13
III	Greek element in the new style. Asiatic influences. Syrian architecture. The Byzantine dome. Abandonment of the Classic Orders. Avoidance of figure sculpture	26
IV	The Greek church and ritual. Marble and Mosaic. The Pulvino. Varieties of Capital	44
V	Constantinople. The walls and Porta Aurea. The churches at Salonica	54
VI	S. Sophia, Constantinople	82
VII	Justinian's other churches	106
VIII	Iconoclasm	114
IX	Later Byzantine architecture	121
X	Italo-Byzantine architecture. The first or pre-Gothic period	145
XI	Italo-Byzantine architecture. The second or Gothic period	161
XII	Italo-Byzantine architecture. The third period under the Exarchate	172
XIII	Rome	186
XIV	The Lombards. Architectural bathos and revival. Rupture between Rome and Constantinople	210
XV	Venice	229
XVI	Pisa. Florence. Lucca	242
XVII	Lombardy	260

LIST OF ILLUSTRATIONS

		Vol. & page	Plate	Cut
AIX-LA-CHAPELLE	Original plan	II. 2		63
	Interior	II. 2	LXXXII	
	Present plan	II. 4		64
ANDERNACH	Exterior (from a photograph)	II. 20	XCIII	
	Carving on doorway	II. 24		73
ANGOULÊME	Plan	II. 40		77
	Capital	II. 47		79
	Exterior (from a photograph)	II. 56	CIII	
ARLES	Sarcophagus in the Museum	II. 30	XCIV	
	S. Trophime. Tower and cloister	II. 66	CIV	
	Do. Portal (from a photograph)	II. 67	CV	
	Do. Cloister, exterior view	II. 72	CVII	
	Do. Do., interior view	II. 73	CVIII	
AUTUN	Bay of nave of Cathedral	II. 109		96
	Porch and west door of do.	II. 111		97
	S. Jean, interior	II. 113		98
AVIGNON	Cupola (from Viollet-le-Duc)	II. 64		87
BARFRESTON	Head of doorway (from a photograph)	II. 246	CLX	
BARNACK	West Tower	II. 192	CXXXVI	
	Pierced stone window	II. 192		120
BATH	Tympanum of Roman Temple	II. 178	CXXXIII	
BEDFORD	Capital of door at S. Peter's	II. 245		143
BERGAMO	Apse and central cupola	I. 250	LXVIII	
BOPPARD	Carving on doorway	II. 26		74
BORGO S. DONNINO	Interior of nave	I. 270		62
	Exterior of apse	I. 269	LXXIX	
	Lion at doorway	I. 272	LXXX	
BRADFORD-ON-AVON	Plan	II. 195		122
	Exterior (from a photograph)	II. 195	CXXXVIII	
	Interior (do.)	II. 196	CXXXIX	
	Angels (do.)	II. 197	CXL	
BRIOUDE	Exterior of east end	II. 130	CXVI	
CAEN	Abbaye aux Hommes. The Towers	II. 153	CXXVII	
	Abbaye aux Dames. Bay of Choir	II. 157		112
	S. Michel de Vaucelles	II. 158	CXXVIII	
CAHORS	Plan	II. 40		77

LIST OF ILLUSTRATIONS   xi

		Vol. & page	Plate	Cut
CAMBRIDGE	Tower arch, S. Bene't's Church (from a photograph)	II. 194	CXXXVII	
CANTERBURY	Plan of the Saxon Cathedral (Willis)	II. 211		127
	Plan of Lanfranc's and later buildings	II. 212		128
	The South Eastern Transept & Tower	II. 212	CXLI	
	The Crypt	II. 213	CXLII	
	Capital in do.	II. 248		146
	S. Pancras. Plan	II. 177		114
CASTOR	Tower	II. 238	CLVI	
	Capitals	II. 243		140
CHAQQA	Construction of the Palace	I. 30		4
CHRISTCHURCH PRIORY	Interior (from a photograph)	II. 234	CLII	
	The Norman turret	II. 235	CLIII	
CIVRAY	West front	II. 48	CI	
CLERMONT-FERRAND	Notre Dame du Port. Plan	II. 132		104
	Do. Exterior of east end	II. 131	CXVII	
	Do. South doorway	II. 134	CXVIII	
	Do. Sections	II. 128		103
COLOGNE	S. Columba. Tower	II. 9	LXXXIV	
	S. Maria in Capitolio. Apse	II. 19	XCII	
	Do. do. Plan	II. 19		71
COMO	S. Fedele. Apse	I. 273	LXXXI	
CONSTANTINOPLE	Gul Djami Mosque. Plan	I. 123		28
	Do. Apses	I. 127		30
	Kahriyeh Djami, Church of the Chora. Plan	I. 131		32
	Do. Exterior (from a photograph)	I. 134	XX	
	Mosque of Mahomet II	I. 143	XXV	
	Phanar, Houses at the	I. 142	XXIV	
	S. John. The Studion. Plan	I. 68		15
	Do. The Narthex	I. 68	X	
	S. Irene. Plan and section	I. 107		26
	Do. View in aisle	I. 108	XVI	
	Do. Exterior view	I. 94	XII	
	S. Saviour, Pantepoptes	I. 129		31
	S. Saviour, Pantocrator. Plan	I. 125		29
	Do. Narthex	I. 124	XVII	
	Do. Apse window	I. 126	XVIII	
	SS. Sergius and Bacchus. Plan	I. 78		19
	Do. Interior	I. 80	XI	
	Do. Architrave of entablature	I. 79		20
	Do. Capital in upper storey	I. 80		21
	S. Sophia. Plan	I. 82		22
	Do. Section	I. 89		23
	Do. Exterior (from a photograph)	I. 94	XII	
	Do. Plan of buttress	I. 92		24

LIST OF ILLUSTRATIONS

		Vol. & page	Plate	Cut
CONSTANTINOPLE	S. Sophia. Plan of piers of dome	I. 97		25
	Do. Interior (from a photograph)	I. 95	XIII	
	Do. Colonnades (from a photograph)	I. 98	XIV	
	Do. Gallery at west end	I. 99	XV	
	S. Theodore the Tiro. Plan	I. 123		27
	Do. Front	I. 127	XIX	
	Tekfur-Serai (from a photograph)	I. 141	XXIII	
	Do. Mosaics	I. 141		35
	Walls. The Porta Aurea	I. 54	IV	
	Do. Capital of do.	I. 55	V	
CONSTRUCTION	Of vaults with and without centering	I. 36		8
	Of domes on pendentives	I. 39		10
	Do. do.	I. 40	I	
DEERHURST	Plan	II. 189		118
	Interior	II. 188		117
DIJON	S. Benigne. Plan and section (from Viollet-le-Duc)	II. 120		102
DURHAM	View of Cathedral from the river (from a photograph)	II. 223	CXLVI	
	Interior of North Transept	II. 225		131
	The nave, triforium and clerestory (from a photograph)	II. 226	CXLVII	
	Interior of Galilee	II. 227	CXLVIII	
	Plan of columns in Galilee	II. 227		132
	Arabesques on monument of Acca, now in Cathedral Library	II. 198		123
EARL'S BARTON	Tower	II. 191	CXXXV	
	Do. West door	II. 191		119
ELSTOW	Interior	II. 230	CL	
ELY CATHEDRAL	Bay of North Transept	II. 219	CXLIV	
	Prior's door (from a photograph)	II. 252	CLXIV	
	Capital in North Transept	II. 244		141
EZRA	Plan	I. 33		6
	Section	I. 33		7
FLORENCE	S. Miniato al Monte. Plan	I. 246		55
	Do. Interior (from a photograph)	I. 246	LXVII	
	Baptistery. Plan and section	I. 248		56
GIGGLESWICK	The dome in construction (from a photograph)	I. 40	I	
GLASTONBURY	S. Mary's Chapel (from a photograph)	II. 237	CLV	
GLOUCESTER	Bay of nave	II. 231	CLI	
IMPOST	With returned entablatures	I. 23		3
ISSOIRE	Plan	II. 134		105
KENCOTT	Norman tympanum	II. 249		147
LAACH	Plan of the Abbey Church	II. 17		70
	Exterior (from a photograph)	II. 17	XC	

LIST OF ILLUSTRATIONS xiii

		Vol. & page	Plate	Cut
LAACH	Atrium cloister	II. 18	XCI	
LAZARITSA	West front (from a photograph)	I. 140	XXII*b*	
LE MANS	Do. (do.)	II. 160	CXXIX	
	Capitals in nave	II. 161	CXXX	
LE PUY	Interior of nave of Cathedral	II. 44	XCVIII	
	Campanile do.	II. 142	CXXIII	
	Capital in Transept	II. 140		107
	Do. in Cloister	II. 140		108
	Cloister (in colour)	II. 138	CXX	
	South Porch	II. 140	CXXI	
	Do., Capitals	II. 141	CXXII	
	S. Michel de l'Aiguille. Doorway	II. 143	CXXIV	
	Do. Interior	II. 144	CXXV	
	Do. Capital	II. 144		110
	Do. do.	II. 144		111
	Do. View of the rock and Chapel (drawing by B. H. J.)	II. 142		109
LESNOVO	East end (from a photograph)	I. 139	XXII*a*	
LOCHES	Exterior (from a photograph)	II. 46	XCIX	
LORSCH	Exterior of the Chapel	II. 8	LXXXIII	
	Capital of do., lower storey	II. 6		65
	Do. do., upper do.	II. 7		66
	Cornice	II. 7		67
LUCCA	Cathedral. Exterior of apse	I. 251	LXIX	
	Do. Capital of apse	I. 251		57
	Do. Scroll on column of façade	I. 255		58
	Do. Inlaid work of façade	I. 252	LXX	
	S. Giusto. Lintel of doorway (from a photograph)	I. 256	LXXIII	
	S. Michele. Exterior (from a photograph)	I. 254	LXXI	
	S. Pietro Somaldi. Façade (from a photograph)	I. 255	LXXII	
LUDLOW CASTLE	Capital from the round chapel	II. 245		142
LYONS	Abbey of Ainée. Exterior	II. 117		100
	Do. Capitals in Chapel of S. Blandina	II. 118		101
MAINZ	Exterior of Cathedral (from a photograph)	II. 15	LXXXVIII	
	Carving in do.	II. 16		69
	Bay of nave and western end	II. 16	LXXXIX	
MALMESBURY	Sculpture in south porch	II. 251	CLXIII	
MANTES	Scroll on west doorway	II. 264		148
MILAN	S. Ambrogio. Plan	I. 262		59
	Do. Atrium	I. 262	LXXV	
	Do. Interior	I. 263	LXXVI	
	Do. Sculptured capital	I. 265		59A
	Do. do.	I. 265		60
	Do. do.	I. 266		61

LIST OF ILLUSTRATIONS

		Vol. & page	Plate	Cut
MILAN	S. Satiro. Tower	I. 268	LXXVIII	
MOISSAC	Porch (from a photograph)	II. 86	CXI	
	Cloister	II. 87	CXII	
MONKWEARMOUTH	Tower	II. 185		115
	West door	II. 186		116
MONTMAJEUR	Chapel of S. Croix. Plan and section	II. 76		88
	Do. Elevation (from Viollet-le-Duc)	II. 77		89
MURANO	Exterior of apse	I. 235	LXIV	
NÎMES	Wall of the Arena	I. 7		1
NORTHAMPTON	S. Peter's. Plan	II. 237		136
	Do. Tower	II. 239	CLVII	
	Do. Capital	II. 241		139
	Do. Detail of tower arch	II. 238		137
	Do. East end	II. 240		138
NORWICH	Cathedral. Nave aisle	II. 222	CXLV	
OXFORD	S. Michael's Tower	II. 193		121
PARENZO	Plan	I. 182		38
	Interior of apse (in colour)	I. 182	XL	
PAVIA	S. Michele. Doorway (from a photograph)	I. 266	LXXVII	
PÉRIGUEUX	S. Front. Plan	II. 35		75
	Do. Interior	II. 36	XCV	
	Bird's eye view of Domes	II. 37	XCV *a*	
	S. Front. Exterior	II. 38		76
PETERBOROUGH	Cushion capitals	II. 230		134
PISA	Duomo. Plan	I. 243		54
	Do. Interior (from a photograph)	I. 242	LXV	
	Do. Exterior (do.)	I. 243	LXVI	
	Baptistery. Scroll on column of doorway	I. 257	LXXIV	
PITTINGTON	Interior of nave	II. 228	CXLIX	
	Capital in nave	II. 229		133
POITIERS	Notre Dame la Grande. Exterior	II. 47	C	
	Do. Capital	II. 47		80
	Temple de S. Jean. Plan	II. 53		82
	Do. Exterior	II. 55		83
	S. Porchaire. Capitals	II. 59		85
	S. Hilaire. Interior	II. 43	XCVII	
POLA	Panel with cross, &c.	I. 218		47
PONTIGNY	Capital	II. 107		95
RAVENNA	Baptistery of Cathedral. Interior (from a photograph)	I. 148	XXVI	
	Do. Mosaics of dome (from do.)	I. 149	XXVII	
	Galla Placidia. Her Mausoleum. Exterior (from a photograph)	I. 152	XXVIII	
	Do. Interior (from do.)	I. 153	XXIX	
	Ivory throne (from do.)	I. 160	XXX	

LIST OF ILLUSTRATIONS

		Vol. & page	Plate	Cut
RAVENNA	S. Apollinare Nuovo. Interior (from a photograph)	I. 161	XXXI	
	Do. Mosaic (from do.)	I. 166	XXXII	
	S. Apollinare in Classe. Interior (from do.)	I. 180	XXXIX	
	S. Giovanni Evang. Capital	I. 154		36
	S. Vitale. Plan	I. 175		37
	Do. Exterior (from a photograph)	I. 172	XXXIV	
	Do. Capitals (from do.)	I. 173	XXXV	
	Do. Interior (in colour)	I. 176	XXXVI	
	Do. Mosaic. Justinian (from a photograph)	I. 178	XXXVII	
	Do. Mosaic. Theodora (from do.)	I. 179	XXXVIII	
	Theodoric, his tomb. La Rotonda (from a photograph)	I. 167	XXXIII	
RECULVER	Plan	II. 201		124
RIEZ	Baptistery. Plan	II. 79		90
ROCHESTER	Bay of nave	II. 236	CLIV	
	West doorway (from a photograph)	II. 250	CLXII	
ROME	S. Clemente Plan	I. 199		45
	Do. Monogram	I. 200		46
	Do. Interior (from a photograph)	I. 200	L	
	S. Costanza. Plan	I. 190		40
	Do. Interior	I. 190	XLIV	
	Do. Mosaic (from a photograph)	I. 191	XLV	
	Do. do. do.	I. 192	XLVI	
	S. Francesca Romana. Tower	I. 209	LIV	
	S. Giorgio in Velabro. Interior (from a photograph)	I. 202	LII	
	SS. Giovanni e Paolo. Apse	I. 201	LI	
	Do. Tower	I. 208	LIII	
	S. Giovanni Laterano. Cloister (drawing by B. H. J.)	I. 188	XLII	
	Do. Pozzo in do.	I. 189	XLIII	
	S. Lorenzo fuori le Mura. Plan	I. 194		42
	Do. Interior (from a photograph)	I. 193	XLVII	
	Do. Cloister	I. 194	XLVIII	
	S. Maria in Cosmedin. Plan	I. 197		44
	S. Maria Maggiore. Interior (from an engraving)	I. 195	XLIX	
	S. Paolo fuori le Mura. Plan	I. 188		39
	Do. Interior (from a lithograph)	I. 186	XLI	
	S. Peter's. Plan of Constantine's Church	I. 19		2
	S. Sabina. Columns of nave	I. 196		43
	Do. Panel with cross, &c.	I. 218		47

LIST OF ILLUSTRATIONS

		Vol. & page	Plate	Cut
ROME	S. Stefano Rotondo. Plan	I. 192		41
S. ANDREW'S	Tower of S. Rule (from a photograph)	II. 190	CXXXIV	
S. AVENTIN	Exterior	II. 86		92
S. BERTRAND DE COMMINGES Cloister		II. 85	CX	
S. DAVID'S	Capital in nave	II. 246		144
S. DENIS	Front (from a photograph)	II. 163	CXXXII	
S. EVREMOND	The Abbey	II. 162	CXXXI	
S. GEORGES DE BOSCHERVILLE	Chapter House doorway (from a photograph)	II. 152	CXXVI	
S. GILLES	Part of the Portal	II. 70	CVI	
S. JUNIEN	Interior	II. 42	XCVI	
	Shrine of S. Junien	II. 48		81
	West front	II. 58		84
S. LEONARD	Plan of Baptistery	II. 60		86
S. LORENZO IN PASENATICO	Pierced window-slab	II. 192		120
S. NECTAIRE	Exterior	II. 136		106
	Interior	II. 135	CXIX	
S. SAVIN	Interior	II. 49	CII	
SALONICA	Eski Djouma. Plan	I. 47		11
	Do. Triplet in narthex (in colour)	I. 56	VI	
	Do. Interior of nave	I. 57	VII	
	Do. Exterior	I. 59		12
	S. Demetrius. Plan	I. 61		13
	Do. Exterior of apse	I. 48	II	
	Do. Blown-leaf Capital	I. 49	III	
	Do. Interior	I. 60	VII*a*	
	Do. Eagle Capital	I. 61	VIII	
	Do. Marble lining (in colour)	I. 64	IX	
	Do. Soffits of arches	I. 63		14
	S. Elias. Plan	I. 136		33
	Do. Exterior	I. 135	XXI	
	S. George. Plan and section	I. 70		16
	S. Sophia. Plan	I. 72		17
	Do. Exterior	I. 74		18
	The Holy Apostles (Souk-Su-Djami). Plan	I. 138		34
	Do. Exterior	I. 138	XXII	
SILCHESTER	Plan of basilica (from *Archaeologia*)	II. 175		113
SOLIGNAC	Interior	II. 41		78
SPALATO	The Porta Ferrea	I. 31		5
SPEYER	The Crypt (from a photograph)	II. 14	LXXXVII	
STAMFORD	S. Leonard's Priory. Façade	II. 253	CLXV	
STOW LONGA	Norman door-head (from a photograph)	II. 243	CLIX	
TEWKESBURY	West front (drawing by R. Davison)	II. 232		135
TORCELLO	Duomo plan	I. 236		52
TOSCANELLA	S. Pietro. Interior (from a photograph)	I. 216	LV	
	Do. Eaves arcading	I. 219		48

LIST OF ILLUSTRATIONS xvii

		Vol. & page	Plate	Cut
TOSCANELLA	S. Pietro. Exterior of apse	I. 217	LVI	
	Do. West front (from a photograph)	I. 220	LVII	
	Do. The Rose window (from do.)	I. 221	LVIII	
	Do. Panel with cross, &c.	I. 218		4
	S. Maria Maggiore. Interior (from a photograph)	I. 222	LIX	
	Do. West front (from do.)	I. 223	LX	
	Do. Details of doorway	I. 223		49
	Do. Pulpit	I. 224		50
TOULOUSE	S. Sernin. Plan	II. 83		91
	Do. Exterior (from a photograph)	II. 84	CIX	
TOURNAI	Interior of nave	II. 23		72
TROMPS AND SQUINCHES		I. 38		9
VALENCE	Interior of nave	II. 115		99
VENICE	S. Mark's. Plan	I. 231		51
	Do. Interior (from a photograph)	I. 232	LXI	
	Do. Capitals (do.)	I. 233	LXII	
	Do. Exterior (do.)	I. 234	LXIII	
	Venetian dentil moulding	I. 238		53
VÉZELAY	Interior (from Viollet-le-Duc)	II. 101		93
	Narthex and west door	II. 104	CXIII	
	Chapter House console	II. 105	CXIV	
	Do. do. vestibule	II. 105		94
VIENNE	Tower of S. Pierre	II. 116	CXV	
WESTMINSTER	Plan of the Confessor's Church	II. 206		125
	Chapel of the Pyx (from *Gleanings* &c.)	II. 207		126
WINCHESTER	Plans of the Norman and present Cathedral	II. 215		129
	Interior of North transept	II. 218	CXLIII	
	Plan of crypts	II. 219		130
	Capital, 2 views	II. 248	CLXI	
	Do.	II. 247		145
WORDWELL	Norman door-head (from a photograph)	II. 242	CLVIII	
WORMS	Plan	II. 12		68
	Interior	II. 13	LXXXVI	
	Western Towers	II. 12	LXXXV	

INTRODUCTION

A NEW book at the present day about by-gone Architecture seems to need an apology. One is met at the outset by the question of the proper relation of art to archaeology and archaeology to art. For at some times architecture seems to have found in archaeology its best friend and at others its worst enemy.

The art of past ages lies of course within the domain of archaeology, but the attempt sometimes made to raise archaeology into the domain of art is fraught with danger and ends in disaster.

In the equipment of the historian archaeology now fills a most important place. History is no longer studied in the old-fashioned way as a mere chronicle of events; these are the dry bones of the subject which must be clothed with the living flesh of the actors. The historic study of art helps to make the past live again for us, and among the remains of our ancestors' handiwork none appeals to us more than their architectural monuments. These silent witnesses of the events that fill our annals bring back the past as nothing else can. To handle the work our forefathers have wrought, to climb the stairs or worship under the vaults they have raised, to pace the streets between buildings on which their eyes have rested seems to make us personally acquainted with them. Even their writings fail to bring them so near.

INTRODUCTION xix

But it need hardly be said that architecture has far other claims on us than those of historical association. The literary and historical view is the accidental one. As distinct from mere building, the primary function of architecture, like that of the other arts, is to please by exciting and satisfying certain aesthetic emotions. Architecture of the past no less than that of today must be judged on aesthetic grounds, and into this aspect of it history does not enter: beauty is for all time and sufficient in itself.

For this reason with many professional architects archaeology and the study of ancient buildings has fallen into disrepute. It is blamed as the parent of that mechanical imitation of by-gone styles which used to be considered the only safe path for an architect to tread. The rigid formulas of the neo-classic school were ridiculed by the neo-Goth, but he in his turn promptly put himself into fetters of his own forging. We were taught to analyse old work " as a German grammarian classes the powers of a preposition; and under this absolute irrefragable authority we are to begin to work, admitting not so much as an alteration in the depth of a cavetto, or the breadth of a fillet[1]." And on this principle the new school worked during the greater part of the last century, producing a vast output of work imitating more or less well, or more or less badly, the architecture of the Middle Ages, and in a few cases it must be confessed rivalling if not surpassing the model in every respect but that of originality.

But if there is one lesson more than another which archaeology teaches us it is this: that art to be worth anything must be modern, and express its own age and

[1] Ruskin, *Seven Lamps of Architecture*, p. 190, ed. 1849.

no other. It has always been so in the past, and it must be so in the future. Imitation, necessary at first, has done its useful work, and the blind worship of precedent is now only capable of doing harm. Archaeology, as Fergusson said long ago, is not art, and a too narrow study of the past may very well stifle the art of the present and future.

There is however a danger of going too far in the opposite direction. To shun slavish imitation is one thing, to reject the lessons of experience is another. Among the *peccant humours* which retard the advancement of learning Bacon places "the extreme affecting of two extremities; the one antiquity, the other novelty; wherein it seemeth the children of time do take after the nature and malice of the father. For as he devoureth his children, so one of them seeketh to devour and suppress the other; while antiquity envieth there should be new additions, and novelty cannot be content to add but must deface. Surely the advice of the prophet is the true direction in this matter; '*state super vias antiquas, et videte quaenam sit via recta et bona, et ambulate in ea.*' Stand ye in the old ways, and see which is the good way, and walk therein. Antiquity deserveth that reverence that men should make a stand thereupon, and discover what is the best way; but when the discovery is well taken then to make progression[1]."

The modern artist therefore still lies under the necessity of studying the art of the past. To shut our eyes to it, as some younger ardent spirits would have us do, would mean the extinction of all tradition, and with it of art itself. For all art, and all science, is based on inherited knowledge, and every step onward is made

[1] Bacon, *Advancement of Learning*, Book I.

INTRODUCTION

from the last vantage won by those who have gone before us and shown the way. Indeed oblivion of the past is impossible. It is said Constable wished he could forget that he had ever seen a picture. If he had had his wish he would not have been Constable. Consciously or unconsciously we form our views from our experience; and our ideas are inevitably shaped in a greater or less measure by what has been done already. But while an architect must take archaeology to some extent into his service he must beware lest it become his master. He must study the art of the past neither as a subject of historical research, nor as a matter for imitation, but in order to learn its principles, taking it as his tutor rather than his model.

It will therefore be the object of the following pages not merely to describe but to try and explain the development of architecture from style to style since the decline of classic art in the 3rd and 4th centuries of our era, down to the dawn of Gothic architecture, by connecting its constructive details and outward features with those social reasons which served to mould them into the forms we know.

From this point of view it is important to compare the rate of progress of the new art in different countries, to mark not only the main current of the movement, but the irregular and unequal advances by which it pushed its way in each instance. For though the general set of the movement was all in one direction it advanced much faster in some places than in others, and in each country it took a distinctive national character. For this purpose the comparative and parallel tables of examples at the end of the book will I hope be found useful.

It is important too to observe the continuity of

architectural history; how one style gave birth to another; for no new style was ever invented, but always grew out of an older one; how this progression from style to style was always unintentional and unconscious: and how revival after depression always began by the attempt to revive an older art, with the result that when art did revive it was always something new, for no dead art was ever made to live again, or ever will be.

These, it seems to me, are the lessons to be learned from considering the by-gone styles of architecture with regard to their bearing on what we have to do in our own day.

CHAPTER I

ROMAN ARCHITECTURE

The Byzantine and Romanesque styles of architecture are the phases into which the art passed from the decay of the styles of ancient Rome : and in order to understand them it is necessary to understand first the character of that art from which they sprang.

In the eyes and judgment of the great masters of the Renaissance in the 15th and 16th centuries Roman architecture was the perfection of human art, and fixed the standard which it was their ambition to reach with that of their own time. At the present day, when the supremacy of Grecian art is insisted upon, Roman art has fallen somewhat into disrepute, and most writers think it proper to treat it apologetically. We are told it is coarse and unrefined. It is the art, Fergusson says, of an Aryan people planted in the midst of other races more artistic than themselves, from whom they were content to borrow what they could not originate; for from the Aryans, according to him, no original art can come.

But if the art of Rome is founded on the art of those more artistic races to which Fergusson refers, and among which the ruling race was established, it had a special direction given to it by Roman genius which made it into an original style, demanding to be judged by a different standard from its predecessors. Properly regarded, Roman architecture stands in no need of apology, and the depreciation with which it has lately been viewed is unjust. That it wants the subtle refinement which the Greek bestowed on his temples and the few public buildings of which we know anything may be granted, but the Roman had to apply his style to an infinite variety of subjects which never presented themselves to the Greek imagination. The Greek had but his own small state with its few temples to think of, and could afford to lavish on them infinite pains, and to treat them with consummate delicacy; but the Roman needed a style that would serve for the great public and private buildings—baths, theatres, basilicas, forums, and aqueducts—with which he filled the capital and enriched the provinces of a vast empire. To have demanded for every building in the Roman world the refinements of the Parthenon would have been ridiculous, had it not been impossible. The true principles of art required a totally different treatment, and by the way in which Roman architecture conformed to the novel requirements of an altered state of Society it satisfied those principles and established its claim to be considered a noble style. If to some its utilitarian element may appear to degrade it to a lower level than that of Greece, to others this loss may seem more than compensated by its greater elasticity and power of adaptation to circumstance.

Although, therefore, there is no doubt that Roman architecture was to a large extent borrowed from the neighbouring peoples in the Peninsula, it possessed certain qualities that made it something new,—something different from the art either of Greece or Etruria,—some principle of life and energy that enabled it to meet the ever increasing and ever novel demands of a new order of Society. And it is in these qualities that we recognize the influence of the Roman mind. The outward forms might be adopted from elsewhere, but the practical temper of the governing race bent them to new uses, and moulded them into new developments to suit the new conditions of a world-wide empire.

It may be admitted that the full-blooded Roman was rarely, if ever, himself an artist. Sprung as he was from a colony of outlaws, refugees, and adventurers, involved in perpetual strife with his neighbours, first of all for existence, afterwards from the passionate love of dominion that carried him to the Empire of the world, the true Roman had indeed little time to cultivate the finer arts of peace. He was content to leave them to the subject races, and to borrow from them what was necessary for his own use. That he should put his hand to actual artistic work was not to be expected: in his eyes it was a mechanical pursuit, to be left to his inferiors. But this contempt for the artist was not peculiar to the Roman. It was felt no less in Greece, even in the days when art itself was most esteemed and reached its highest achievements. Plutarch tells us how Philip asked his son Alexander whether he was not ashamed to sing so well. No well-born youth, he continues, would be inspired by the statue of Olympian Zeus to desire to be a Phidias, or by that of Hera at Argos to be a Polyclitus[1]. These prejudices survived to the days of Lord Chesterfield, and to some extent survive still. Readers of *I miei ricordi* will remember the consternation of the family of the Marquis D'Azeglio when his son announced his intention of being a painter.

To the Roman of the ruling caste the arts of the conquered races were valuable as ornaments of the

[1] Plutarch, *Life of Pericles*. "Many times when we are pleased with the work we slight and set little by the workman or artist himself."

triumph of the conqueror. To have engaged in them personally would have been a degradation, and it seems to have been the fashion to speak of them contemptuously and pretend not to understand them[1]. Cicero, though himself a man of taste, and a collector of works of art, thinks it proper when addressing a jury of Roman Senators to assume an air of indulgent pity for the art-loving Greek[2]. "It is strange," he says, "what delight the Greeks take in those things which we despise. Our forefathers readily let them keep all they pleased, that they might be well adorned and flourishing under our empire; while to the subject and tributary races they left these things which seem to us trifles as an amusement and solace in their servitude."

He affects to be himself a poor judge of matters of the kind[3]; he pretends he has only learned the names of Praxiteles and Myron while hunting up evidence in Sicily for the prosecution of Verres; and he has to be prompted before he can remember that of Polyclitus[4]. This, which in Cicero was mere stage-play, was evidently in his opinion the attitude of his hearers towards the arts. The greatness of Rome rested on far different grounds. The stern idea of Roman destiny breathes in the splendid words of prophecy which Virgil puts into the mouth of the legendary founder of the race. War and empire were to be the arts of Rome, and she might leave it to others to outshine her in sculpture, rhetoric, and science[5].

It was then from her Etruscan neighbours on one side, and the great and flourishing cities of Magna Graecia

---

[1] The histrionic performances of Nero, in which noble youths were forced to join, gave the bitterest blow to Roman dignity.
[2] Cicero, *In Verrem*, Act. II. Lib. iv. Cap. 60.
[3] Nos qui rudes harum rerum sumus. *In Verr.* II. ii. 35.
[4] *Ibid.* II. iv. Cap. 2. 3.
[5] Excudent alii spirantia mollius aera, &c., &c. *Æn.* VI. 848.

on the other in the main that the architecture and sister arts of Rome took their origin. Pliny[1] says the early temples of Rome were all Tuscan. The advent of plastic art he traces to Demaratus the Corinthian refugee who founded the family of Tarquin, and brought with him the artists Eucheir and Eugrammos,—him of the deft hand, and him of the cunning pencil. The myth points evidently to the influence of the older civilization of Etruria, and the splendour of the great Greek cities of the South, which were populous and powerful states when Rome was an obscure nest of robbers on the Palatine. Greek architects appear frequently in later times. Cyrus, a Greek, was employed by Cicero in building or altering his villa[2], and Diphilus, about whom he writes to his brother Quintus, seems from his name to have been Greek also. Vitruvius gives the Greek terms for his principles of architecture, Apollodorus who fell a victim to the jealousy of Hadrian was a Syrian Greek, and Trajan writes to Pliny the younger in Asia, that he need not send to Rome for architects, but would easily get one in Greece, whence Rome itself was constantly supplied with them[3]. Horace's recommendation of Greek models to the Poets might have been addressed as well to the Artists[4].

But, as we have said, if the Roman of the old Latin stock was rarely if ever an architect himself, it was his influence that gave to the architecture of the Roman world that special practical and utilitarian character which distinguishes it from all preceding styles, and in which

---

[1] Plin. *Nat. Hist.* XXXI. 12.
[2] Cic. *ad Atticum*, XVIII.; *ad Quintum Fratrem*, III. 1.
[3] Trajan to Pliny, *Lett.* XLIX.
[4] ......vos exemplaria Graeca
nocturna versate manu, versate diurna. *Ars Poet.*

consists its chief merit. For his temples the Greek or Etruscan type sufficed, and survived with certain modifications to the last; but for the various requirements of a larger civic life, a vast and ever growing population, and a more complex state of society something very different was wanted, something less costly in labour and material, less rigid in detail, and admitting of ample liberty in plan and construction. The solution was found in the art of Etruria and not in that of Greece; in the frank adoption of the arch, not only as an element in construction, but also as an element of design; and this was the greatest innovation in architecture since the days of the Pharaohs.

Not of course that the use of the arch was a new discovery. It had always been understood from the earliest times. To ask when it was invented is like asking the same of the wedge, the lever, or the wheel. It must have been found out by the earliest people that began to put stones or bricks together into a wall. Accident, if nothing else, would have suggested it. Arches of construction, and arched vaulting in brick or stone are found in the tombs and pyramids of Egypt as far back as four thousand years before Christ. The granaries of Rameses II at Thebes are vaulted in brick, and arched drains and vaults occur in the substructure of the palaces of Nineveh. But though the arch had long been employed as a useful expedient in construction it is the glory of Roman architecture to have raised it into the region of art. Without it the theatres, amphitheatres, aqueducts, baths, basilicas, and bridges of the Roman world would have been impossible. It is to the practical turn of the Roman mind that we must credit its adoption, while on the other hand it is probably due to the versatility of the artists, mostly Greek or Greco-Roman, to whom the direction had been given by their Roman masters, that we must attribute the development

Fig. 1.

of what originated in mere considerations of utility into a consistent and novel style of architecture.

It has been objected to the Roman architects that

whereas, except in porticos of temples where Greek tradition survived, they rejected the principles of trabeate construction, they nevertheless continued to use its forms. In such buildings as the Theatre of Marcellus, and all the amphitheatres known to us from Nîmes in the west to Pola in the east (Fig. 1), the real construction is by arches, but yet the architectural effect depends largely on the columns and entablatures in which the arches are, as it were, framed. It is contended that to apply the constructional forms of a trabeated style to an arcuated fabric as a mere surface decoration is a sham; and as such it stands self-condemned in the eyes of the Gothic Purist and worshipper of absolute truth.

There is an element of justice in the accusation: things should be what they seem, and it must be admitted that columns and entablatures were invented for a different purpose from that to which they are applied in the Colosseum. It is also quite true that ornament rises in value in proportion as it illustrates and emphasizes the construction; and the converse is also true that ornament is indefensible when it falsifies or conceals it.

But to the latter charge, at all events, the Roman architect need not plead guilty: his wall decoration by columns and entablatures deceives nobody: no one would take them for the main supports of the building. Columns separated by seven or eight times the width of their diameter, of which a fourth part is lost in the wall to which they are attached, make no pretence to carry a serviceable lintel; and entablatures tailed and bonded into the main wall are obviously only string courses, to divide the storeys, and give perspective lines to the composition.

It does not do to apply the canon of utility too rigidly

to every decorative feature in architecture. The objection which is raised against Roman architecture on Ruskinite principles might with equal force be taken to much that we admire in Gothic. The blank arcading of the fronts of Salisbury, Wells, or Lincoln, or that in the aisles of Westminster or Winchester is quite as devoid of any constructional purpose as the orders which divide and surmount the arches of the arenas at Nîmes or Arles. It may be said that the pediments over Inigo Jones's windows at Whitehall are absurd because a pediment is properly the gable end of a roof: but they are not more indefensible than the steep gablets that surmount so gracefully the clerestory windows at Amiens which have no constructional meaning whatever. The Gothic spire itself is an extravagance if we look merely to its original function as a covering to the tower. While on the one hand we should try to make decoration as significant as we can, it is clear that if the test of utility is pedantically enforced there will be an end of architecture altogether.

The adoption of the arch as a leading element in construction opened the way at once to fresh forms of design. The principles of trabeated architecture, naturally adapted to construction of wood, when applied to stone, which has no tensile strength, required narrow intercolumniations such as could be spanned by stone lintels short enough not to snap under their load. The arch removed this difficulty; wide spaces could now be spanned without intermediate support. The arch was followed by the vault, which is only the arch prolonged sideways, and by the dome which is the arch rotated on its axis. Economy led to the use of brick and concrete, which made possible the vast Baths of Caracalla, the Pantheon, the Palatine, and the Basilica of Maxentius, works such as the world had never seen before, which still amaze us by their scale and solidity. These simple constructions of rude materials invited decoration in colour, which was given at first by painting and afterwards by linings of coloured materials and mosaic. And as under the later Republic and the Empire luxury and extravagance superseded more and more the plainer life of older times, Roman taste, less alive to the delicacies of art, ran riot in ornament, a sure sign of weaker artistic sensibility. Coloured marbles by their splendour and costliness lent themselves admirably to that display of wealth and power which the Roman loved. Pliny[1] complains that the Alps, intended by nature to fence in countries and direct the course of rivers, which Hannibal and the Cimbri had crossed to the astonishment of the Romans of old, were now being quarried and carted away that their degenerate successors might sleep within walls of parti-coloured stones; a kind of adornment which displaced the older and more artistic decoration by painting[2].

The passion for splendour and ostentation appears also in the profuse enrichment of the entablature by ornaments of a conventional kind. The Greeks, except where they touched them with colour, kept the mouldings of their cornices and architraves plain, and reserved themselves for the more perfect decoration of the frieze by fine sculpture. But the Romans often enriched every moulding with egg and dart, bead and reel, and leaf ornaments, confusing the severity of the outline, and disturbing the breadth of light and shade. The result is a certain gorgeousness of effect, purchased too dearly

---

[1] Plin. *Nat. Hist.* XXXVI. 1.

[2] Et Hercules non fuisset picturae honos ullus, non modo tantus, in aliqua marmorum auctoritate. *Ibid.* XXXVI. 6.

at the cost of simplicity. But one must admit the admirable technical execution of these ornaments and their skilful adaptation for due effect in position; and in this we may I think detect the touch of the true artist, while in the dictation of extravagance in amount of decoration we may read the vulgarity and insolence of wealth in his master.

We need not shut our eyes against these defects, but they are not enough to obscure the merits of an architectural style which has given us perhaps the grandest, and some of the most beautiful buildings in the world. Above all we must recognize its admirable suitability to the purposes it had to fulfil; and also its elasticity and power of adaptation to novel requirements, in which quality it surpassed Greek architecture as much as it was itself surpassed by the styles that succeeded it. It was this quality that fitted it to become the parent of all the styles of modern Europe, and it is out of Roman architecture that they have all arisen. For practical purposes, apart from archaeology, it is the only ancient style with which the modern architect need trouble himself. The styles of Egypt, Assyria, Persia, India, and China, admirable as they are in their several ways, are alien to our temperament, and have no direct bearing on our modern use. They illustrate indeed, so far as they are good, that dependence of design on sound construction which is the very soul of all good architecture wherever and whenever we find it. But the circumstances amid which they arose and by which they were shaped are so different from our own that they teach us no other lesson, and for the practical architect they are dead. It takes some courage to say the same of the styles of ancient Greece: but supreme as we admit Hellenic art to be, especially in sculpture, it has limitations, and for the British architect at all events it is as dead as Assyrian. The attempt of Sir John Soane and others to revive it in the 19th century under an English sky resulted in the most frigid and desperately dull work of modern times. It is with the architecture of Rome that we first begin to feel at home, because in it we find the seeds of all subsequent architectural growth during the dark and middle ages, the period of the Renaissance, and down even to our own day.

CHAPTER II

DECAY OF ROMAN ARCHITECTURE. FOUNDATION OF CONSTANTINOPLE. THE BASILICAN PLAN

THE extent of Roman architecture was limited only by that of the Empire itself. Wherever the Roman carried his arms he took with him the arts and civilization of the capital. In every part, from Britain in the north to the shores of Africa in the south, and the sands of Baalbec and Palmyra in the east, Roman architecture is to be found, varying no doubt in degrees of scale and execution but bearing everywhere the impress of the same character; and it was from the examples that adorned each country that their several native styles arose in later times, however widely they differed among themselves in their development. {Roman architecture co-extensive with the Empire}

There is a certain likeness to the life of man in the history of all great schools of art. From crude beginnings they struggle through a vigorous youth, full of promise and unrealized yearnings to a period of what is, within their own limits, perfection. Beyond that they cannot go, and it is followed, not perhaps at once, but in the end none the less surely by a period of decline which sooner or later brings about dissolution, and makes way for something different. They are like an author who has written himself out, or a teacher who has said all that there is in him to say, and for whom the time has come to stand aside and be silent.

Decay of Roman art

The art of Rome furnishes no exception to this rule. From the time of Augustus and the early Caesars it steadily declined in purity though still retaining many fine qualities. The sculpture of Trajan and the Antonines was becoming dry and inexpressive, though it had still about it a fair classic grace. But by the time of Diocletian and Constantine it had become gross and barbarous. On Constantine's arch at Rome, besides figure subjects of his own time, are some parts of an older arch of Trajan, and the contrast between the two kinds is remarkable.

> "What sculpture raised
> To Trajan's glory, following triumphs stole,
> And mixed with Gothic forms, the chisel's shame,
> On that triumphal arch the forms of Greece[1]."

By the middle of the 4th century after Christ, Roman classic architecture, as Vitruvius would have understood it, may be considered to have sunk into decay and come to an end.

It is from the decay of older styles that new styles of art have their beginning, and Roman architecture at its death left behind it a successor ready to take its place, and better adapted to the altered conditions of the time.

Removal of the Capital

As the frontiers of the Empire became more and more threatened by surrounding nations the later emperors moved the seats of government nearer to the scene of danger. Rome was no longer the centre of empire, and was deserted for Nicomedia and Milan. In 324 Constantine founded a new Rome on the shores of the Bosphorus, and was rarely seen in the old capital of the world afterwards.

Constantinople founded

To these new capitals all the architectural resources of the Empire were directed, and especially to the last:

---

[1] Thomson's *Liberty*, III. 509.

but we read that in the "decline of the arts the skill as well as the numbers of the emperor's architects bore a very unequal proportion to the greatness of his designs[1]." Schools were founded, and professors appointed to instruct ingenuous youths in the principles of architecture; but schools of art are not formed in a hurry, nor could the impatience of the emperor endure delay. Byzantium seems to have possessed already some fine buildings of Greek architecture: the baths of Zeuxippus were preserved and decorated afresh; but for new buildings the emperor had to depend on such artists as were forthcoming. Nevertheless, in less than 10 years New Rome was ready to be dedicated by a solemn festival, though many of the structures with which it was furnished bore signs of haste, and even threatened ruin.

Among other works in this new capital, which was destined to bear his name, we read that Constantine built two churches, dedicated respectively to Peace—Irene— and to the Apostles[2]. For the Empire had now become Christian, and with the new creed came the demand for suitable places of worship. The temples of the older faith were sometimes, as the Pagan creeds declined, converted into churches, but their small interior cella was ill-suited to the Christian congregation, and the basilica suggested a better type for the accommodation of large bodies of worshippers. The first church of S. Sophia at Constantinople which, according to Socrates, was built by the Emperor Constantius and consecrated in the tenth year of his reign by the patriarch Eudoxius[3], is reported

Constantine's churches at Constantinople

---

[1] Gibbon, cap. XVII.
[2] καὶ ἐν ταύτῃ τῇ πόλει δύο μὲν οἰκοδομήσας ἐκκλησίας μίαν ἐπωνόμασεν Εἰρήνην, ἑτέραν δὲ τὴν τῶν Ἀποστόλων ἐπώνυμον. Soc. *Hist. Eccl.* c. 45.
[3] *Ibid.* cc. 93 and 160.

to have been of the basilican type (ναὸς δρομικός) with a wooden roof.

The basilica

The basilica, στοὰ βασίλειος, introduced to Rome from Greece under the later Republic, was a public building consisting of a long central court sometimes but not always covered, between colonnaded porticos, serving like the Royal Exchange in London for gatherings of merchants on business. Adjoining it, or actually as at Pompeii at one end, was the tribunal of the Praetor where he sat with the Judices to try cases, separated by cancelli or railings from the body of the hall. Frequently this tribunal was an apse with a hemicycle of seats for the magistrate and others concerned. Whether many basilicas were actually used as churches is doubtful. Texier and Pullan say that though many temples are known to have been turned into churches, the Licinian basilica at Rome is the only law-court known to have been used for Christian worship[1]. One writer points out that basilicas would have been wanted for their original purposes just as much after the establishment of Christianity as before[2]. But however this may be it is clear that the basilican form recommended itself as convenient to the Christian architects so soon as they were free to build without fear of persecution[3].

[1] Texier and Pullan (*Byzantine Architecture*, p. 12). It is suggested this is a mistake for the *Basilica Sicinini*, or S. Maria Maggiore. Rushforth in *English Historical Review*, July, 1913. v. Gibbon, ch. xxv., note.

[2] *History of English Church Architecture* by G. G. Scott, Jun., 1881.

[3] Though the term basilican is misleading if taken to imply too close a connexion between one kind of church and the Roman basilica, its use is convenient to describe a certain class of Byzantine and Romanesque buildings, the ναὸς δρομικός, for which another general term is wanting, and it will be so used in what follows. It should be observed however that the old writers use the word "Basilica" for any form of church: Agnellus calls the octagonal church of S. Vitale at Ravenna a basilica, and Eginhardt calls

There had, of course, been Christian churches before the time of Constantine. The number of believers must soon have outgrown the accommodation of one or two rooms in a private house, which had sufficed at first. When milder counsels in their rulers prevailed the Christians crept forth from the holes and caves, the catacombs and rock hewn oratories, to which they had been driven for the celebration of their rites, and built themselves churches above ground. Edicts from time to time swept these buildings away when the imperial temper veered round towards persecution. Some of them seem to have been on a splendid scale. The church at Nicomedia which was destroyed under the edict of Diocletian is said to have towered above the imperial palace and to have provoked the envy and jealousy of the Gentiles[1]. Eusebius describing the church at Tyre rebuilt by Constantine after the destruction of its predecessor under the same edict mentions that the new church followed, though in a more splendid fashion, the form of the older building.

This form was what we call basilican: a nave consisting of a long parallelogram, ending in an apse; divided from an aisle on each side by rows of columns carrying either lintels or arches, above which was a clerestory, with windows that looked over the aisle roofs. The roofs were of wood, except that of the apse, which was a semi-dome of brick or stone. In front of the church was generally a court or atrium surrounded by a cloister

---

the round church at Aix-la-Chapelle by that name. As used by them the word has no reference to the form of the Roman Basilica—"Basilicae prius vocabantur regum habitacula; nunc autem ideo basilicae divina templa nominantur, quia ibi Regi omnium Deo cultus et sacrificia offeruntur." Isid. *Orig.* v. (7th century), cited Milman.

[1] Lactantius, cited by Gibbon, ch. XVI.

such as we see at S. Ambrogio in Milan, S. Clemente in Rome and Parenzo in Istria. The altar was placed on the chord of the apse, and round the hemicycle of the apse behind it were seats for the presbyters with the bishop's throne in the middle, as may still be seen at Torcello, Aquileja, Parenzo and Grado. The altar and its apse were at the west end of the church, and the main entrance at the east, so that the ministering priest stood behind the altar looking eastward and facing the congregation, as he still does at Parenzo and at S. Peter's and several other churches in Rome and as he did in the original cathedral of Canterbury.

Simple construction of basilica

This seems to have been the type of all Constantine's churches, and among them that of S. Peter's at Rome (Fig. 2), where however the plan was complicated by the addition of an outer or second aisle on each side, and by a transept at the end next the apse, such as we may see in the church of S. Paolo fuori le Mura. The construction of these churches was light and simple, requiring very little architectural skill, challenging no constructional problems, and dispensing entirely with the vault and the dome which had played so important a part in the later Roman architecture. The very materials themselves were often taken ready-made from Pagan buildings, and columns and capitals were stolen without scruple from older structures. The Roman world was sacked by Constantine for the adornment of his new capital.

S. Peter's at Rome

S. Peter's was the first Christian church built in Rome by Constantine after his conversion. It stood on the Vatican near the Circus of Nero, the reputed scene of the Apostle's martyrdom. This, the oldest and largest of the Roman basilican churches, has disappeared to make way for the greatest church in Christendom, but

Fig. 2.

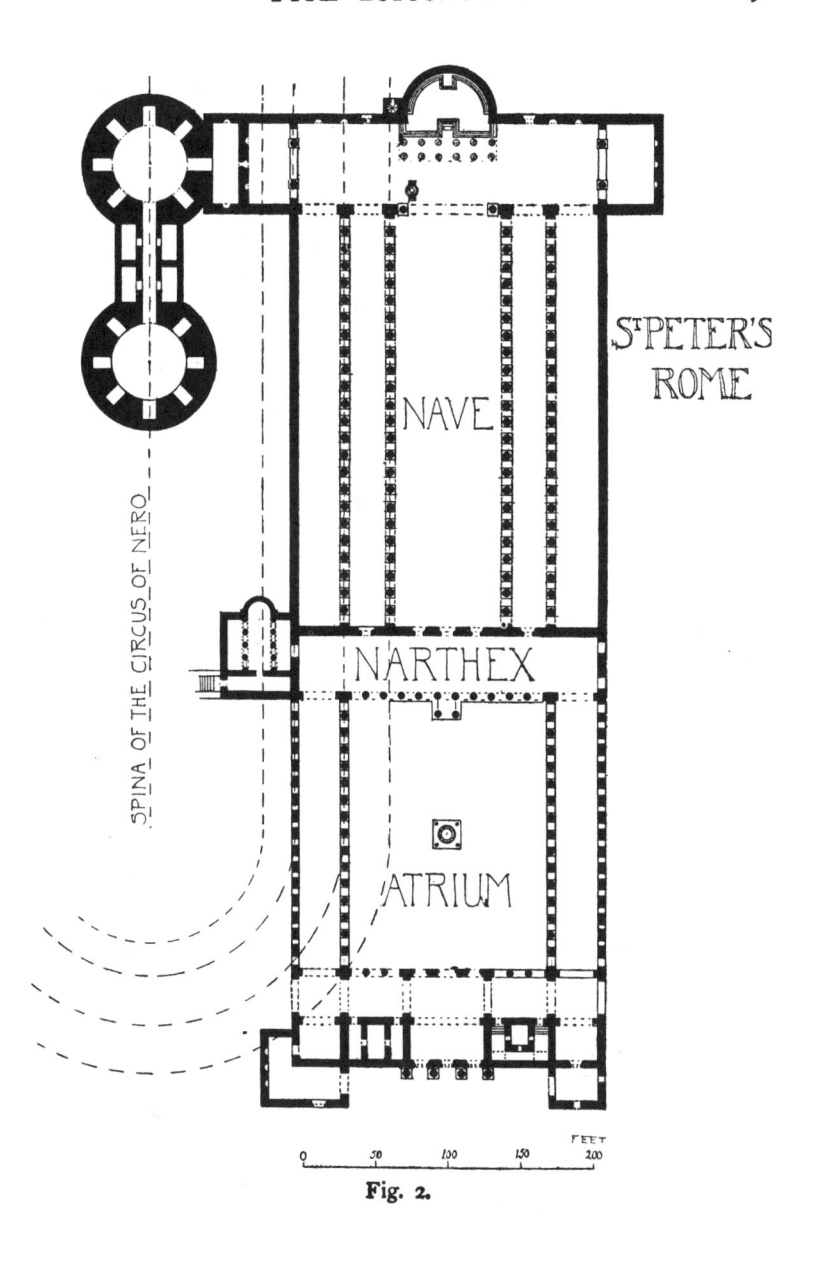

we know what it was like from drawings made before its destruction. From them we learn that even at the beginning of the 4th century, when the fiery trial of the last persecution was only just abated, the Church had already begun to rival the outworn creeds in the magnificence of her ritual and ecclesiastical system. The simple republicanism and equality of the primitive congregation had yielded to the growth of a hierarchy, which demanded the separation of clergy and laity. At first the tribune in the apse, then the dais in front of it on which the altar stood was railed off by cancelli or railings; in other words a chancel was formed; and later a choir was enclosed within the nave by a low wall within which the clergy were seated and on each side were ambones or pulpits whence the gospel and epistle were read.

The choir

At S. Peter's the five aisled body of the church was 380 ft. long by 212 ft. wide, the central nave having a span of 80 ft. The Western transept extended one way to two round Mausolea placed on the axis of Nero's circus, supposed at one time to be the tombs of the Apostles, and now those of the Theodosian Emperors. The apse was 58 ft. wide by 35 deep, and the altar was surmounted by a ciborium or baldacchino. The seat of the chief Pontiff like that of the Praetor was in the centre of the tribune, and the chief clergy, the embryo Cardinals, sat like the Roman judices to his right and left in a semicircle. In a crypt below were the tombs of Roman bishops. At the east end of the church the entrance was preceded by a splendid atrium or cloistered court measuring 265 ft. by 122, in front of which was a portico with two towers.

The nave

The apse

The atrium

The principal or triumphal arch divided the nave from the Western transept. Before the steps of the bema or sanctuary stood twelve ancient columns of Parian marble,

The sanctuary

spirally twisted and adorned with vine leaves, fabled to have belonged to Solomon's Temple[1]. A low wall between them enclosed the presbytery, and on them rested beams or entablatures supporting images, candelabra, and other ornaments.

The side walls in the nave below the clerestory windows were adorned with pictures either painted or in mosaic, but the exterior of the church was of simple brickwork, plain and not plastered. *Mural decoration*

Such was the type of Constantine's churches, and it is strange to think that S. Peter's was built only 16 years later than his final victory at the Milvian bridge, which is commemorated by a triumphal arch, showing indeed in its sculpture the degradation of Roman art, but nevertheless designed in the orthodox classical style of the triumphal arches of his predecessors.

It was natural that the churches of the new religion, making demands of a novel kind on the architect, should break more decidedly with the old classic rules than civil structures. But there too change had already set in before the time of Constantine. When Diocletian resolved on abdicating the imperial diadem, which he had been the first to wear, he prepared for himself a splendid retreat in Dalmatia, the country where he had been born, and where his parents, if not he himself, had been slaves. His villa near Salona sufficed in the middle ages to contain the whole city of Spalato, of which its mighty walls formed the defence against Slavs and Tartars; and it still remains the most perfect example that the Romans have left us of their domestic architecture on the grandest scale. Hither Diocletian came in 303; here he planted the *Palace at Spalato*

---

[1] These probably suggested to Raffaelle the twisted columns in his cartoon of the Beautiful Gate of the Temple.

famous cabbages, the cultivation of which he preferred to the cares of empire; and here he died in 313.

<small>New details in architecture</small>

In the details of this building we can see the beginnings of many changes which resulted in the subsequent forms of Byzantine and Romanesque art. There are entablatures of two members only, the frieze being omitted: the cornices are diminished till they are not much more than the Gothic string course: the whole entablature of architrave frieze and cornice springs into an arch over the central intercolumniation of the vestibule; miniature arcading on colonnettes makes its appearance as a wall decoration over the Porta Aurea, anticipating that on the fronts at Pisa; new sections are given to mouldings, and new ornaments such as zigzags are seen for the first time, which afterwards played so large a part in Norman architecture.

<small>Liberation of arch from entablature</small>

But the most important novelty in the work at Spalato is the way in which the arches of the great peristyle are made to spring directly from the capitals of the pillars without the intervention of an entablature. According to Greek tradition the column and the entablature were inseparable, and could not be combined with arches. In purely engineering works, aqueducts and bridges, the orders were left out altogether, and the arches sprang from simple piers. And when they had to be used together, as in the Colosseum or the Theatre of Marcellus the arches were kept clear of the orders which preserved the appearance of trabeation above them (Fig. 1, *supra*). The arches did the work and the orders supplied the ornament. This did not answer when, as sometimes happened, the arch had to be raised above the entablature; and in that case by a rather absurd extravagance of logic a fragment of the entablature corresponding to the diameter of the column was placed upon it with all the mouldings and members returned round the sides, as at the Baths of Antonine and those of Diocletian at Rome, and the arch was made to spring from the top of this fragment which formed a sort of pedestal above the capital (Fig. 3). The only instance M. Choisy can quote of arches springing directly from columns before the age of the later Empire is an unimportant one at Pompeii[1]. "The first placing of the arcade on columns," he says, in monumental construction, "occurs at Spalatro, and dates from the time of Diocletian[2]."

Entablature returned as impost

Fig. 3.

The step thus taken in dispensing with the inconvenient and unnecessary entablature opened the way for all subsequent arched design, and was one of the greatest ever taken in the history of our art. From the arcades of Diocletian's peristyle at Spalato naturally followed all those of the Romanesque, Byzantine, and Gothic styles. It marked the last stage in the liberation of architecture from the fetters of strict classic rule. Henceforth it was free to develop itself on new lines, adapting itself to the altered conditions of the Roman world, and the requirements of the new religion.

Effect of the change at Spalato

The rectangular basilican type prevailed at first in all parts of the newly Christianized empire, as the proper ecclesiastical plan. It is found in Palestine, in Syria, in

Prevalence of basilican plan

---

[1] Choisy, *Hist. d'Archit.* vol. I. p. 514.
[2] *Ibid.* vol. II. p. 5.

Prevalence of basilican plan

Africa, as well as in the central provinces. Constantine's churches are all of that form. His five-aisled basilica at Bethlehem still remains, though that he built at Jerusalem at or near the Holy Sepulchre has disappeared. The great church of S. Paolo fuori le Mura at Rome has been burned and rebuilt, but it preserves the original basilican form, with the addition of a transept at the upper end like that in old S. Peter's. Rome is full of early churches conforming to the same plan. It was adopted for all the churches at Ravenna, when the seat of government was shifted thither, and prevailed until the fall of the Western Empire. And although modified in a hundred ways by circumstance it still forms the basis of ordinary church planning in our own day and in our own country.

In a few instances the old tradition of trabeation survived, and the colonnades of Constantine's church at Bethlehem, and those of S. Maria Maggiore, and S. Maria in Trastevere at Rome carry horizontal lintels instead of arches. Constantine's church of S. Peter did the same in the central nave, though the outer colonnades carried arches. But these were the exceptions. In nearly every case the liberty first won at Spalato was not forgotten, and the colonnades carry arches from capital to capital.

Basilican architecture unprogressive

To this class of buildings we will return later. It continued for some centuries with but little variety. Designed, as has been said already, in the simplest way, without challenging any difficulties of construction, no fresh expedients were called for, no new problems of statics presented themselves to be solved, and therefore no suggestions from his work occurred to the architect to force new methods on his attention. His walls were of the rudest brickwork, and the exterior hardly deserved to be called architecture at all. Ancient monuments, especially the deserted temples of the older faiths, furnished him with an endless supply of ready-made columns and capitals. Old marbles could be sliced up for wall linings and pavements, and made the labour of quarrying unnecessary. The timber roofs of both nave and aisles had no thrust and could be carried by thin walls, and the only feature that required any skill beyond ordinary bricklaying was the semi-dome of the apse, which after all was not a very serious affair. Use of old materials

It was therefore an unprogressive style, and the basilican churches of the 10th and 11th centuries differ but little, except in details of ornamentation, from those of the 4th. It was a disastrous period in the history of Italy. The unsettled state of society which followed the tide of barbarian inroad and conquest, the fall of the Western Empire, and the establishment of foreign rulers were obviously unfavourable to any artistic growth, and we must look to the comparatively settled and better ordered lands of the Eastern Empire for the first signs of any fresh departure in architecture. Basilican style stationary

CHAPTER III

GREEK ELEMENT IN THE NEW STYLE. ASIATIC INFLUENCES. SYRIAN ARCHITECTURE. THE BYZANTINE DOME. ABANDONMENT OF THE ORDERS. AVOIDANCE OF FIGURE SCULPTURE

Division of Empire between Greek and Latin

THE final partition of the Empire between the sons of Theodosius only set the seal on that division between Greek and Latin which had long existed in reality. Throughout the whole of the eastern part of the Empire of the Caesars, both in Europe and Asia, Greek culture and the Greek tongue had always prevailed. In Palestine, in the times of the Apostles, Greek seems to have been spoken side by side with the vernacular Aramaic, and the earliest Christian literature was composed in that language. The coast cities of Asia Minor were Greek, and their influence had spread among the barbarians of the interior. The new Rome on the shores of the Bosphorus was in fact a Greek city, and Greek was the official language of the first great council of the Church in the neighbouring city of Nicaea. Constantine indeed was more at home in Latin, though he could muster Greek enough to address the assembled Fathers in that language[1]: but his nephew, the Emperor Julian, was more thoroughly Hellenic, and had only a competent knowledge of the Latin tongue[2].

Constantinople a Greek city

---

[1] ἑλληνίζων τὲ τῇ φωνῇ ὅτι μηδὲ ταύτης ἀμαθῶς εἶχε. Euseb., cited Socrates, XX.

[2] Aderat Latine quoque disserenti sufficiens sermo. Ammianus, cited Gibbon, ch. XIX.

BYZANTINE CHRISTIANITY

It was in the Greek half of the Empire that Christianity triumphed more completely during the 4th century. The penal laws against paganism, by which the Christian Church, when it gained the upper hand, turned the weapon of persecution against its old oppressors, were enforced with difficulty, or not at all, in Italy, where the Roman senate still observed the ancient rites, and listened unmoved, and even replied to the arguments with which Theodosius exhorted them to embrace the new and better faith[1]. On the other hand, Constantinople had never been a pagan city, and its churches were enriched with the spoils, and the actual materials of countless pagan temples that had been ransacked and ruined to embellish them. In vain were appeals made for their preservation as monuments of national greatness and art, and fruitless were the edicts of emperors against their destruction. It is fortunate indeed that many of them were turned into churches, and to that happy circumstance it is that we owe the survival among others of the temples at Athens and those at Nîmes and Vienne in Gaul.

Greater progress of Christianity in the East

At the time of the division of the Empire then towards the end of the 4th century the Greek half had broken more decidedly with the past than the Latin, and new principles of social and religious life invited new methods of architecture to suit them. There was less disturbance also from without, for the Eastern Empire remained unshaken when the Western fell before the barbarian, and this comparative peace and security favoured the growth and development of the arts. Another influence, fertile in suggestions of new modes of construction and

Asiatic influence

---

[1] Zosimus, cited Dill, *Roman Society in the last century of the Western Empire*, p. 37.

Asiatic influence design, was exerted by the eastern provinces of the Empire, and especially Syria.

For though the capital was a Greek city on the European side of the Bosphorus, the bulk of the Empire was Asiatic; and though Greek culture had long before permeated the Asiatic provinces, it was in its turn subject to Oriental influence, and the Byzantine school, mainly Greek, was largely affected by the traditional arts of the East.

Syria Syria had been the seat of the Greek kingdom of the Seleucidae, and under the Romans Antioch, the ancient capital, became the third city of the Empire. Under their firmer rule the interior districts, which had till then been swept by the restless nomad hordes of the desert, became settled and civilized. Numerous towns sprang up on all sides, adorned with temples, theatres, aqueducts, and triumphal arches. The style of their architecture was "Greek, modified by certain local influences, by the traditions of older arts or by the nature of the materials employed[1]."

Cities of Syria The district known as the Haouran between the desert and the mountains of the Mediterranean littoral, together with its continuation northwards towards Aleppo, is full of ancient remains. M. de Vogüé counted more than 100 cities within a space of from 30 to 40 leagues. The buildings date from the 4th to the 7th century; they were all abandoned at the same time, at the Mussulman conquest, and have remained as they were left ever since, many of them in so perfect a state that they can hardly be called ruins. Where not damaged by earthquakes, says M. de Vogüé, they want nothing but their roofs to present the appearance of a Syrian town in the 7th century.

[1] Le Comte de Vogüé, *Syrie Centrale*, 1865–1877.

The peculiarities of the district suggested fresh principles of design. The Haouran grows no timber, and the only available material is stone—a hard and stubborn basalt. Driven by necessity the builders learned to make everything of stone, not only walls but actually doors, windows, shutters, and roofs. This involved new systems of construction; the arch played a principal part, and large halls were covered with slabs laid across between parallel arches. When the span was too great for slabs the builders resorted to cupolas. This mode of construction depended of course on stability of abutment, and the building resolved itself into a framework of arches, slabs, and buttresses, while the intervening walls became mere curtains, thus anticipating in a manner, as M. de Vogüé remarks, the principle of Gothic construction[1] by equilibrium of forces.

A very typical example of this mode of construction is afforded by the palace at Chaqqa (Fig. 4) which dates from a time when the Empire was still Pagan[2]. It consists of several halls, of which the largest measures 130 ft. by 36 ft., and is spanned by eight arches of solid stone on the back of which walls are carried up level with the crown of the arch. Across the intervals between these walls, varying from 6 to 10 ft., are laid slabs of stone forming a flat ceiling and roof in one. On the top of the walls corbel courses are laid in order to diminish the bearing of these roofing slabs. The thrust of the arches is encountered partly by bringing the springing forward on interior piers, and partly by exterior buttresses, perhaps the earliest instance of their use. The whole of the masonry is put together without mortar.

[1] *Op. cit*, p. 7.
[2] De Vogüé, p. 47 and Plates VIII, IX, X.

In other examples the roofing of slabs, instead of being flat as at Chaqqa, is laid with a pitch on a gabled wall resting on the cross arches.

Fig. 4.

CHAQQA after De Vogüé.

The entrance doorway of the great hall that has been just described is square, with a complete entablature for its head and a round arch above, the lunette between the two being left open as a window. Additional height is given to this arch by making it a horseshoe instead of stilting it in the western way.

It is remarkable that some of these features of Syrian architecture occur in Diocletian's palace at Spalato. There too in the peristyle of the larger temple we have slabs of

Syria and Spalato

Fig. 5.

stone laid across from the entablature of the colonnade to the central cella. There also in the two remaining gateways, the Porta Aurea, and the Porta Ferrea, the square opening has a straight lintel surmounted by an open lunette within a round arch (Fig. 5). There also over the smaller temple is a semicircular vault, roof and ceiling in one, formed of huge slabs between the two end walls. At Spalato also, both in the crypto porticus and

32   SYRIAN ARCHITECTURE   [CH. III

Greek workmen at Spalato — in the vestibule, the entablature rises into an arch from column to column as it does at Baalbec. From these instances of resemblance it has been conjectured that the palace of Spalato was built by Syro-Greeks, probably from Antioch[1]. That it was built by Greeks, may be assumed with tolerable certainty, but it is not necessary to suppose they came from Syria. Roofing with slabs was not confined to the East, though the scarcity of timber made it a convenient method both in Syria and Dalmatia. It is found in many countries and both in Roman and mediaeval times. There is a well-known example of it in the vault of the graceful temple of Diana at Nîmes, and there are corridors covered with flat slabs in the Roman buildings in that town and also at Arles. The interesting cathedral of Sebenico in Dalmatia was roofed by Giorgio Orsini in the 15th century in a similar manner, with slabs of stone carried on cross ribs of the same material, and on small scale there are instances of this construction in England.

Influence of material on Syrian style — In these peculiarities of Syrian architecture we have an admirable instance of the influence of local circumstances on architectural style. The scarcity of wood drove the architect to adopt such modes of construction as admitted of the use of stone instead. His earlier churches were basilican, and for the nave he was unable to dispense with the use of timber, but the aisles were roofed with stone as at Souaideh, and partly at Quennaouât[2]. The basilican plan was in some cases abandoned, *The dome* the later churches were domed, and in them the use of timber was entirely avoided. The church in these

---

[1] Strzygowski, *Orient oder Rom*. I am indebted to Mr Phené Spiers for this reference.
[2] De Vogüé, I. pp. 60, 61, Plates XIX, XX.

CH. III] SYRIAN ARCHITECTURE 33

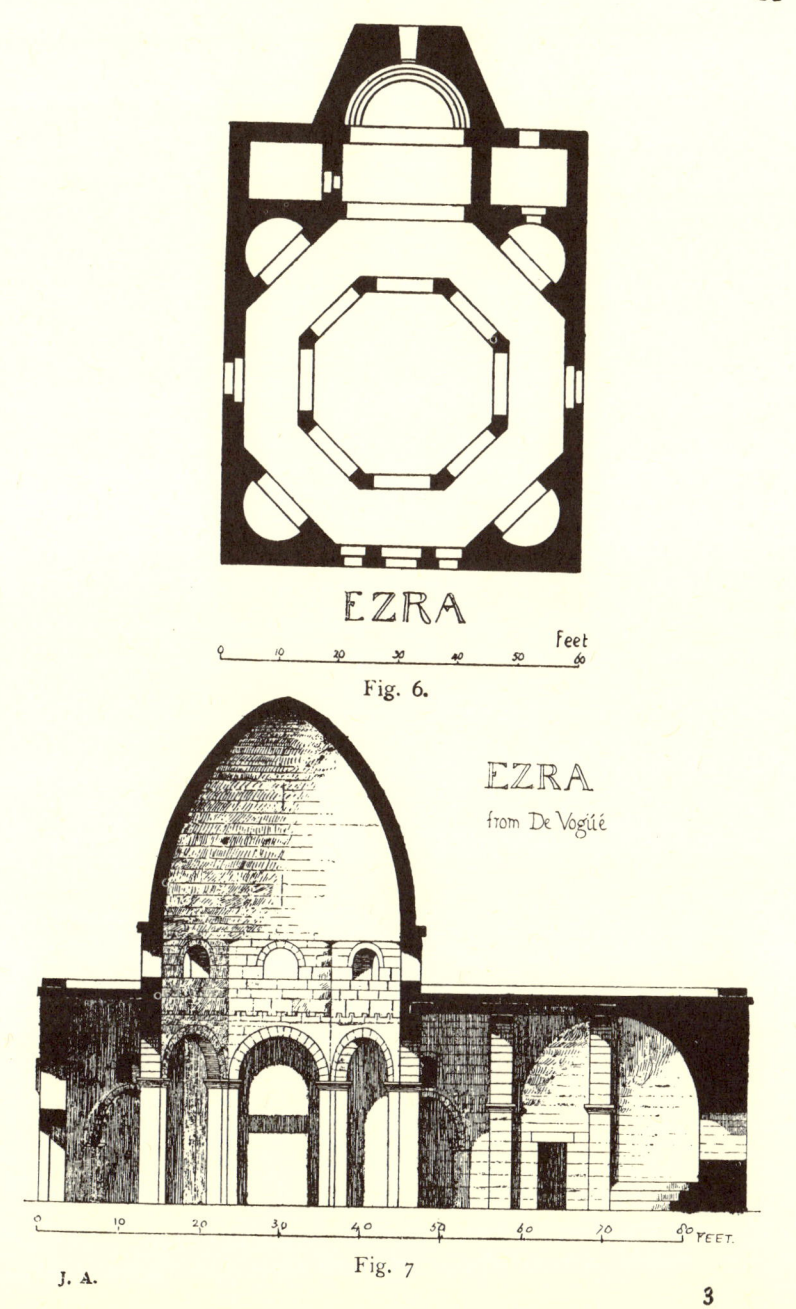

EZRA

Fig. 6.

EZRA
from De Vogüé

Fig. 7

cases became square, with a projecting apse for the sanctuary. The angles of the square were filled internally with exedrae or semicircular niches which brought it into an octagon. Within that was a smaller octagon of eight piers on which the cupola rested, surrounded by an aisle between the inner and outer octagons. A very perfect example of this is the church at Ezra (Figs. 6, 7), of which M. de Vogüé gives a plan and sections[1]. The surrounding aisle is covered by slabs, and the prolongation forming the sanctuary and ending with an apse has the cross arches and slab covering of the palace at Chaqqa. This most interesting church, which is still perfect and in use, is dated by an inscription A.D. 515

Church at Ezra

The ovoid form of the dome is remarkable, and was probably adopted as easier to construct without centering, which, on account of the scarcity of wood, had to be dispensed with as much as possible.

The whole is constructed of wrought stone put together without mortar.

Eastern origin of dome

The dome probably took its origin in the East, though M. Choisy says that cupolas are to be seen in the Egyptian paintings[2]. They appear in Assyrian bas-reliefs, sometimes hemispherical and sometimes stilted, and are found in the buildings of the Sassanian rulers of Persia in the 4th and 5th centuries of the Christian era at Serbistan and Firouzabad[3].

It was of course long before the latter date that the dome found its way to Italy. The great baths of the

[1] De Vogüé I. p. 61, Plate XXI. The Cathedral at Bosra, which he also illustrates, was similar in plan but of double the dimensions and the dome seems to have fallen in soon after it was built. A smaller basilican church was then formed in the interior.
[2] Choisy, *Hist. d'Archit.* I. 124.
[3] R. Phené Spiers, *Architecture East and West*, p. 60, &c.

early Empire had domed halls, and the mightiest dome of all time is that of the Pantheon of Rome. Domes of a certain kind exist in the primeval buildings of Greece, in the building known as the Treasury of Atreus and others. But the construction of all these differed widely from that of the domes we are now about to consider. *The Roman dome*

The subterranean Treasury of Atreus at Mycenae is formed by horizontal courses of stone gradually projected inwards on a curved line; in fact by a system of corbelling, consisting of a series of horizontal rings, each smaller than the one below, and coming together in a point at the top. Each ring has the strength of an arch laterally, to resist the pressure of the incumbent earth, but there is no arch construction vertically, and therefore this is not a true dome. *Mycenaean dome*

The great Roman domes on the other hand may be said to be moulded rather than constructed, for they are made of concrete, and are solid monolithic masses, with little or no thrust. To construct these of course centering was necessary, and in the East, the true home of the dome, timber for centering was not generally available, and some mode had to be found for doing without it. *Concrete domes*

The same difficulty applied to the construction of vaults in treeless countries, and led to various expedients. The ordinary way of building a vault is to lay the bricks or stones in horizontal courses with their beds radiating from a centre (Fig. 8 *a*). This of course involves a centering of timber on the back of which the arch stones are laid, and without this support an arch so constructed could not stand till it was joined and keyed together at the crown. The problem was to find some way of keeping the bricks or stones from falling during construction if there were no centering. It was solved in early *Vaults without centering*

36   DOMES AND VAULTS   [CH. III

Vaults without centering

times both in Egypt and Assyria in a very curious manner (Fig. 8 *b*), by laying the courses of bricks vertically instead of horizontally, so that the vault consisted of a series of rings or arches side by side, of which the joints and not the beds radiated from the centre. More than this, the rings were not exactly vertical, but inclined backwards, so that each partly rested on the one behind it. Each brick therefore as it was placed and bedded in clay against the hinder ring had adhesion enough to stick in its place till the new ring was finished

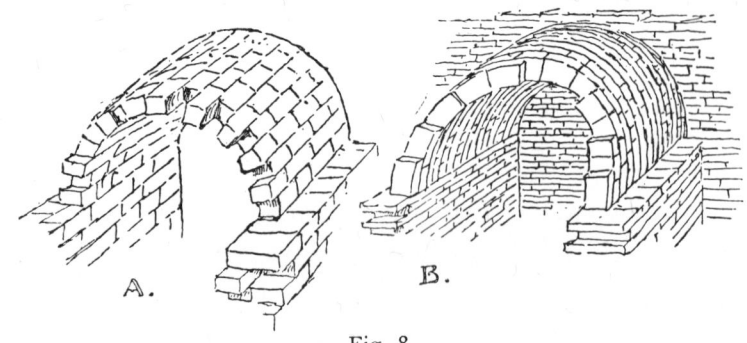

Fig. 8.

and so by being keyed became secure. It is in this way that the granaries of Rameses II at Thebes are constructed, and also the galleries at Khorsabad. The same method is adopted in the Palace of Ctesiphon, built by Chosroes II about A.D. 550, where the enormous barrel vault of the central hall, with a span of 86 ft. and a height of 105, is constructed of brickwork laid in this fashion, but in this case set in excellent mortar[1]. It should be added that this method requires an end wall

Sassanian vaults

[1] Spiers, *op. cit.* p. 77. The lower part of the arch for about half way up is laid with horizontal courses, and the section of the vault is elliptical, with the long diameter upwards, which of course reduced the inclination of the courses and made them less likely to fall before the ring was keyed.

CH. III]   DOMES AND VAULTS   37

from which to start. I have observed the same method of vaulting in the remains of the Carian portico of A.D. 587, in the harbour walls of Constantinople, and in the Yedi-Kuleh built after the Moslem conquest.

It has been already explained that the ovoid form of the dome at Ezra and the vault at Ctesiphon made it possible to lay bricks without centering for at all events the greater part of the height; the bed being less inclined to the horizon than it would have been in a semicircular arch, and the bricks therefore being less liable to slip. The same plan of inclining the beds at a less angle to the horizon than the radius of the dome or vault allowed the construction of hemispherical domes and semicircular vaults without centering or with very little. To construct a dome a central post was fixed upright with two arms or trammels capable of moving in every direction as radii, one for the soffit or intrados and one for the extrados or back of the shell. Every stone or brick was set to this radius, but with its bed to a slighter inclination, so that the adhesion of the mortar and the comparatively gentle slope of the bed was sufficient to keep it in its place till the course was completed. I think it probable a small centering must have been necessary for closing the crown where the beds would be too steeply inclined for the bricks to stay without support, but it would be very small, resting on the part already gathered over. By using interlocking bricks I have myself built a dome in this way without centering[1], and it is said that interlocking courses occur in the Eastern domes, to form a chain annihilating the thrust.

Dome construction without centering

[1] In this case at Giggleswick in Yorkshire (Plate I) no centering was used even near the crown, for when the beds towards the top became very steep the bricks were held back by clips of iron to the course below them till the ring was completed, when the irons were taken away.

Domes over a square plan

But the greatest achievement of the Eastern and Byzantine dome-builders, was to place a hemispherical dome over a square chamber. The Roman domes, of which the Pantheon is the greatest example, were placed over round buildings, so that the junction of the two presented no geometrical difficulties. But a circle inscribed in a square only touches it at four points and the problem was how to fill the four triangular spaces left at the corners in such a way as to carry the dome between those points, or in other words how to bring the square plan to a circle. M. Choisy says that the first instance of a dome on a base not round is to be found in Persia, where the corners are filled by what he calls "tromps,"

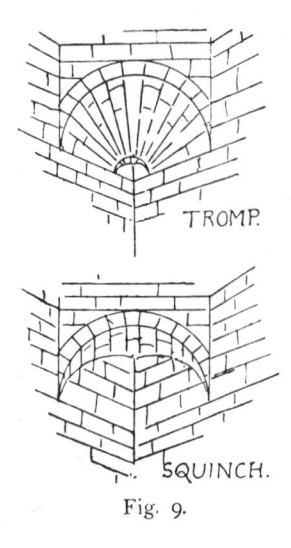

Fig. 9.

Domes on squinches

that is conical squinches (Fig. 9) which brought the square to an octagon[1]. This is the way adopted at Serbistan and Firouzabad, and still followed in that country. On the octagon it was not difficult to place a circular dome, which would be constructed without centering in the manner already described.

Domes on corbelling

In Syria another method was adopted. Large flat stones were laid across the angles, bringing the square to an octagon, and other stones across the angles of the octagon bringing the plan to 16 sides, which might if necessary be again divided so as to approach to a circular plan very closely.

[1] Choisy, *Hist. d'Archit.* I. 125.

DOMES AND VAULTS

A far more scientific and beautiful way was by the spherical pendentive, the discovery of which, or at all events its use on a serious scale, constitutes the triumph of Byzantine architecture. It is arrived at in this manner. *ABCD* (Fig. 10) is the square and the *inscribed* circle *E*

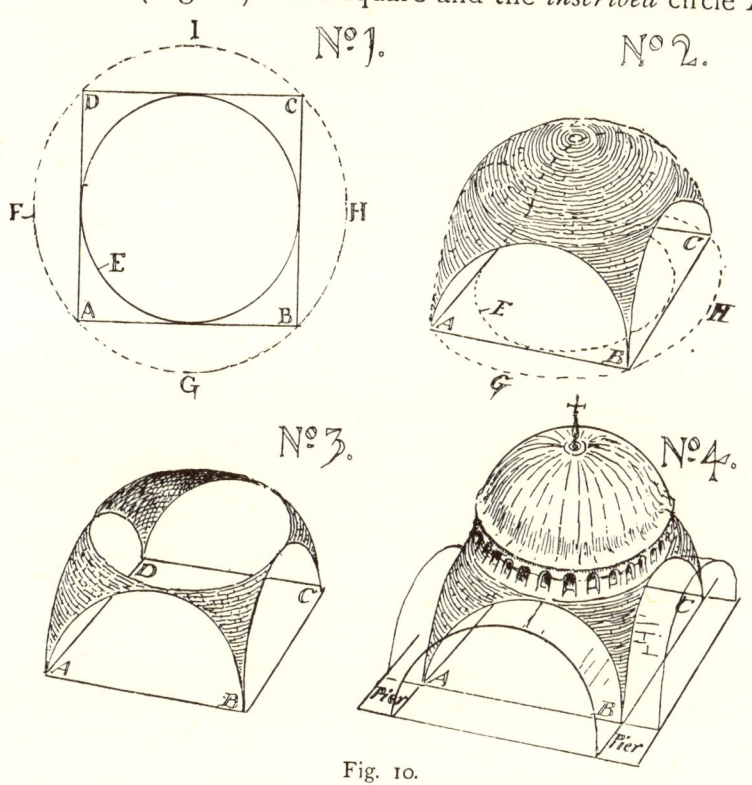

The spherical pendentive

Fig. 10.

the dome to be placed over it. Imagine a larger dome *FGHI circumscribed* about the square. Then if the four segments *ABG*, *BCH* and the other two are cut off vertically on the lines *AB*, *BC*, etc. we get the imperfect dome shown by Fig. 10, No. 2. This is in fact the vault over the crossing of the cruciform mausoleum of Galla Placidia at Ravenna, and occurs in many parts of S. Sophia.

The spherical pendentive

These are not real domes on pendentives, though some writers speak of them as if they were, but only imperfect domes. To form the real dome on pendentives it is necessary to slice off the top of this imperfect dome on a plane level with the crown of the four side arches (Fig. 10, No. 3), and from the circular ring thus formed to spring the dome. The four spherical triangles on which the dome rests,—relics of the imaginary dome *FGHI*,—are the pendentives, the strength of which lies in their being arched in two directions both horizontally and vertically, and they are supported by being wedged in between the four arches of the square (Fig. 10, No. 4). Plate I shows such a dome in actual process of construction at the period when the ring is just formed, as in Fig. 10, No. 3.

Its first appearance at S. Sophia

Although there may have been tentative approaches to this method of construction before, the first real appearance of it on a grand scale was in Justinian's great church of S. Sophia, the Holy Wisdom, at Constantinople, which was begun in A.D. 532; and the credit of it is fairly due to his architects from the Greek Ionian cities of Asia Minor, Anthemius of Tralles, and Isidorus of Miletus.

The Syrian dome

In Syria, however, they never arrived at this method, and the junction of square and circle was managed in the simpler way already described, which sufficed for moderate domes, but would have been inapplicable on a large scale. And indeed the cupola does not play a very large part in Syrian churches, which never quite abandoned the basilican plan. There are many interesting peculiarities about these Syrian buildings, which show that a fresh departure was being made in architecture. Above all it should be noted that the classic orders have disappeared. There is no pretence of decoration with the columns and entablatures of the Colosseum. Columns

The Roman orders abandoned

Plate I

THE DOME IN CONSTRUCTION

and piers are used abundantly, but they are all working members of the construction. Here and there, as at Qualb-Louzet, colonnettes are used for exterior decoration[1], but they are exceptional, and on a miniature scale like those over the Porta Aurea at Spalato, or the blank arcadings of Gothic architecture, and they are perhaps the least attractive of the examples of Syrian architecture illustrated by M. de Vogüé.

The church at Tourmanin which dates from the 6th century, and that at Qualb-Louzet[2], have dumpy towers at the west end which stand in front of the main building with a porch between them. It is curious that the same feature occurs twice in Dalmatia, in the 13th century cathedral at Traü, and in that at Cattaro, also at the cathedral of Cefalù in Sicily, and was originally adopted at Chartres. I may mention another instance of correspondence in design between Syria and Dalmatia which is afforded by the remarkable cornices over Syrian doorways, enriched with elaborate sculpture, which find a parallel on a humble scale in Byzantine doorways at Ragusa and Nona[3] that are very unlike doorways elsewhere.

Church at Tourmanin

Syria and Dalmatia

It is remarkable that among all the illustrations of sculptured ornament given in M. de Vogüé's admirable volumes there is scarcely any representation of animal life and none of human. This avoidance of figure sculpture runs through all Byzantine work from the earliest

Absence of figure sculpture in Syria

---

[1] De Vogüé, vol. II. Plate CXXIV.

[2] De Vogüé, *Qualb-Louzet*, vol. II. Plates CXXIII–CXXIX.

Tourmanin, vol. II. Plates CXXXII–CXXXV. This church unfortunately no longer exists. A note in M. Diehl's *Manuel d'Art Byzantin* tells us that it has been demolished to build a military post and a village.

[3] v. De Vogüé, vol. I. Plates XXXI, XLV, LXII, LXVIII, and my *Dalmatia, the Quarnero, and Istria*, Plate I, Fig. 2 and chap. XX. Fig. 62.

time, long before the iconoclastic movement took place. The representation of the human figure was reserved for mural decoration in painting and mosaic.

Civil architecture in Syria

Syria is rich not only in churches but also in civil and domestic buildings, all dating from a time before the Saracen conquest in the 7th century when the province was deserted by the old inhabitants. Many of these remain in almost perfect preservation, and they are valuable as among the very few surviving examples of domestic work in the Byzantine period. They are largely columnar, with open loggias and porticos, and are remarkable for the same extensive use of stone and lack of timber as the churches.

Vitality of Syrian work

M. de Vogüé observes that "while in the West the sentiment of art was expiring little by little under the barbarian rule, in the East, at least in Syria, there existed an intelligent school which maintained good traditions, and rejuvenated them by happy innovations." This remark may be extended to all Byzantine architecture, of which the Syrian school should be regarded as a part. Though inspired by Greek traditions it adopted and carried forward on new lines the Roman system of arched construction, and advanced it to the development of forms and principles, both of construction and decoration, that were entirely novel, and resulted in revolutionizing architecture.

Influence of Syria on Western art

In estimating the influence on Byzantine architecture of the school of Syrian art about which we have been speaking, one must remember the special circumstances under which it arose. The same difficulties of material did not present themselves in other countries of the Empire, and therefore many of the more marked peculiarities of the Syrian style did not travel westwards, there being no occasion for them. We may, however, recognize an Oriental influence in the gradual adoption in Constantinople and the nearer provinces of the domed church, on a plan more or less square, in preference to the older basilican type; and this influence may be traced back through Asia Minor to the older Greek kingdom of the Seleucidae, which was in its turn affected by the neighbouring schools of Persia and the East. It was also perhaps the Syrian schools and those of Asia Minor that set the example of frank abandonment of the strict classic orders. Constantine no doubt brought with him from Rome and Italy to his new capital the traditions of Vitruvius, or those that we associate with that name. His own triumphal arch at Rome is in the same classical style as those of his predecessors Titus and Severus. But if he began to build the new Rome in the style of the old, it is certain that the fashion did not last for long: the earliest buildings of the eastern part of the Empire which have come down to us are very far removed from classic example; and in shaping those differences which distinguish them from the arts of Rome the influence of oriental art certainly played a not inconsiderable part.

Whatever influence, however, the East had on the development of Byzantine architecture, it must be remembered that it was all filtered through a Greek medium, and that the prevalent character of the style was Hellenic as distinct from Roman. Therein it differs from the styles of Europe further west, in which, though Byzantine influence may be traced to a very considerable extent, the general character is distinctly Romanesque. *Syrian art acted through Greek medium*

CHAPTER IV

THE GREEK CHURCH AND RITUAL. MARBLE AND MOSAIC. THE PULVINO. VARIETIES OF CAPITAL

<small>Growth of ritual</small>

THE church architecture of the eastern part of the Roman Empire reflects the internal changes that had taken place in the religion itself. With the establishment of Christianity as the State creed came inevitably the taste for greater splendour of ritual. With the intention of making the passage from paganism more easy the heathen festivals were continued under a new Christian attribution, and the temples themselves with their sumptuous adornment were often converted into churches, and re-dedicated with allusion to the old Divinity. Thus the Parthenon at Athens, the shrine of Pallas Athene, the wise goddess, became the church of the ἁγία Σοφία, the Holy Wisdom: the temple of Theseus, the slayer of the Minotaur, was dedicated afresh to S. George, the vanquisher of the dragon: the temple of the Magna Mater at Ancyra became the church of the Θεοτόκος, the Mother of God[1]. The Pantheon at Rome,—Temple of all the Gods,—was re-consecrated to the Virgin Mary and all Saints and Martyrs, so that "where assemblies of dæmons used to be gathered there

<small>Re-dedication of temples</small>

---

[1] Cedrenus cited Texier, p. 42. It has been remarked that "the land which introduced the mother of the Gods to the Roman world also gave the name θεοτόκος (mother of God) to the church." Glover, *Conflict of Religions in the Early Roman Empire*, p. 21.

the memory of all saints and of God's Elect should be revered¹."

As with the buildings, so with the ritual. The services of the Church, now dominant, imitated and vied in splendour with the pagan ceremonies; and in proportion as greater importance was attached to the Church offices the dignity of the clergy was magnified, and elevated them into a hierarchy. The older religion of Rome can hardly be said to have had a clergy. The Pontifices, with the Emperor at their head and the Caesars in their ranks, were after all laymen. But the eastern cults, that with their more emotional and spiritual influences had largely superseded the older Latin worship, possessed a sacerdotal caste, and ceremonies and sacraments, so like those of the Church that Tertullian² and other early Apologists thought they were invented by the devil to parody the Christian rites. A recent writer observes that "the Christians readily recognized the parallel between their rites and those of the heathen, but no one seems to have perceived the real connexion between them. Quite naively they suggest the exact opposite: it was the daemons who foresaw what the Christian rites ($\iota\epsilon\rho\acute{a}$) would be and forestalled them with all sorts of pagan parodies³."

The new hierarchy

In the Church sacerdotal ideas were now firmly established. From the simple meal of the Early Communion the administration of the Sacrament had in the

---

¹ Agnellus, *vita Johannis*.
² Tertullian, *de Praescriptionibus*, cap. XL. qui (diabolus) ipsas quoque res sacramentorum divinorum idolorum mysterio aemulatur...Mithra signat illic in frontibus milites suos, celebrat et panis oblationem...habet et virgines, habet continentes.
³ Glover, *Conflict of Religions in the Early Roman Empire*, p. 159.

2nd century passed into the hands of the clergy[1], and become a mystic rite which in the Eastern church had to be secluded from the eyes of the laity. The sanctuary where the sacred functions were performed was accessible to the priests alone: and this affected very considerably the architecture of the churches.

Plan of Greek churches

The Greek church, when the ritual arrangement was fully developed, consisted of three parts. At the entrance was the narthex, a long porch or ante-church extending all across the front, beyond which during divine service, catechumens and penitents were not allowed to pass. Three or more doors led from the narthex into the ναός, nave, or body of the church where the congregation were placed, and beyond that was the bema, or platform reserved for the officiating clergy. The plan was completed by three apses, which were concealed by the iconostasis or screen with three gates in it. In the middle were the holy gates, admitting to the principal apse, where was the altar, "a name which insensibly became familiar to Christian ears," and the two side gates admitted to the lesser apses, the prothesis on one side, where the elements for the sacrament were prepared, and the diaconicon or skeuophylacion on the other, where the church vessels were kept. This, which was the final plan of the Greek church, was not arrived at all at once. The earlier churches of S. George (Fig. 16) and the Eski Djouma (Fig. 11) at Salonica are simpler, the latter being of the ordinary basilican type, and it was perhaps not till the time of Justinian that the ceremonial of Greek Christianity was finally regulated.

---

[1] Tertullian, *de Corona*, cap. III. contrasting rites based on tradition with those resting on Scripture,—Eucharistiae Sacramentum, et in tempore victus, et omnibus mandatum a Domino, etiam antelucanis coetibus, nec de aliorum manu quam praesidentium sumimus.

CH. IV] **GREEK CHURCH ARCHITECTURE** 47

These churches had no bell-towers, for they had no bells, and the congregations were summoned by beating with a wooden mallet on a long thin board or plate of metal,—a semantron, or symbolon,—which may still be heard at some places in the East.

Unlike the Latins, the Greeks separated the sexes in their services. In large churches the women sat in the *The gynae-conitis*

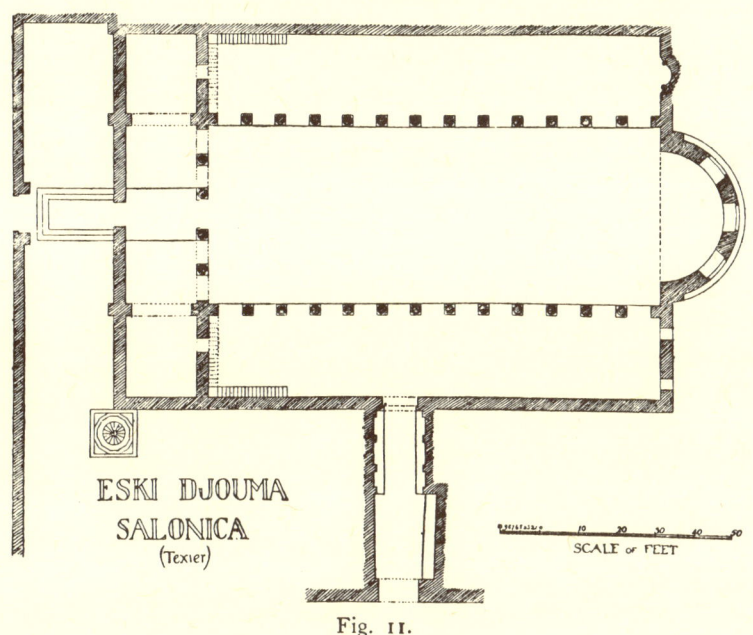

ESKI DJOUMA
SALONICA
(Texier)

SCALE of FEET

Fig. 11.

triforium gallery, reached by stairs from the narthex; where there was no triforium, in the narthex; and where there was neither narthex nor triforium they sat on one side of the nave and the men on the other.

The exterior of the buildings was of plain brickwork, sometimes, though not generally, plastered, with little or no architectural decoration; at the utmost columns and capitals between the apse windows carrying arches over *Plain exteriors* them as at S. Demetrius, Salonica (Plate II). The roofs of timber were covered with half-round tiles, the Italian *coppi*. All splendour of adornment was reserved for the inside. This was magnificent enough; the columns and capitals were of fine marble, with which the very walls were also encrusted, and the apse and dome were lined with mosaic of glass. The result was that strange mysterious beauty which invests these Byzantine churches with a character and a charm that is all their own. The effect on the imagination is to remove them, as it were, from the ordinary field of criticism, and to place them in a category by themselves, which one regards almost as one does the beauties of nature.

<small>Splendour of interior</small>

For their adornment an unlimited supply of marble was furnished by the spoils of temples, which, now that pagan worship had become illegal, were rifled without scruple. The aid of persecution had been invoked to stamp out the worship of the heathen deities, but though their adherents complained when their own weapon was turned against themselves, and found an eloquent advocate in the orator Libanius, paganism has no martyrs to celebrate. The temples were deserted. S. Jerome writes exultingly that the gilded Capitol lies in squalor, and all the temples in Rome are hung with cobwebs. S. Augustine, who approved the capital punishment of idolaters, describes the temples as partly sinking into disrepair, partly destroyed, and partly closed[1]. Their materials served as an almost inexhaustible quarry for the buildings of the new State religion, and the supply was supplemented by the waste of private and civil structures. For under the Empire the amount of marble that was

<small>Use of old materials</small>

---

[1] v. Dill, *Roman Society in the last century of the Western Empire*, p. 38. Gibbon, ch. XXVIII.

S. DEMETRIUS—SALONICA

Plate III

S. DEMETRIUS—SALONICA

quarried and imported had been enormous. Pliny tells us that M. Scaurus when Ædile, B.C. 58, had 360 columns set up in his temporary theatre, which lasted barely a single month[1]. The spendthrift Mamurra, whom Catullus and Horace ridicule, set the fashion of lining the whole of his walls with precious slabs, and making every column of solid marble, and his example was followed and surpassed by others[2]. And in the 4th century, besides the supply from the spoliation of older buildings, we are told that the marble quarries were still being worked.

The Byzantine mosaic is made of glass. According to Pliny the art of glass mosaic is as old as the time of Augustus[3], and he suggests Agrippa, or Scaurus, as among the first to use it. Under the later Empire it seems to have been practised chiefly, if not exclusively, by Greeks, and in their hands it attained a degree of perfection that has never been surpassed. A close study of their technique discovers various refinements of execution, from ignorance or disregard of which most modern attempts have lamentably failed. *Byzantine mosaic*

In Byzantine mosaic the treatment is broad and simple: the ground, whether of ultramarine blue or gold, is left largely uncovered; the figures are treated very flatly, shaded with restraint, and sometimes defined on one side and in folds of drapery by dark lines. They are generally spaced widely apart, and very rarely grouped, and when joined together they are still arranged with some distinction. Those of the 5th century are drawn with considerable remains of the old classic grace, which *Its breadth of treatment*

---

[1] Plin., *Nat. Hist.* XXXVI. i.   [2] *Ibid.* cap. vi.

[3] *Ibid.* XXXVI. cap. xxv. Pulsa deinde ex humo pavimenta in cameras transiere e vitro. Evelyn saw remains of gold mosaic in a vault at Baiae (*Diary*, 1645.)

in Justinian's time was in a measure lost, the figures of that time being often very ill drawn, not to say barbarous, though preserving all the beauty of colour to which the art owes its principal charm. Little regard is paid to architectural lines. As a rule the mosaic of the wall is carried round the edges of arches and under their soffit, without any hard and sharp line in stonework to define their form. This helps to give that strange, archaic, undesigned effect of which we are conscious in the interior of S. Mark's at Venice. For full display of colour, and especially to get the greatest value of the gold which plays so important a part in the treatment, mosaic is used preferably on curved surfaces such as apses and domes and vaults, where the gold passes from a brilliant glitter in the full light to a lovely soft and liquid brown in the half lights and shades. The superiority of mosaics thus placed to the same on a flat surface may be appreciated by comparing the brilliancy of those in the apses and domes at Ravenna, with that of the processions on each side of the nave of S. Apollinare nuovo in the same city. It would take too long to dwell on the various minor technicalities to which the old mosaics owe so much; on the ingenuity with which the workman would stick his little half inch or quarter inch cube of glass, always with the fractured edge to the front, into the cement so as to catch the light at the best angle; how he would follow the outline of the figure in arranging the tesserae of the ground, and employ various other devices which occur only to the actual handicraftsman or to those who are in the habit of designing for and with him. Working on the spot, with only a few lines traced on the surface to guide him, it is evident the mosaicist would have something of the freedom of the fresco painter.

He followed, of course the traditions of his art and the style of contemporary painting and he had fortunately only a limited palette of colours to work with, and this ensured a certain uniformity of design and standard in all the work of that school[1].

The sculpture in Byzantine churches did not, as has been said already, deal with representation of the human form. It was confined to the capitals of the pillars and the plutei, or dwarf partitions, and altar frontals, which were carved with interlacing patterns, peacocks and other birds, and geometrical figures, in very shallow relief, and sometimes pierced. The capitals underwent a new development. In strict classic usage the load on the abacus should not be wider than the top diameter of the column, and the corners of the Corinthian capital which extended beyond this were pierced and undercut in a manner that unfitted them to bear any weight at all. The load therefore which rested on the abacus, whether lintel or arch, had to be no thicker than the width of the column below the capital. It was obvious that when the lofty wall and clerestory of the Christian basilica had to be placed over the columns this thickness would not suffice for stability, and the problem was how to reconcile a thick wall with a capital intended only to carry a thin one: for in many cases actual Corinthian capitals from ancient buildings were used, and where new ones were provided they imitated the old. The device of the Greek artists was not only ingenious but audacious in its simplicity (Plate III). On the capital they placed a block of stone

Byzantine sculpture

The pulvino

[1] From this will be understood the hopelessness of the plan common in modern times, of tracing the pattern reversed on linen and glueing the tesserae face downwards on it, and then pressing the whole into the cement, so that till the mosaic is set and the linen removed the artist never sees the face of his work.

spreading upwards from the width of the column where it rested on the abacus, to the width of the wall above, and from the top of this stone they sprang their arch, of the full thickness of the wall. This dosseret, pulvino, or impost block is an entirely novel feature. It has been supposed by some to have been suggested by the fragments of entablature on the coupled columns of the church of S. Costanza at Rome (Plate XLIV), the mausoleum built by Constantine for the Princess Constantia, but it is more likely that the feature originated in the brain of some master-builder who was puzzled how to carry his wider wall on the slender column he had pilfered from an ancient building, and did it by interposing a tapered block to reduce the area of the load. One admires his audacity. It will be discussed later whether the pulvino appeared first in Italy, or began in the Byzantine school, which broke more completely with classic tradition than the contemporary schools of Italy[1]. Nothing can be more opposed to classic rule than the pulvino.

Invention of the Pulvino

Having got this new feature, based absolutely on utility, they set to work like true artists to decorate it. Preserving the solid geometrical outline on which its usefulness depends they carved its surface with leaves, and enriched it with sacred monograms in a circle on the front, or with the cypher of bishop or donor, or sometimes perhaps of the architect[2], and sometimes merely with a simple cross.

The new capital

The capitals themselves, when new ones were worked, for the use of old ones was more common in the West than in the East, underwent a great change in the direction of solidity. The influence of classic models was not lost, and though the delicate undercutting and modelling of the Corinthian capital was abandoned, the hollow abacus, the volutes and rosette survived, and the acanthus leaf was em-

---

[1] v. p. 171, inf.   [2] My *Dalmatia*, &c. vol. III. p. 361.

ployed for the foliage, generally arranged alternately in two tiers as in the ancient examples, but sometimes twisted as if blown by the wind in a very curious fashion, of which there are examples in the churches of S. Demetrius at Salonica where the leaves in the two tiers are blown in opposite directions (Plate III) and S. Sophia in the same city where they are both blown the same way, and at S. Apollinare in Classe at Ravenna where they are blown flat open.

The Byzantine leaf was not modelled so artificially as the Roman, but treated as a flat surface on which the pipings were represented by shallow lines, and the raffling by sharply cut perforations and a plentiful use of the drill. The result is curiously precious and delicate and reminds one of the shell of the sea-echinus, which is enriched with similar perforations. *[margin: Flat treatment of Byzantine foliage]*

But besides these capitals, based on the antique Corinthian, another type, quite new and original, made its appearance. The shape is that of a solid block, square above, tapered to a circle below to fit the column, and the four sides are enriched with delicate surface carving kept quite flat, and often undercut and pierced through behind, forming a sort of network of foliage over the solid block inside. In some cases the upper part is not square but retains the tradition of the Corinthian hollow abacus which gives the capital a fluted appearance like a melon. In others the horns of the Corinthian capital survive, and are sometimes turned into figures of birds and animals[1]. In short, having broken with ancient rule, there was no limit to the fancy and invention of the Greek artists in this field of decoration. *[margin: Varieties of Byzantine capital]*

---

[1] See Plate XXXV in chapter XII from S. Vitale at Ravenna and those from S. Mark's, Venice, in chapter XV.

CHAPTER V

CONSTANTINOPLE. THE WALLS AND PORTA AUREA. THE CHURCHES AT SALONICA

Of the buildings with which Constantine adorned his new capital there is nothing now to be seen above ground but a shattered and blackened column of porphyry standing on a pedestal which is disfigured and encased in rude masonry of a later date. The "burnt column," as it is generally called, stood in the "Mese" or main central street which led from the Augusteum to the Golden Gate, the triumphal way of Constantinople; and in a chamber below it, if tradition be true, lies the Palladium brought from the Old Rome when the seat of Empire was transferred to the New.

The walls of Constantinople

It is in the walls of Theodosius II, the grandson of Theodosius the Great, that the earliest examples of Byzantine art are to be found. These mighty bulwarks, consisting of an inner and outer wall and a wide moat and breastwork which, with their triple line of defence, saved Constantinople from the barbarian for a thousand years, and which still, though shattered and broken down in places, surround the city on all sides, were erected in 413 and 447 for the most part, though additions were made at the end next the Golden Horn by the Comnenian Emperors, and various repairs were carried out elsewhere from time to time.

PORTA AUREA—CONSTANTINOPLE

Plate V

CAPITAL OF PORTA AUREA—CONSTANTINOPLE

GATES OF CONSTANTINOPLE

The Porta Aurea, or triumphal gate, near the sea of Marmora (Plate IV), is the most interesting feature from an architectural point of view. It consists really of two gates, one on each line of wall. The inner is now supposed to have been a triumphal arch built by Theodosius the Great after his victory over Maximus, and to have stood at first alone outside the wall of Constantine. It would then, if this be true, have been a triple arch like those at Rome, and it is recorded to have been decorated with sculpture and statuary. When Theodosius II enclosed the city within a larger circuit his inner wall was joined on to this arch, its wide openings were reduced to defensible proportions, and it became one of the town gates. At the same time a second gateway was formed in the outer wall which remains more in its original state, though shorn of its marble facings, and of the sculptured panels of classical mythology which once adorned it. The archway is flanked by two columns of marble with very characteristic capitals (Plate V). Birds take the place of volutes at the angles, the lip of the bell is widely exposed, and is surrounded with a delicate little frill of acanthus foliage; and there are two rows of eight leaves each, in which the drill is used almost to excess. Still the Theodosian capital is a very fine one, and it marks a new departure from strict classic example, which thenceforward receded more and more into the background.

Porta Aurea

None of the other gates possess much architectural character; nor in their present state do they show much evidence of strength, being mere archways through the wall, the outer covering defences having been removed. The gate of Rhegium is the finest of them, and bears many inscriptions, one recording that the Prefect

The other gates

Constantine built it in 60 days. This was probably a repair, for the work is very hastily put together with odds and ends of masonry. Two marble columns laid flat form the lintel, and one jamb has a regular Byzantine capital taken from an older building, while its fellow has a small Ionic capital from a different source. The old iron-plated doors still hang in most of the gateways[1].

Of the Byzantine churches some followed the basilican plan and some were grouped round a central dome, though the latter plan gradually prevailed over the former. A fine example of the basilican type is the church at Salonica, now known as the ESKI DJOUMA DJAMI, or "old Friday mosque," the original Christian dedication being forgotten, which dates from early in the 5th century. It is a simple basilica (Fig. 11, p. 47 *supra*), with a nave ending in an apse, and a single aisle on each side in two storeys, the upper storey, or triforium, being the gynaeconitis or gallery for women. The proportions are considerable, the nave being about 120 ft. long with a span of nearly 50 ft. from centre to centre of the columns. The side aisles are each about 23 ft. wide from the wall to the same point. The columns have a bottom diameter of 1′ 11½″ and are about 7 diameters in height; the length of the bays from centre to centre is 9′ 5″. At the west end is a double narthex, of which the outer or exo-narthex is now very ruinous, but retains its original door into the street with marble jambs and lintel. From this a central doorway now leads into the eso-narthex; but this opening is not original, for it cuts through two small blank arches of brick which when perfect would have met in the middle, so that there

[1] Professor Van Millingen's admirable work *Byzantine Constantinople* gives an exhaustive account of the walls.

Plate VI

ESKI DJOUMA—SALONICA
Triple light between exo- and eso-narthex

Plate VII

ESKI DJOUMA—SALONICA

could have been no doorway there. Right and left are two large archways, now built up, which probably formed the original entrances. In the wall over the modern central opening is a very fine triplet (Plate VI) with deep shafts tapering from base to necking, and long fluted capitals through the wall. The wide soffits of the three arches retain their lining of mosaic, which no doubt was continued over the face of the wall above, the whole construction being of simple brickwork, now in great measure exposed. *The Eski Djouma*

The inner or eso-narthex, which is as it were a return of the aisles across the west end, opens to the nave with a triple arcade that ranges with those of the aisles. The triforium originally consisted of colonnades with round arches like those below, but with the exception of three at the west end on the south side, the columns are encased in brick piers carrying smaller and lower arches, inserted probably to steady the original construction, for the old arches can be traced in the wall above. There is no clerestory. *The eso-narthex* *The gynaeconitis*

The capitals of the nave arcades (Plate VII), which are all alike, show a Byzantine version of composite, with hollow abacus, angle volutes, and two rows of crisply raffled acanthus leaves. The bell is crowned by a frill of little acanthus leaves, like that of the capitals at the Porta Aurea in the Theodosian walls, and the necking is adorned with the same reversed. The two capitals of the western triplet leading to the narthex are nearer to the strict classic type. All have the pulvino fully developed, carved on the end, and plain at the side. The shafts are of cipollino. *The capitals*

The capitals of the upper storey or triforium are only rudely chopped out into a semblance of Ionic.

The Eski Djouma

The contrast between the principal capitals of the great arcades, which are beautifully executed, and the rudeness of the secondary capitals of windows and triforia runs through most of the Byzantine churches, and will be noticed elsewhere. It would seem that the splendid capitals of the main arcades, both here and at Constantinople, and also at Ravenna, and later at S. Mark's in Venice, were a special production of the capital, and were exported from Proconnesus, or wherever else they were carved, to churches throughout the East and the nearer shores of Italy; while the less important capitals of the upper storeys were chopped out as well as local talent permitted.

Production of Byzantine capitals

The mosaic

The soffits of the arches both in nave and triforium retain their fine mosaic lining on the soffits, though in a sadly decayed state, but that on the face of the walls is gone. The patterns consist of floral diapers, scrolls, and arabesques in colour on gold grounds, within a border which originally no doubt was doubled round the arris of the arch on to the wall face in the manner usual in Byzantine work.

The windows at Eski Djouma

The aisles are lighted by a nearly continuous arcade of round headed windows high up in the walls interrupted at intervals by solid piers. The mullion shafts are tapered from base to necking and carry simple capitals through the wall. A similar series of window arcades higher in the wall lights the triforium gallery (Fig. 12). The windows probably had wooden frames to hold the glass, for there are traces of some method of fixing them[1].

[1] Both these tiers of windows seem to have been discovered lately, for they do not appear in Signor Rivoira's illustration, of 1901. At present the windows are open to the air, for the mosque is disused, and is under repair, a new roof having lately been put on; and the floor is encumbered with huge timbers the debris of the old one, which I understand was damaged by fire.

CH. V] CHURCHES AT SALONICA

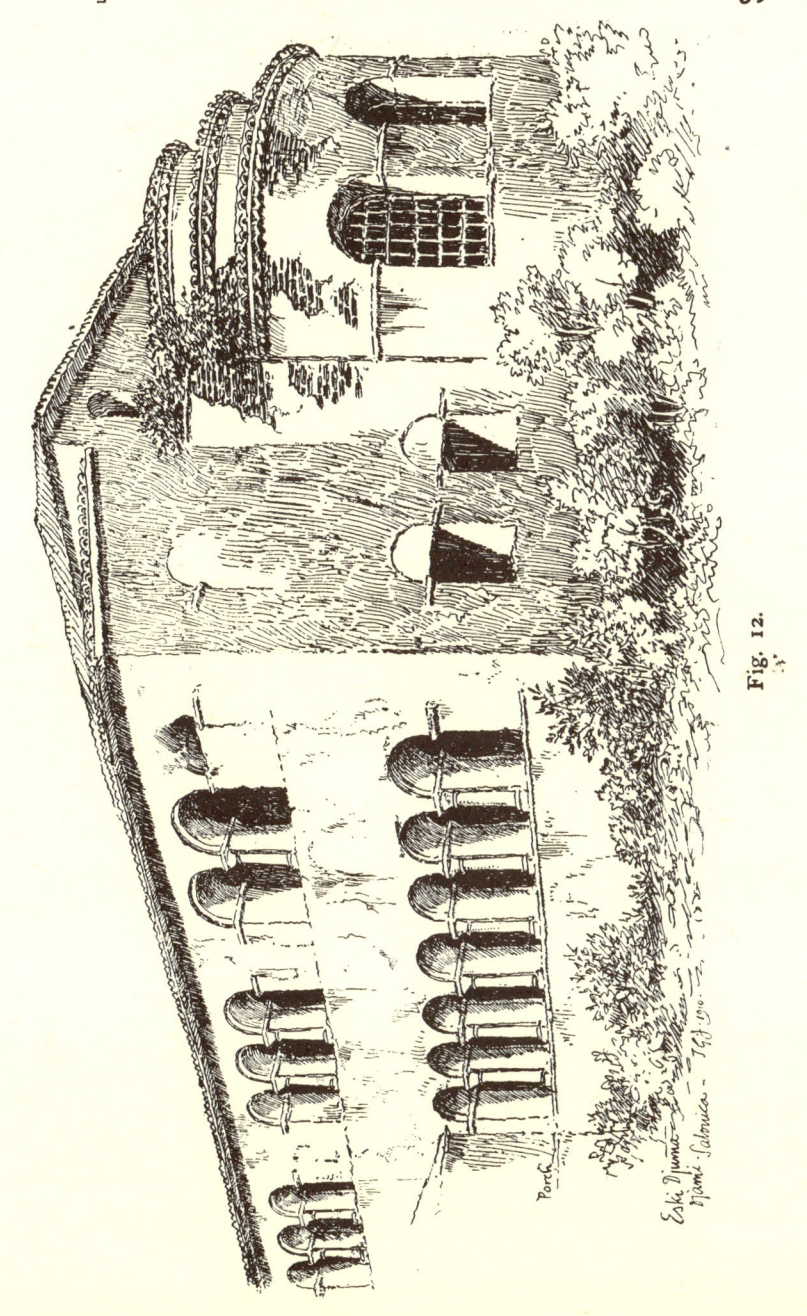

Fig. 12.

Eski Djouma, Salonica

Besides the western entrance the Eski Djouma has a south porch with a barrel vault springing from dwarf pilasters with flat Byzantine capitals; a very interesting feature of the building.

The apse at Eski Djouma

The apse (Fig. 12), which is semicircular both inside and out, is lighted by three very large round headed windows, and has no architectural feature outside but a simple moulding at the impost level of the window arches. Inside, the semi-dome was decorated with fresco painting, as were also the soffits of the aisle windows, which were painted in patterns like mosaic, inside and outside of a line which marks the place of the window frame.

It is characteristic of the early date of this church that it is without the triple arrangement at the east end of the later Byzantine ritual; and has, besides the single great apse, only a small niche at the end of the north aisle, which perhaps served as a skeuophylacion.

This ancient church at Salonica has been described at length because it is the earliest, and in its prime must have been one of the finest of its class both in scale and richness of adornment. But in its present state of decay and neglect it was far surpassed in beauty by its better preserved neighbour S. DEMETRIUS.

S. Demetrius, Salonica

The latter church, though like the rest of the Christian buildings it was turned into a mosque, had been well cared for by the Turks. It has now[1], to the irreparable loss of art, been destroyed by fire, and we are told only bare walls remain. The exterior, as is usual with the Byzantine churches, has little to commend it; but the interior (Plate VII A) was perhaps the most beautiful of them all, and with the exception of S. Sophia at Constantinople, no other was so well preserved. It is a five-aisled basilica (Fig. 13), with a nave some 25 ft. longer than that at Eski Djouma, but narrower by about 12 ft., the span from centre to centre

[1] In Aug. 1917.

*Plate VII*A

T. G. J.   SALONICA—S. Demetrius

Plate VIII

S. DEMETRIUS—SALONICA

CH. V] CHURCHES AT SALONICA 61

of columns being about 38 ft., and each of the aisles being S. De-
about 16 ft. wide. Both aisles had galleries at different metrius
levels, the outer and lower one looking into the inner
aisle through an upper colonnade which carried the floor
of the gallery over the inner aisle; which gallery in its
turn looked into the nave through another upper colonnade
at a higher level. The nave walls, and the walls dividing
the outer and inner aisles, therefore consist each of two
storeys of colonnades of different heights, over which in
the nave is a clerestory.

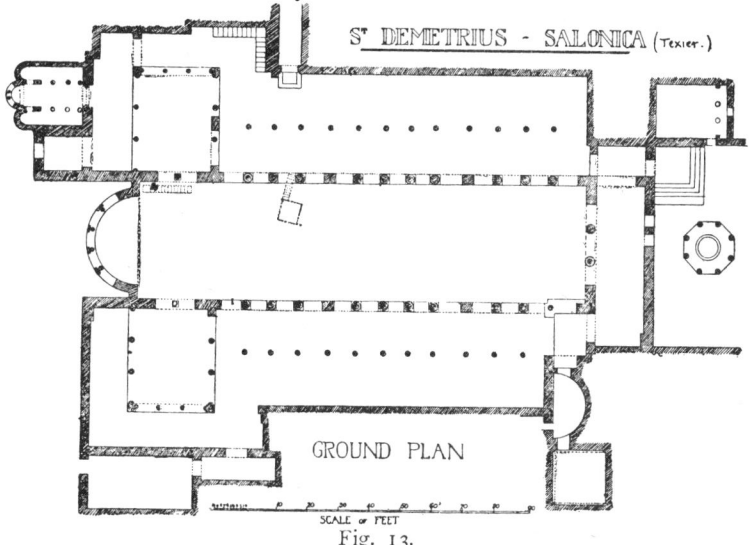

ST DEMETRIUS - SALONICA (Texier.)

GROUND PLAN

SCALE OF FEET
Fig. 13.

The nave consists of twelve bays in length, which The nave
are divided into groups of three, five, and four by two
piers, a feature new to the style. Eastward it is prolonged by the intervention of a transept before the apse.
This evidently once opened to the nave on each side by
a lofty arch, which in consequence perhaps of some signs
of failure is now supported by sub-arches and piers. The
two-storey aisle is carried round the sides and ends of

S. Demetrius

the transept and a carved cornice surrounds the apse at its springing.

The columns of the nave arcade have shafts with a lower diameter of 1' 8¼", and about nine diameters high, but they are of all lengths, some mounted on rather tall pedestals and some without any, as if they were spoils of an older building. They are all of marble, the four in the middle group and the two of the western triplet opening to the narthex being of verd' antico from Thessaly, the rest of cipollino. Their capitals are of the very finest Byzantine work, and nothing better has ever been done in that school. They are of various kinds; there is the "blown-leaf" type (Plate III), and there are others of the more ordinary quasi-composite form: there are examples of the "melon" variety, and there are others with birds at the angles instead of volutes. One in particular with imperial eagles, now, alas! headless, surmounting a basket-shaped bell, is a triumph of Byzantine art. The wreath surrounding it is formed with a scroll of acanthus, undercut and standing away from the bell, surmounted by a ring on which the birds' feet rest (Plate VIII).

The capitals

The arches spring from a pulvino, or impost block of grey stone with a circle, containing a figure perhaps representing the Labarum.

The triforium

The upper storey, or triforium, has a marble colonnade, and a simple marble parapet divided by slight lines into panels. The capitals, as in the Eski Djouma, are very simple, some rudely Ionic, some only blocked out at each corner, pulvino and capital in one. The clerestory above consisted of wide arched windows with small shafts and piers alternately, but most of the openings are now blocked.

CH. V] CHURCHES AT SALONICA 63

The whole of the arches in both storeys and their spandrils were lined with marble slabs (Plate IX). On the arches they were arranged like voussoirs, dark and light alternately, though as they are all full of figure the alternation is not very regular or pronounced, and the effect is not forced. The spandrils and walls up to the first floor were faced with fine figured marbles in slabs, and

The marble linings

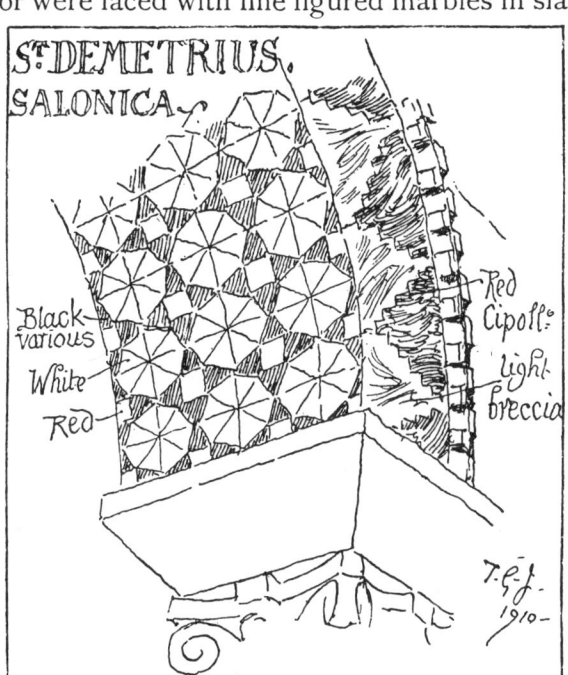

Fig. 14.

a square of marble mosaic occupied the middle of each spandril over the column. Above, at the first floor level, was a singular band of marble mosaic representing in perspective a modillion cornice, the modillions at certain intervals changing their perspective direction. It is perhaps a ridiculous freak, but it does not produce any illusion, and tells simply as a band of colour. The extrados of the voussoirs has a narrow red marble label with the double

Marble mosaic

dentil, front and back, which the Venetians used so much in later times, and which occurs also at S. Sophia in Constantinople. A red marble cornice finishes this storey.

The arches and spandrils of the upper storey were faced with marble like those below. The splendour of these walls was almost beyond belief. Very little if any of it now remains.

The soffits of the side arches of the nave are now of plain plaster, but they were originally lined with marble like their faces. The arches of the western triplet still retained their marble soffits, those in the side arches formed with veined marble, split and opened to compose a figure, and that in the middle arch with a pattern in mosaic (Fig. 14). The soffit did not project in the manner followed afterwards at Venice to receive the facing slab of the voussoirs, but the two seemed to be mitred together at the edge of the arch. One of the arches in the south transept also retained its soffit of grey marble, split and opened to form a pattern.

From a small piece of marble facing remaining on the outside of the apse it may be supposed that the exterior of the church was partly at all events veneered with marble like the nave. At present the exterior brickwork is plastered and brilliantly whitewashed.

In the interior the marble facing was confined to the nave. The lesser arcades dividing the aisles were decorated with glass mosaics, which have only recently been discovered below the plaster. Those that have been exposed are believed to be all that remain, for so far from hiding these decorations, the Turks have made careful search for more by removing plaster elsewhere, but without success. They were mostly confined to a part of the secondary arcade dividing the two north aisles, and occupied the soffits and spandrils of the arches, but there were also panels of

Plate IX

S. DEMETRIUS—SALONICA

mosaic on the responds of both main arcades. In beauty of execution these works will bear comparison with any of those at Ravenna or Parenzo. They represented various saints, there was the Virgin between two angels, and in many cases there were little figures to represent the donors of the several panels. One of those on the responds of the great arcade had S. Demetrius between the figures of a bishop and a civic dignitary, whom an inscription in four iambic lines described as the founders of the church:—

S. Demetrius. The mosaics

The founders' picture

ΚΤΙCΤΑC ΘΕѠΡΕΙC ΤΟΥ ΠΑΝΕΝΔΟΞΟΥ ΔΟΜȢ
ΕΚΕΙΘΕΝ ΕΝΘΕΝ ΜΑΡΤΥΡΟC ΔΗΜΗΤΡΙΟΥ
ΤΟ ΒΑΡΒΑΡΟΝ ΚΑΥΔѠΝΑ ΒΑΡΒΑΡѠΝ CΤΟΛѠ
ΜΕΤΑΤΡΕΠΟΝΤΟC ΚΑΙ ΠΟΛΙΝ ΛΥΤΡΟΥΜΕΝΟΥ[1].

The figures were evidently portraits, but unfortunately they were not named, or we should be able to fix the exact date of the church. For the civilian M. Diehl suggests the Prefect Leontius, who is recorded to have repaired and adorned the chapel of S. Demetrius, to whom he attributed his recovery from an illness in 412–413. But the architecture will not bear so early a date: the piers dividing the nave colonnade into groups, and the decoration of the apse with columns and capitals on the outside must be referred to a later period than that of the Eski Djouma. The reference to the defeat of the barbarians seems to throw some light on the matter. In 584 the city was attacked by Slavs or Avars whom the citizens defeated with the help of the Saviour and S. Demetrius, as the old records have it, and this is almost exactly the date of the very similar

[1] In this and other Greek inscriptions the words are not divided. I have divided them for clearness. For καυδωνα, which is unintelligible, my friend the late Vice-Provost of Eton suggested κλυδωνα. MM. Diehl and de Tourneau read cτολων but there is no final ν in the inscription. v. Illustration in M. Diehl's *Manuel*, p. 191.

J. A.

S. Demetrius

mosaics in S. Apollinare Nuovo at Ravenna after its re-consecration to Catholic use. As the founders appear in the mosaics and are shown with the square nimbus one may fairly conclude that the pictures and the church are coeval. This would make the church of S. Demetrius

Its date

a little later than that of Parenzo which was built by the Bishop Euphrasius between 535 and 543, and contemporary with that of Grado by the Patriarch Elias between 571 and 586, and the style of the architecture seems to me to point to that conclusion.

Amid these mosaics at S. Demetrius however are three medallions representing the saint between a priest on his right holding a book, and an archbishop with the pallium also holding a book on his left. An inscription below reads thus, in an iambic distich :—

Its early restoration

✠ ΕΠΙ ΧΡΟΝΟΝ ΛΕΟΝΤΟC ΗΒΟΟΝΤΑ ΒΛΕΠΕΙC
ΚΑΥΘΕΝΤΑ ΤΟ ΠΡΙΝ ΤΟΝ ΝΑΟΝ ΔΗΜΗΤΡΙΟΥ.

"Of Leo's time in youthful bloom is seen
Demetrius' fane, which burned before had been."

The question is to which Emperor Leo and to what fire this refers. There was a fire in 584 from which the citizens were called away to repel the barbarian attack, and there was another fire in 690 which does not seem to have been so serious. The two first Leos in the 5th century are too early. M. Diehl refers the inscription to Leo III (717–741) the Isaurian, but Leo III and Leo IV were iconoclasts and surely would not have allowed their names to be associated with an image. There remain Leo the Armenian (813–820), and Leo the Philosopher (886–911), to one of whom it would seem the inscription refers, for there is no doubt it is of a different date from the other mosaics into the middle of which it has been inserted. If the inscription may be taken to imply that the Emperor helped to restore the church that would be consistent with the character of Leo V the Armenian, who helped the Venetians to build their church of S. Zaccaria, and sent them "excellent masters in architecture." But he too was an iconoclast, and it is probably Leo VI who is meant. Or again, Leo may have been a bishop, and not an Emperor.

S. Demetrius, Salonica

On the north wall near the west end is a large mural monument with a long inscription in hexameters to the memory of Lucas Spantouna who died in 1480. As this was 50 years after the final capture of Salonica by the Turks under Murad II in 1430 it shows that the Christians were not at first dispossessed of the church[1].

At Constantinople there is but one church of the basilican type, and that is on a small scale and now unfortunately in ruins. The church of S. JOHN THE BAPTIST, now the Mir Akhor Djami (Fig. 15), in the Psammatia quarter, was founded in 463 by a wealthy Roman named Studius. It has a nave with side aisles, over which was once a triforium gallery, opening to the nave by another colonnade. In the side walls two tiers of windows light the aisle and gallery respectively. The single apse has had the upper part re-built by the Turks. The nave is eight bays long, and is now roofless, but in Salzenberg's time it seems to have been perfect. At present the narthex is the only part covered and in use as a mosque. This is a beautiful piece of work, with a strong classic feeling in the wide spreading composite

S. John of Studius, Constantinople

---

[1] A communication from Salonica that has just reached me (Nov. 1917) describes a crypt that has been discovered since the recent fire, under the Eastern chapel of S. Demetrius. It contains frescoes (? mosaics) dated 6811, i.e. A.D. 1303, and therefore coeval with those at the Church of the Chora at Constantinople which they appear to resemble. See preface.

S. John the Baptist

capitals of the columns, which support a level entablature without arches, as does also the lower range of columns in the interior. The entablature of the narthex (Plate X) however is far removed from pure classic, and so closely resembles that of the church of SS. Sergius and Bacchus (Fig. 19) which was built in the reign of the Emperor Justin I (518–527) by his nephew Justinian, that it must be attributed to that date rather than, as most writers have done, to the original foundation of the church and convent

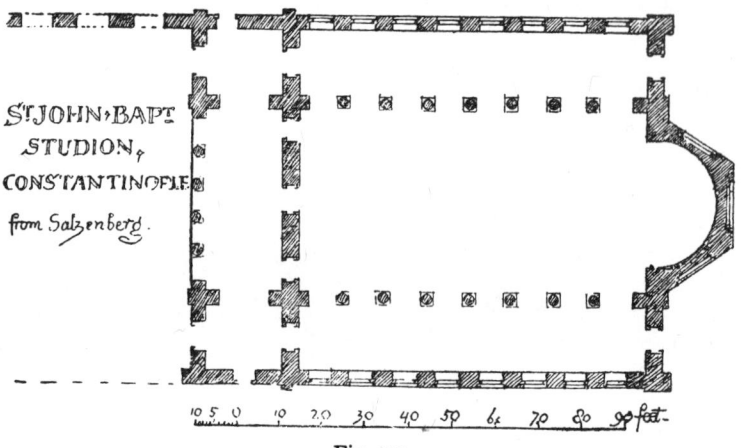

Fig. 15.

The sculpture of the façade

by Studius in 463. It has the same pulvinated frieze of delicate undercut Byzantine foliage, now nearly all broken away, but retaining enough to show what it was, and the same cornice above. The corona has disappeared from the profile, and the modillions and other features are so smothered with ovolos, beads and reels, and such-like conventional ornaments that their architectural propriety suffers. The modillions in particular are little more than lumps of confused ornament. The intercolumniations of this portico are now filled with sashes, but originally they

Plate X

S. JOHN BAPTIST, CONSTANTINOPLE

had marble door-cases fitted between the pillars, two of which exist, and the part over the lintel would have been open, up to the entablature.

The building was preceded by an atrium, of which the walls partly remain, and contain marble door-cases now blocked up, one of which, if I understood my Turkish informant aright, is credited with saintly if not miraculous properties.

But coincidently with these basilican churches the dome made its appearance in the European provinces of the Eastern Empire. The church of S. GEORGE at Salonica (Fig. 16), now the Orta Sultan Osman Djamisi, is a round church with a choir and apse projected eastward, and the nave is covered by a dome with a span of 80 ft. The plan and the dome, however, are both rather Roman than Byzantine. The wall of the round part is of immense thickness, and contains, besides a lofty arch opening to the choir, seven arched recesses under barrel vaults over which are round-headed windows. The dome which springs above them is also lit by small semi-circular openings. The wall, 18 ft. thick on the ground floor, is reduced from the outside to about half that thickness at the level from which the dome springs, and it is carried up as a drum, level with the top of the dome, to support a flat pyramidal roof of timber. The plan being circular presents no difficulty to the construction of the dome, which is steadied not only by the great thickness of the outside wall, but by the weight of the brick drum that surrounds and conceals it. Though constructed probably at the end of the 4th century, and not much before the Eski Djouma, it retains much more of the character of Roman art. The plan, and the recesses in the wall, forcibly recall the Pantheon

S. George, Salonica

ST GEORGE
SALONICA
(Texier)

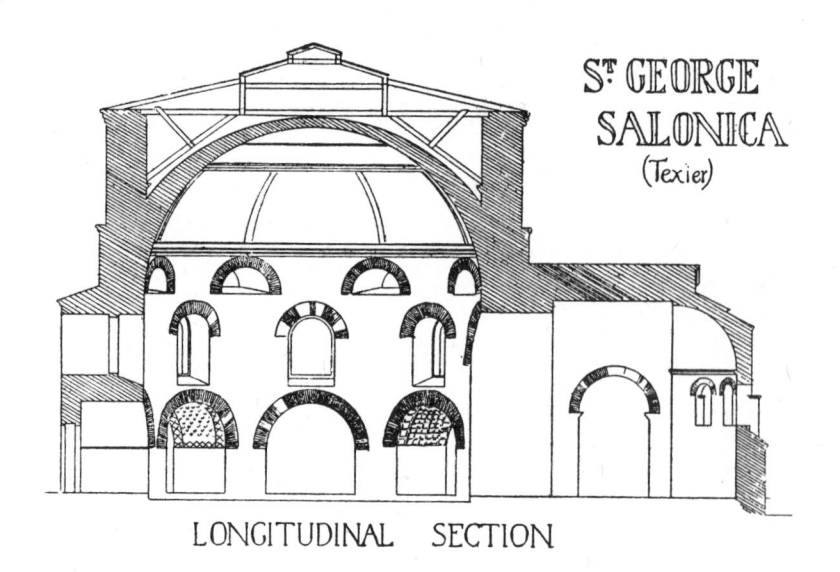

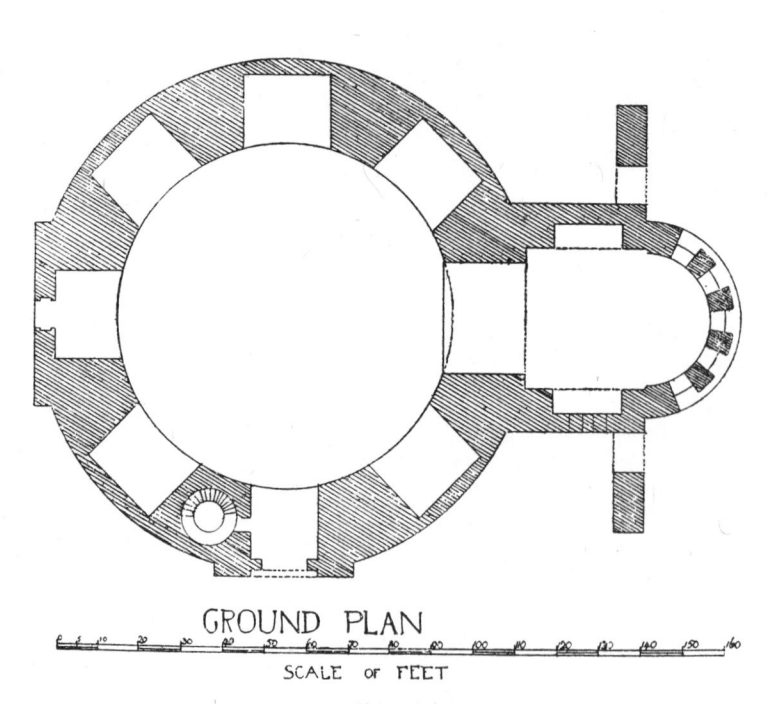

LONGITUDINAL SECTION

GROUND PLAN

SCALE OF FEET

Fig. 16.

at Rome; and the drum that hides the dome, with its pyramidal roof, resembles Diocletian's Temple of Jupiter, now the Duomo of Spalato, which preceded it by nearly a century. The apse is like that of the Eski Djouma, quite plain on the outside, with wide round-headed windows, and nothing but a slight impost moulding at their springing.

S. George

The chapels or recesses in the side walls have their barrel vaults decorated with mosaic, a good deal patched with painted plaster. One of them is very pretty,—a sort of diaper of birds at regular intervals alternating with rosettes of flowers, resembling slightly a mosaic in the vault of the archbishop's chapel at Ravenna. It has also some resemblance to the mosaics on the annular vault of S. Costanza at Rome. Most of the others are imitations of coffering, with the mouldings shaded illusively, and the effect is uninteresting.

The mosaics

The dome has retained a fine mosaic all round it, and half way up; but the central disc has been destroyed, and is now finished with plain white plaster. The surface, of which the circumference, as M. Texier says, is more than 72 yards, is divided into eight compartments, in each of which are figures of saints standing in front of an architectural composition, representing in a conventional way churches with apses, hanging lamps, altars and domes, flanked by towers, and adorned with curtains, while peacocks and storks perch in some of the niches. The ground is of gold. The saints have their hands extended in attitude of prayer; they have no nimbus, and their names are inscribed, with the month of their festival.

The dome

These mosaics, which have been very highly praised, seem to me less interesting than is usual with Byzantine

72   SALONICA   [CH. V

S. George
The
mosaics
of the
dome

work of the kind. Architecture even when treated as it is here, and in the wall decoration of Pompeii, in an abstract and conventional way, never rises to a high level of ornament: and here it certainly gives a dullness to the design. It is difficult to derive any pleasure from these fantastic impossible structures, with tabernacle insecurely perched on tabernacle and pavements in false

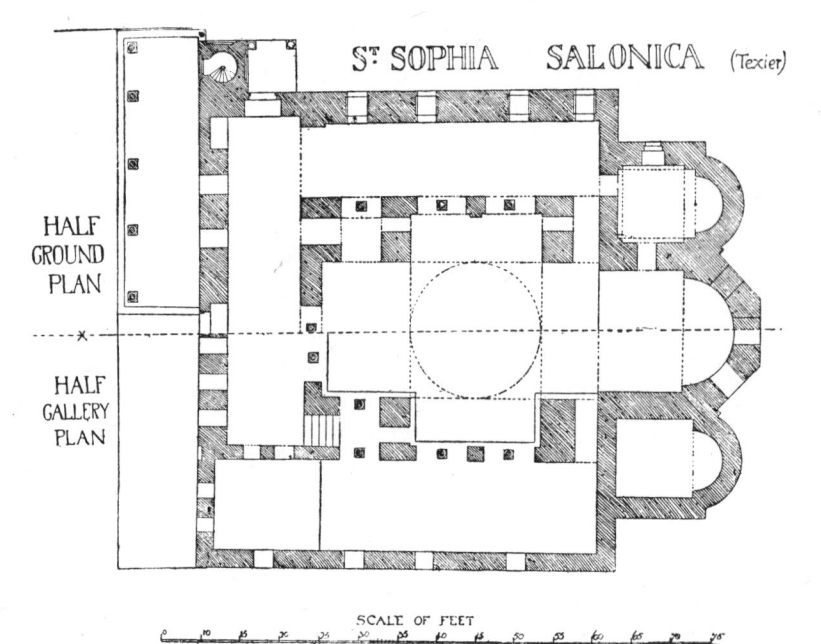

Fig. 17 (from Texier).

perspective. Nor do architectural forms lend themselves well to display of colour, for which the draperies of figures and the foliage of trees give such splendid opportunities in other mosaics at Salonica; and it is to magnificence of colour that the art of the mosaicist must trust for its supreme effects.

As bearing upon the antiquity of these mosaics,

M. Texier observes that all the saints commemorated lived before the reign of Constantine.

It is in the old cathedral of S. SOPHIA at Salonica (Fig. 17) that we first get the domical church on a square plan instead of the long basilica, and in its arrangements there is something tentative, as if it were an experiment. The central part of the church consists of a Greek cross, with a dome over the crossing and four barrel vaults over the arms. The eastern arm is prolonged by one bay, and finishes with an apse, which is semicircular within and polygonal without. A screen of columns fills the outer arches of the transepts. Outside is a wide aisle with a gallery above it, which runs round the three sides, north, west, and south, and the plan is completed by two lateral apses at the east end, which however do not correspond with the aisles. The plan is thus brought to a square, with the three apses projected eastwards.

The dome springs from pendentives; it is not however a true circle, but rather a square with the corners rounded off, so that the pendentives are small and only imperfectly developed. On the outside the square base of the dome is carried some way up the curve of the hemisphere, and forms a drum pierced with windows, and at the angles are diagonal buttresses running back to the shell of the cupola (Fig. 18). All this looks as if the architect were attempting a form of construction with which he was not familiar, and this disposes of the tradition that the church was built by Anthemius, fresh from the triumphant construction of the other S. Sophia at Constantinople. The cathedral of Salonica is no doubt the older of the two, though perhaps not by much. The latest authorities date it about 495.

S. Sophia The screen walls in the transepts have four marble columns with "blown leaf" capitals, and in these it is interesting to observe the survival of the Corinthian

Fig. 18.

caulicoli, which are lost in that at S. Demetrius (Plate III). Another capital of a column in the north-west of the nave has a beautiful veil of Byzantine foliage pierced and undercut, which is now unfortunately a good deal damaged.   *S. Sophia*

S. Sophia is remarkable for its mosaics, which have only lately been fully exposed, and have provoked much discussion among archaeologists. In 1890 the church was seriously injured by a fire, and remained in a half-ruined state till 1908 when the French Government commissioned M. Le Tourneau to examine and report on the Byzantine monuments at Salonica. Since then the restoration of the church has been undertaken by the Ottoman Government, and when I saw it was approaching completion. The mosaics of the dome were illustrated by M. Texier in 1864, but his reproductions are very conventional and give little idea of the original. M. Le Tourneau had the advantage of examining them from scaffolding during the process of cleaning and exposure, by which they are now restored to view in all their original brilliance[1].   *The mosaics*

On the apse is a figure of the Virgin enthroned with the infant Christ on her lap, and placed on a field of gold. Her purple dress is elaborate, and beautifully varied, and the figure of the child is vested in gold and stretches out an arm to bless with the happiest effect. The Virgin's nimbus is represented by a line on the gold ground. Round the front rim or arch of the semi-dome is a rich border of colour, and a text from the 65th Psalm:—   *The apse mosaic*

✠ ΠΛΗΘΗϹΟΜΕΘΑ ΕΝ ΤΟΙϹ ΑΓΑΘΟΙϹ
ΤΟΥ ΟΙΚΟΥ ϹΟΥ ΑΓΙΟϹ Ο ΝΑΟϹ
ϹΟΥ ΘΑΥΜΑϹΤΟϹ ΕΝ ΔΙΚΑΙΟϹΥΝΗ ✠

---

[1] The expense of cleaning and exposing them was borne by the French Government. Messrs Diehl and Le Tourneau have published an illustrated monograph on these mosaics of S. Sophia in the *Monuments et Mémoires de l'Académie des Inscriptions et Belles-Lettres*, Tom. XVI. Fascicule I.

S. Sophia The mosaic

At the lower margin of the semi-dome is another inscription which is imperfect, being interrupted by the feet and pavement of the seated Madonna:—

✠ ĶOΘC̄TωNΠPωNHMωNCTEPEωCONTON
OIKONTOYTONEωCTHCCYNTEΛEI * * * *
* * TONΠPOCΔOΞANCHNKAIMONOΓENOYC
COYỸYKAITOYΠANAΓIOYCOYP̄NC.

which with the abbreviations expanded reads thus:—

✠ κύριε ὁ Θεὸς τῶν πατέρων ἡμῶν στερέωσον τὸν οἶκον τοῦτον ἕως τῆς συντελεί * * * * * * τὸν πρὸς δόξαν σὴν καὶ μονογενοῦς σου υἱοῦ καὶ τοῦ παναγίου σου πνεύματος[1].

Later insertion of the Madonna

It is evident from this that the figure of the Madonna is a later insertion into an older mosaic, and M. Le Tourneau found traces in the gold ground of a large cross, which as at S. Irene in Constantinople probably formed the original subject without any figure. He observes in confirmation of this that the same text from the Psalms appears in connexion with the cross at S. Irene. From the nature of the technique he attributes the figure of the Virgin to the 8th century after the end of the iconoclastic movement and the restoration of image worship.

The barrel vault that precedes the apse is finely decorated with a cross in a blue circle on the crown of the arch, and two broad bands of ornament at the springing, the rest of the surface being of plain gold.

The mosaics of the dome

The mosaics of the dome, which are almost perfect, represent the Ascension, by a seated figure of our Lord in a circle at the crown, and round the lower part are

---

[1] Messrs Diehl and Le Tourneau suggest for the lacuna συντελε(σεως καὶ σῶσον αὐ)τόν, but the first word should surely be συντελείας or συντελειώσεως.

figures of the Virgin standing in the attitude of prayer between two angels, and the twelve apostles. Two flying angels support the central circle, and below them is the text from the Acts, ΑΝΔΡΕC ΓΑΛΙΛΑΙΟΙ ΤΙ ΕCΤΗΚΑΤΕ, &c., &c. The effect of the whole leaves an impression of pearly greys and blues, and faint tones of colour on a gold ground, and I know no other mosaic so beautiful. The draperies are not much shaded or modelled, but the folds are drawn with lines. The attitudes of the figures are a good deal varied. Some rest their heads on their hands, others look up with an arm thrown over the head, some stand front face, others sideways, and this attempt at expression and individuality speaks of a much later date than that of the fabric. In fact, M. Le Tourneau has observed traces of alteration and has satisfied himself that though the figure of our Lord is probably part of the original decoration in the 5th or 6th century, together with some fragments of inscriptions that remain, the 15 figures and the trees that divide them, with the rest of the design, were inserted into the old field of gold in the 10th or early in the 11th century: a conclusion which is disputed by a later writer[1], who assigns them to the end of the 9th. I think the latter is nearer the truth.

The Virgin and her attendant angels have the nimbus, but the apostles have none.

In front of the church was an open portico carried on ancient columns, some of which were of verd' antico. They supported pointed arches of Turkish work, and capitals of the same, but may originally have carried a Byzantine arcade on Byzantine capitals. This portico is shown in Messrs Texier and Pullan's book. When

[1] Smirnoff, cited in Dalton's *Byzantine art and archaeology*, p. 377.

S. Sophia I was there the columns and capitals lay on the ground, the effect no doubt of the fire, but it was about to be re-built as part of the restoration.

Before the church is now a large open space, littered with building materials, where no doubt there was originally an atrium, of which however no traces remain.

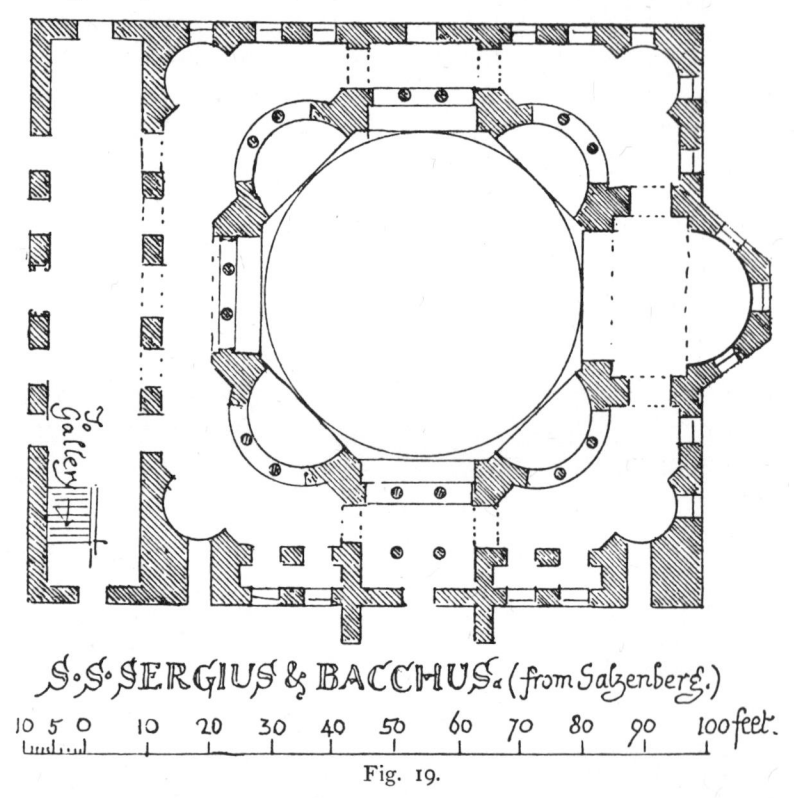

SS. SERGIUS & BACCHUS. (from Salzenberg.)

Fig. 19.

SS. Sergius and Bacchus, Constantinople
In the church of SS. Sergius and Bacchus—which Mahomet the conqueror called Kuchuk Aya Sofia, or little S. Sophia,—at Constantinople, we find a more developed example of a domed church, square in plan, designed by a surer hand, and a little later in date

CONSTANTINOPLE

than S. Sophia at Salonica. It is one of the many churches which Procopius says was built by Justinian in the reign of his uncle Justin I, during which he had a large share in the administration[1]. Side by side with the church of SS. Sergius and Bacchus, in the same enclosure and with the same approach, Justinian built another church, equal to it in splendour, "the two outshining the sun with the brilliancy of their stones." This second church, which has disappeared, was basilican, having its pillars κατ' εὐθύ, while in the other they were mostly ἐν ἡμικύκλῳ. The irregularity in plan of

SS. Sergius and Bacchus

The vanished basilica

Fig. 20.

S. Sergius on the south side seems to suggest the place of contact with its twin structure (Fig. 19).

The plan

The surrounding aisle, which is of two storeys is brought into an irregular octagon by semicircular niches in the four angles, which are semi-domed both below and above the gallery floor. Eight piers within this figure form a true octagon, and four exedrae with pillars ἐν ἡμικύκλῳ fill out the oblique angles. Of the other four sides that to the east is prolonged with an apse beyond the square outline, and the other three have two columns each κατ' εὐθύ. These 14 columns carry a horizontal

[1] Procop. *de Aedif.* Lib. I. ταῦτα γὰρ ἅπαντα οὗτος ὁ βασιλεὺς ἐπὶ τοῦ θείου Ἰουστίνου βασιλεύοντος ἐκ θεμελίων ἐδείματο.

SS. Sergius and Bacchus

entablature which supports the gallery floor (Plate XI); its design has travelled far from the classic model, and in its detail is almost identical with that of the Studion which has been already described. The pulvinated frieze with its undercut and pierced foliage (Fig. 20) is very beautiful, but the modillion cornice, overloaded with conventional ornament, is undeniably clumsy. The "melon-formed" capitals of this storey are admirable examples of a type

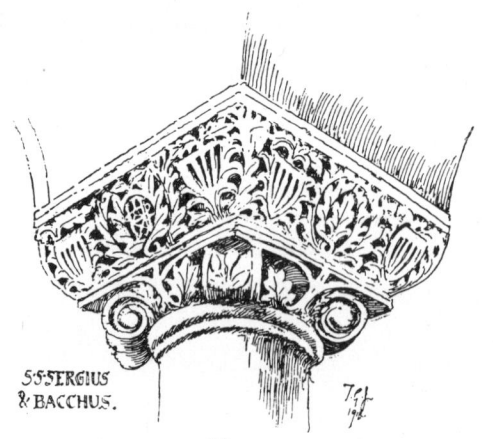

Fig. 21.

which occurs also at Ravenna, Salonica, and Parenzo. Those of the upper storey have a quasi-pulvino (Fig. 21) which has descended and become merged in an Ionic capital with rude and almost barbarous volutes. The gallery runs all round, except where interrupted on the east side by the opening to the apse which occupies both storeys. The aisle and gallery above it are each ceiled with an annular vault, like the aisle of S. Costanza at Rome, and in this way the awkwardness of the protrusion of the exedrae into the aisle is avoided, which causes such confusion in the aisle vaults of S. Vitale at Ravenna.

SS. SERGIUS AND BACCHUS—CONSTANTINOPLE

CONSTANTINOPLE

The dome, with a diameter of 52 ft., springs from the octagon and has no pendentives, but 16 ribs, two on each face, and the panel between them is arched from rib to rib. The angle of the octagon comes in the centre of a panel and runs up and loses itself in a rather artless manner. There are eight windows in the dome, one over each face of the octagon.

SS. Sergius and Bacchus

An inscription in hexameter verse in white letters on a blue ground runs round the church on the upper part of the frieze: the beginning is hidden by the mimbar:—

(ΑΛΛΟΙ ΜΕΝ ΒΑ)ϹΙΛΗΕϹ ΕΤΙΜΗϹΑΝΤΟ ΘΑΝΟΝΤΑϹ
ΑΝΕΡΑΣ ѠΝ ΑΝΟΝΗΤΟϹ ΕΗΝ ΠΟΝΟϹ ΗΜΕΤΕΡΟϹΔΕ
ΕΥϹΕΒΙΗΝ ϹΚΗΠΤΟΥΧΟϹ ΙΟΥϹΤΙΝΙΑΝΟϹ ΑΕΞѠΝ
ϹΕΡΓΙΟΝ ΑΙΓΛΗΕΝΤΙ ΔΟΜѠΙ ΘΕΡΑΠΟΝΤΑ ΓΕΡΑΙΡΕΙ
ΧΡΙϹΤΟΥ ΠΑΓΓΕΝΕΤΑΟ ΤΟΝ ΟΥ ΠΥΡΟϹ ΑΤΜΟϹ ΑΝΑΠΤѠΝ
ΟΥ ΞΙΦΟϹ ΟΥΧ ΕΤΕΡΗ ΒΑϹΑΝѠΝ ΕΤΑΡΑΞΕΝ ΑΝΑΓΚΗ
ΑΛΛΑ ΘΕΟΥ ΤΕΤΛΗΚΕΝ ΥΠΕΡ ΧΡΙϹΤΟΙΟ ΔΑΜΗΝΑΙ
ΑΙΜΑΤΙ ΚΕΡΔΑΙΝѠΝ ΔΟΜΟΝ ΟΥΡΑΝΟΥ ΑΛΛ ΕΝΙ ΠΑϹΙΝ
ΚΟΙΡΑΝΙΗΝ ΒΑϹΙΛΗΟϹ ΑΚΟΙΝΗΤΟΙΟ ΦΥΛΑΞΟΙ
ΚΑΙ ΚΡΑΤΟϹ ΑΥΞΗϹΕΙΕ ΘΕΟϹΤΕΦΕΟϹ ΘΕΟΔѠΡΗϹ
ΗϹ ΝΟΟϹ ΕΥϹΕΒΙΗΙ ΦΑΙΔΡΥΝΕΤΑΙ ΗϹ ΠΟΝΟϹ ΑΙΕΙ
ΑΚΤΕΑΝѠΝ ΘΡΕΠΤΗΡΕϹ ΑΦΕΙΔΕΕϹ ΕΙϹΙΝ ΑΓѠΝΕϹ

From this it would seem that this inscription was written after Justinian's accession in 527, so that the church was probably finished a short time after the death of the Emperor Justin I[1].

A certain similarity may be noticed between the plan of S. Sergius and that of Ezra (Fig. 6, p. 33) and some other Syrian churches illustrated by de Vogüé, which is suggestive of the oriental element in Byzantine art.

[1] This inscription is very inaccurately quoted in the *Constantiade* of the Patriarch Constantius in 1846, and also by Salzenberg. I take the word παγγενεταο on the authority of my friend Professor Van Millingen: I did not so read it but can make no sense of what I took down. The blue ground has been painted in lately and some letters may have suffered.

J. A.

CHAPTER VI

S. SOPHIA, CONSTANTINOPLE

Sedition of Nika

IN the year 532 Constantinople was disturbed by the violence of the Blue and Green factions of the Circus, known from the war cry of the rioters as the Sedition of Nika,—conquer. A large part of the city was set on fire, and Constantine's church of S. Irene, his son's church of S. Sophia, and many other public buildings perished in the flames. Their re-construction was immediately undertaken, and Procopius in his book *de Aedificiis* has given a lively account of the re-building of the cathedral of S. Sophia[1]. The architects whom Justinian summoned to the task were Anthemius of Tralles, who surpassed in constructive skill[2] all his contemporaries and predecessors, and Isidorus of Miletus, both of them—be it observed—from the Asiatic part of the Empire. For the description of the plan, which was quite novel, and has never been rivalled or repeated, we cannot do better than follow the account given by Procopius[3] who watched the building as it rose (Fig. 22). At the east end is a semicircular apse—"what those who know about such things call a half cylinder," covered by a semi-dome. Right and left are pillars set in semi-circles "like dancers in a chorus," forming the two

Re-building of S. Sophia, Constantinople

The apse

---

[1] As the plans for the new church were ready, and the building was begun only 39 days after the fire, M. Antoniades suggests that the new church had been intended and prepared for previously. Ἔκφρασις τῆς Ἁγίας Σοφίας. Vol. I. p. 13.

[2] ἐπὶ σοφίᾳ τῇ καλουμένῃ μηχανικῇ λογιώτατος, Procop. *de Aedif.* i. 1.

[3] Procopius was Secretary to Belisarius. His praises of that hero in his histories roused the jealousy of Justinian, and the book, *de Aedificiis*, was written to atone for this indiscretion.

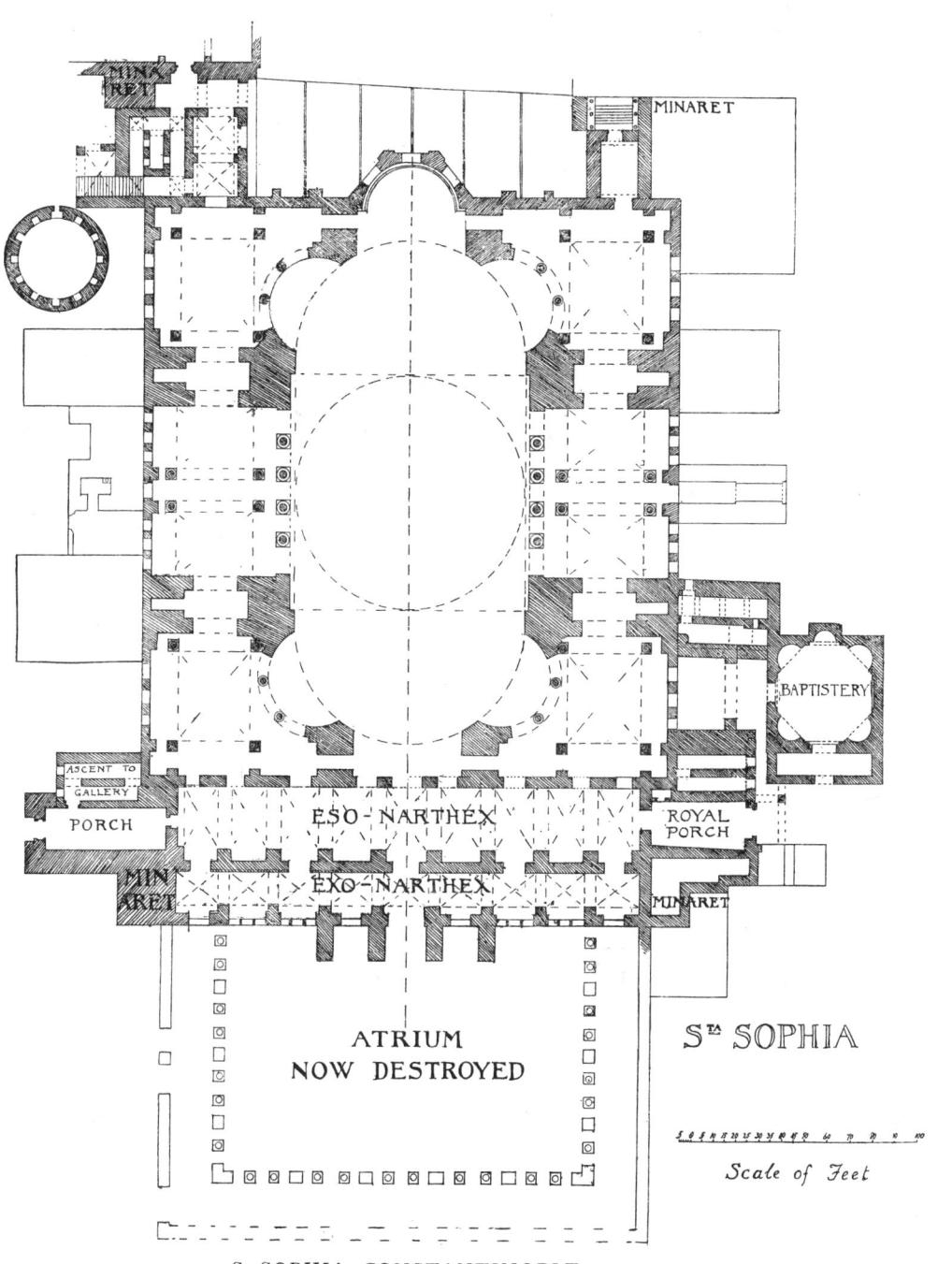

S. SOPHIA, CONSTANTINOPLE
Fig. 22

CH. VI] S. SOPHIA, CONSTANTINOPLE 83

exedrae. At the west end are the entrances similarly flanked by pillars. In the middle of the church are four piers, "two on the north and two on the south opposite and equal to one another, having four columns between each pair. But the piers are put together with huge stones, carefully selected and skilfully fitted to one another by the masons (λιθολόγοι), and they reach to a great height. You might fancy them precipitous cliffs." *The four piers*

"On these rest four arches (ἀψῖδες) square ways... two stand in empty air towards the east and west, and the others have a wall and little pillars carefully placed below them."

He then describes the windows over these pillars, "through which the daylight first smiles, for it overtops, I think, the whole country....Thus far, I think, the description is not beyond the powers of a lisping and stammering tongue." *The upper windows*

The description of the four spherical pendentives follows (v. *sup.* p. 39, Fig. 10, No. 4), which finish in a circular ring on which is raised the dome (σφαιροειδὴς θόλος) and this "owing to the contraction of the structure[1] seems not to rest on solid construction but hanging by a golden cord from heaven to cover the space." *The pendentives*

"All these joined together, beyond belief, in mid-air, springing from one another, and resting simply on those parts next to them, make a single and most lovely harmony of the work. The beholders cannot let their sight rest fondly on any one point, for each attracts the eye and makes it travel easily to itself...and thus those who have studied every part, and bent their brows over

---

[1] I understand this to mean the gathering in of the pendentives from the square plan to the round. δοκεῖ δὲ οὐκ ἐπὶ στερρᾶς τῆς οἰκοδομίας διὰ τὸ παρειμένον τῆς οἰκοδομίας ἱστάναι, &c., &c.

them all, fail to understand the art, but go away struck by what to the sight is incomprehensible."

"The four great pillars were joined not with quicklime[1] nor with asphalt, the boast of Semiramis at Babylon, nor anything else of the kind, but with lead poured into the joints and travelling everywhere between them...."

The women's gallery

"But who can describe the upper storey of the women's gallery (γυναικωνῖτις) or the numerous porches and colonnaded courts with which the church is encompassed? Or who can reckon up the splendour of pillars and stones with which the fane is adorned? One might fancy oneself to have happened on a lovely mead of flowers. One might duly admire of some the purple, of others the green; and in some the bloom of crimson, and in some white flashes out, while nature, like a painter, tricks out the rest with contrasting tints. And when one goes there to pray he straightway understands that it is not by human power or art but by the influence of God that this work has been fashioned: and his mind lifted Godwards walks the air, not thinking him afar off, but rather that it pleases him to dwell with his elect. And this not at the first time of seeing it only, but every man continually feels the same as if he had never seen it before. No one ever tired of the spectacle, but men rejoice in what they see when present in the temple and extol it in their talk when they go away."

The treasures

"Further, it is impossible to tell accurately the treasures of the church, and the things of gold and silver and precious stones which the Emperor Justinian offered there. From one thing only I let you guess what I have mentioned. The most sacred part of the church, into which only priests enter, which they call the sanctuary (θυσιαστήριον), has 40,000 pounds weight of silver."

[1] τίτανος ἥνπερ ἄσβεστον ὀνομάζουσιν

Justinian is represented as constantly on the works, dressed in white linen with a staff in his hand, and a kerchief round his head, and Procopius adds two anecdotes illustrating the skill and wonderful inspiration of the Emperor in the direction of the building, which he protests he is quite unequal to describe at length. When the eastern arch (ἁψίς) of those on which the dome was to rest was nearly finished, but not yet keyed, the piers from which it sprang began to split and give way. The architects in alarm ran to Justinian who, says our author, "by whom guided I know not, but by God I think, for he is not skilled in construction (μηχανικός) told them to finish turning the arch. For it, said he, supported by itself will no longer have any need of the piers." {Justinian's part in the building}

This advice was followed, and Procopius tells us the structure was made stable. It is obvious that it would not have been made anything of the kind if the piers had really given way, for they would not have been relieved by the keying of the arch. On the contrary, if it had been the centering which had given way the result really would have been attained, for the arch when keyed could do without the centres. Procopius seems to have misunderstood what took place.

At another time while the masonry was green, the other arches settled and the columns below flaked off. Again recourse was had to Justinian, who directed part of the load to be removed and not re-built till the walls were dry[1].

Thus far Procopius, whose account is interesting as being that of a contemporary spectator of the building, though not an expert in architecture. He does not

[1] The settlement in Byzantine brickwork must have been considerable, the mortar joints being as thick as the brick. Consequently the marble columns not being able to sink with the walls to which they were attached crushed under the pressure.

Later legends

indulge us with any miracles in connexion with the building, without which according to legend no church seems to have been erected in the earlier middle ages. But the deficiency was supplied some centuries later by an anonymous author whose date is variously fixed in the 10th or the 14th century[1]. There we learn how during the workmens' dinner hour an angel sent the boy who was watching their tools to fetch them back, and incautiously promised to take his place till he returned; and how the Emperor, to secure the constant care of this heavenly guardian, entrapped him by sending the boy with a rich present to the Cyclades, so that he should not come back at all. How when the architect was debating whether to put one or two lights in the apse, an angel personating the Emperor came and told him to put three in honour of the Trinity, a direction which the real Emperor confirmed. All these and many other tales however belong to a much later age.

The dedication A.D. 537

The solemn dedication took place on Dec. 26, 537, five years and ten months after the laying of the first stone in February, 532. Justinian walked alone to the ambo, and stretching out his hands exclaimed, "Glory be to God who has thought me worthy to finish this work. I have surpassed thee O Solomon[2]." The dedication to ΑΓΙΑ ΣΟΦΙΑ, Holy Wisdom, refers to Christ the "Wisdom of God[3]." (1 Cor. i. 24.)

Fall of the first dome A.D. 558

Twenty-one years after the consecration, in 558, misfortune overtook the Great Church. An earthquake

---

[1] The anonymous of Combesis. Cited Lethaby and Swainson, p. 128.

[2] A later writer says Justinian erected a statue of Solomon regarding the Church and gnashing his teeth with envy.

[3] Exstruxit quoque idem Princeps intra urbem Constantinopolim Christo Domino, qui est Sapientia Dei Patris, templum quod Graeco vocabulo ΑΓΙΑΝ ϹΟΦΙΑΝ, id est Sanctam Sapientiam, nominavit. Paul. Diac. IV. 25.

A church at York was dedicated to the *Alma Sophia* in 999. Willis, *York Cathedral*.

caused the fall of the eastern part, which involved the destruction of the interior fittings. Theophanes, who died in 818, writing more than 250 years after the catastrophe, says that while the Isaurian workmen were repairing the rents caused by previous earthquakes the eastern part of the vault over the sanctuary fell, destroying the ciborium, the holy table, and the ambo. It is not quite clear what was the extent of this collapse. Paul, the Silentiary, who wrote a poetical description of S. Sophia immediately after the subsequent restoration, says that what fell was the top of the eastern vault, and part of the dome itself, of which part lay on the ground and part hung insecurely suspended in the air "a wonder to be seen[1]." The piers of Anthemius themselves, he says, remained firm and were commended by Justinian, who hurried to the spot disregarding all the usual ceremonies of attendants. It appears that the eastern semi-dome fell, together with the great eastern arch and the part of the dome next that side. The dome being constructed with ribs, and consisting of independent sections, it is conceivable that part might fall without the rest. The great ambo stood under the dome, and was involved in its ruin, but the ciborium was in the eastern apse, and therefore it would seem that the semi-dome of that apse fell as well as the larger semi-dome.

Extent of the collapse

---

[1]   σφαίρης ἡμιτόμοιο κατήριπε θέσκελος ἄντυξ,
. . . .
οὐδὲ μὲν εὐρύστερνος ὑπώκλασε μέχρι θεμείλων
νηός, ἀριστώδινος ἐελμένος ἅμμασι τέχνης
ἀλλὰ μιῆς ἀψῖδος ἀπωλίσθησε κεραίη
ἀντολική, σφαίρης τε λάχος κονίησιν ἐμίχθη.
ἦν δὲ τὸ μὲν δαπέδοισι, τὸ δ' εἰσέτι, θαμβὸς ἰδέσθαι
οἷάπερ ἀστήρικον ὁμίλεεν ἐκκρεμὲς αὔραις.
          Paul. Silent. v. 187–203.

The rebuilding by Isidorus the younger

But if the extent of the disaster is uncertain, the extent of the subsequent re-building and alteration is still more difficult to ascertain. Justinian set to work at once on the repair. Anthemius, we are told by Agathias, another contemporary writer, was now dead, but the younger Isidorus, nephew it would appear of him of Miletus, advised the Emperor as to the mode of re-construction. All agree that Justinian strengthened the supports, and raised the dome some 20 or 25 ft.[1] He must therefore have taken down the rest of the dome which had escaped the earthquake. Probably it was so much shaken that it could not safely be left standing. Theophanes says the architects were blamed for having made passages through the piers instead of making them solid, in order to save expense[2], and that the "most pious king raised other piers, and supported the dome, and thus it was built, being raised more than 20 feet upwards above the original structure." This seems to imply that Justinian re-built the two eastern piers[3], but that is inconsistent with the contemporary account of Paulus, and would have involved so much interference with the whole anatomy of the building, which bears no signs of such heroic treatment, that it is hardly credible. The later Byzantine historians copy Theophanes almost word for word, but often bring in a little fresh matter. Cedrenus, writing in the 11th century, after repeating the account of Theophanes almost verbatim, says Justinian built opposite the interior piers four winding staircases by which you could mount as high as the dome, "making them

---

[1] Agathias, v. 9. ἐπὶ μεῖζον ὕψος ἐξῆρε.

[2] φυγόντες τὴν ἔξοδον.

[3] Λοιπὸν συνιδὼν ὁ εὐσεβέστατος βασιλεὺς ἤγειρεν ἄλλους πινσούς, καὶ ἐδέξατο τὸν τροῦλλον.

Theoph. ann. mundi 6051.

CH. VI] S. SOPHIA, CONSTANTINOPLE

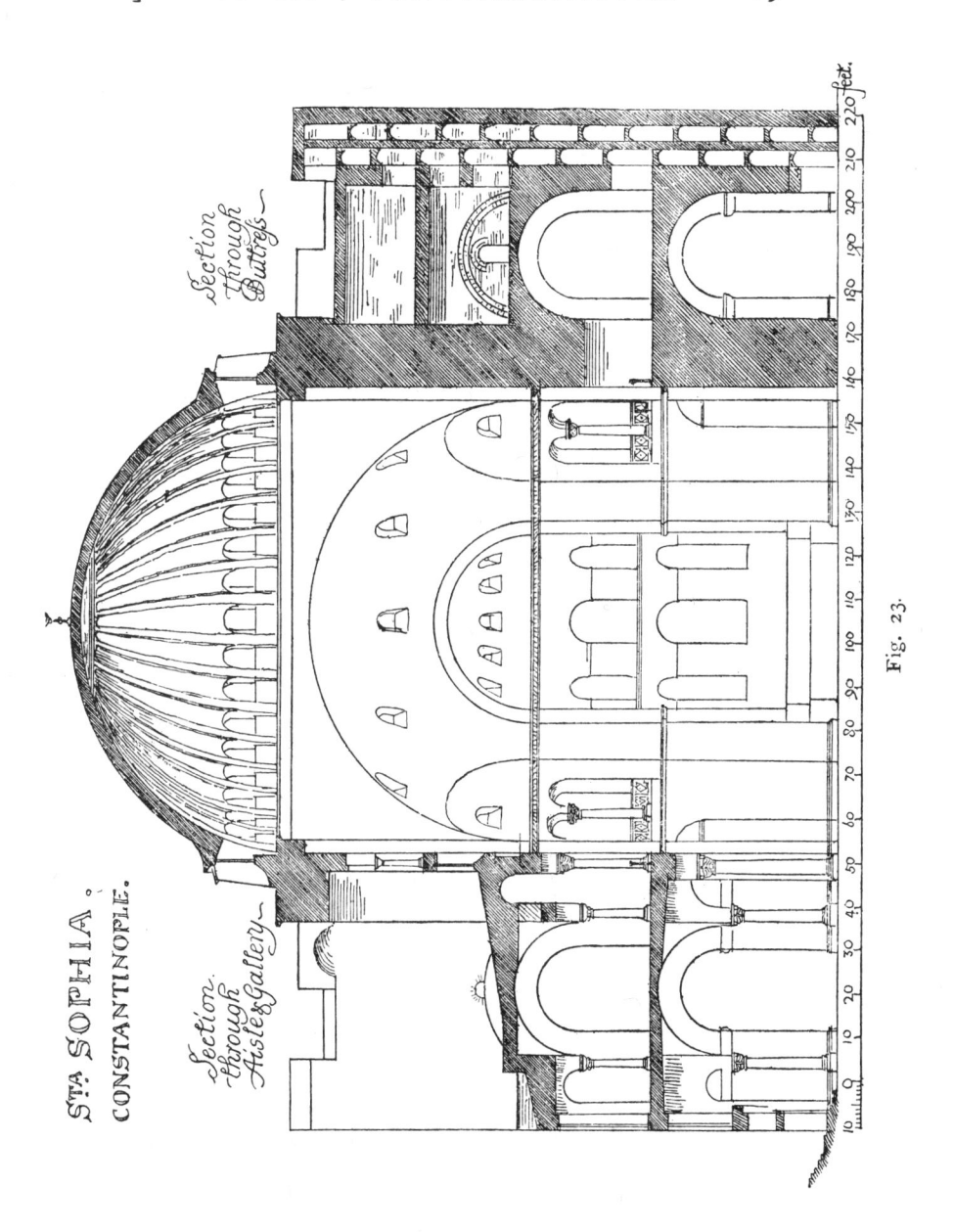

Fig. 23.

STA SOPHIA. CONSTANTINOPLE.

Section through Aisle & Gallery.

Section through Buttress.

The rebuilding of the eastern part

a support of the great arches¹." This seems to imply additions to the four great exterior buttresses of the north and south sides to afford a better abutment to the east and west arches (ἀψῖδες) that supported the dome. Can these additions be the other piers of which Theophanes speaks? Here, however, it is impossible to believe that these buttress piers were originally shorter on plan than they are now, for they must always have reached the outer walls of the church (Fig. 23). If Justinian at this time added to them it must have been in the upper part only: of this, however, we must speak hereafter. Zonaras, writing in the 12th century, also repeats Theophanes's words, but says distinctly that Justinian is said to have had the dome taken down and re-built 25 ft. higher².

Additional height given to the dome

These accounts, written by statesmen and monks, copying a good deal from one another, and with one exception long after the event, are not very intelligible in point of detail, nor can we expect from them more than a general idea of what happened: it seems probable that the eastern semi-dome fell, together with the semi-dome of the apse and part of the great dome, shaking the adjoining parts so much that the great dome itself had to be rebuilt; that Justinian's architect took the opportunity of giving it more rise, and a more stable curve than that of the original dome, which was much flatter; and that something was done to strengthen the abutments.

During the 14 centuries that have since elapsed

---

¹ ἐπόνησε δὲ καὶ τοῖς ἔξω τοῦ ναοῦ κατέναντι τῶν ἔσω πιυσῶν τέσσαρας κοχλίας, οὓς ἀπὸ γῆς φυτεύσας μέχρι τοῦ τρούλλου ἀνεβίβασεν, ἔρεισμα τούτους τῶν ἀψίδων κατεργάσμενος.   Cedrenus, *Hist. Comp.*

² λέγεται καὶ τὸν τροῦλλον προστάξει τοῦ βασιλέως καταιρεθῆναι καὶ αὖθις ἀνεγερθῆναι.   Zonaras, *Annales.*

CH. VI] S. SOPHIA, CONSTANTINOPLE 91

various repairs have been needed from time to time, occasioned by the earthquakes to which Constantinople is subject; and the present condition of the fabric is such as to cause anxiety, for both dome and supports bear sad evidence to the shakings they have undergone[1].

The original design of the construction is admirable, and the best testimony to its excellence is the fact that it has for so many centuries withstood the violence of nature and of man. The weight of the dome is taken by the four great arches and the pendentives between them, with a resultant bearing on the four massive piers at the angles of the central square of the nave. On the east and west these arches are supported by the great semi-domes, which are fitted against them, and form in fact continuations of their soffits. On the north and south sides the support is less continuous between the great buttresses which are placed outside in the plane of the east and west arches. The architect trusted for resisting the thrust of the dome northward and southward to the thickness of the arches which have a soffit of over 15 ft., and to the squinch arches[2] thrown across the angle formed by the buttresses with the wall, and as no bulging is apparent between the buttresses his confidence is justified (Fig. 23).

Principles of its construction

The great buttresses consist each of two parallel walls, varying from 4' 6" to 7' in thickness and 10' 6" apart (Fig. 24): they are pierced by large arches 20 ft. wide in the ground and gallery storeys, over which two barrel-vaulted chambers occupy the interval between them, which is therefore vaulted across four times in the height. In the outer part is a narrow staircase winding

The four great buttresses

[1] See Appendix to this chapter
[2] From these squinch or oblique arches flying buttresses formerly sprang to the dome. They were removed by Fossati when he put his iron girdle round the dome. v. Antoniades, Ἔκφρασις &c. Plate KΓ'.

92   S. SOPHIA, CONSTANTINOPLE [CH. VI

The four great buttresses

round a brick newel, which probably in all cases once reached from the ground to the level of the gallery round the dome, though now some of the lower flights are blocked, or destroyed.

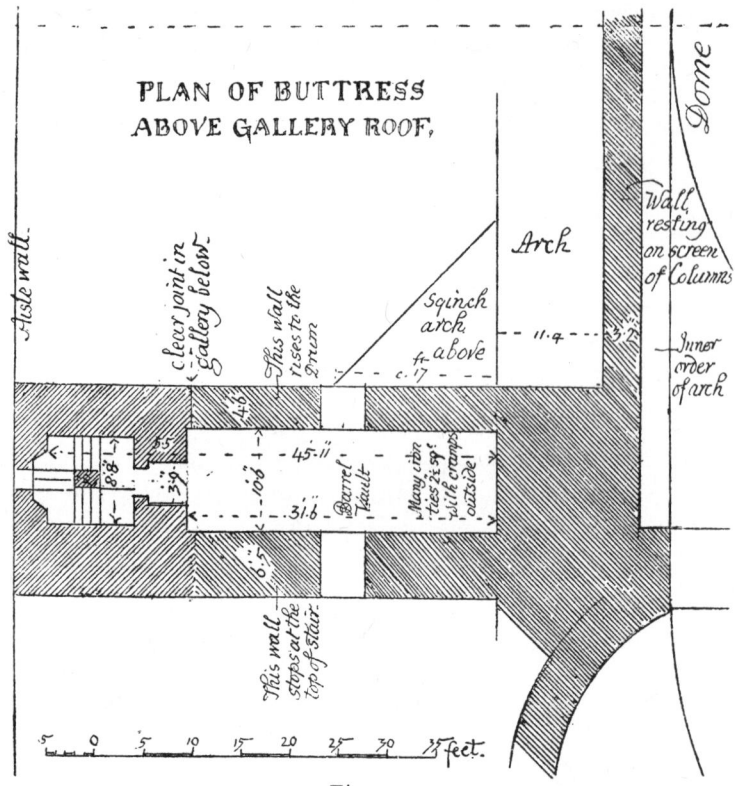

Fig. 24.

The effect of piercing these buttresses with arches in the gallery floor and that below is to convert them into flying buttresses; and their strength depends on their abutment, which is the stair turret and the short respond walls of the gallery arches. Strange to say removal of plaster for the purpose of examination has revealed the fact that in one case at all events the stair turret was not bonded to the

CH. VI] S. SOPHIA, CONSTANTINOPLE 93

rest, but was separated by a clear joint[1]. Should this be the case throughout it constitutes a structural defect. The buttresses

The aisles and galleries are both vaulted, the middle bays with the Roman cross-vault, the angle bays with the pseudo-dome of Galla Placidia's mausoleum (Fig. 10, No. 2, p. 39). Their thrust laterally is taken by barrel vaults forming arches parallel to the nave and side walls which relieve the outside walls on one hand, and the nave arcades on the other from all pressure. The vaults

The stability therefore of the whole structure depends on the four great piers, and the stability of the piers on that of the exterior buttresses; and the construction in a measure anticipates that equilibrium of forces which was the principle of Gothic art some centuries later.

The exterior (Plate XII), like that of most Byzantine churches, seems to have been little studied. It is now plastered over, but probably at first showed the naked brickwork. The cloistered atrium that preceded the façade is now gone, with the exception of the eastern walk which forms the exo-narthex. Gone too is the colossal statue in bronze of Justinian on horseback, which stood hard by in the square of the Augusteum. Ruy Gonzalez de Clavijo, who saw it in 1403, says it was placed on a wonderful high column, and was four times the size of life. The horse was "very well made, and had one fore and one hind leg raised as if in the act of prancing." The knight on its back had his right arm raised with the hand open, the reins in his left hand, and a great plume on his head resembling the tail of a peacock[2]. Exterior plainness
The atrium
Justinian's statue

---

[1] This seems to have some bearing on what Cedrenus says about the construction of *cochleae*, winding stairs, by Justinian at his re-building in 558. See above, p. 88.

[2] Journal of Ruy Gonzalez de Clavijo of his embassy from the King of Spain to Timour, at Samarcand, 1403-6. Hakluyt Soc. vol. 26.

94 S. SOPHIA, CONSTANTINOPLE [CH. VI

The façades

The façade of the church towards the atrium consists of the two nartheces, the first of one storey in height, the second of two storeys overtopping the first, and showing like it a range of large mullioned windows, behind which rises the great western semi-dome. In a side view the two great buttress-piers, rising squarely as high as the springing of the dome, are certainly not beautiful, and one doubts at first whether that can have been their original form. Salzenberg thinks they originally rose only as high as the top of the gynaeconitis, or triforium storey; but as that would not have afforded sufficient abutment for the great east and west arches, one may perhaps imagine them continued with a backward rake from that level up to the necessary height, or possibly with a series of steps like those in the post-conquest mosques of Mahomet II and Suleiman, and the rest, which were confessedly imitated from S. Sophia. This brings us back to the four corkscrew stairs which Cedrenus says Justinian added to them, and the clear joint that has been discovered seems to have some bearing on the matter. And yet without the block containing the staircase there would be no abutment sufficient for the flying arches across the gallery and no strength in the buttresses. They must from the first have reached the outer wall and so have contained the lower flights of the newel-stair up to the roof of the triforium. This, together with the stepped buttressing we have imagined, if it ever existed, may have proved too weak, and what Justinian did may have been to raise the whole pier by the two chambers above, which would have brought it to the present form, at the same time carrying the cochlea to the new level.

Original form of buttresses

Possibly altered by Justinian

The four Moslem minarets which have been added, though not so beautiful as many of their kind, certainly add grace and dignity to the outside view of the building.

Plate XII

S. Irene   S. Sophia

CONSTANTINOPLE

Plate XIII

S. SOPHIA—CONSTANTINOPLE

The windows contribute little to the beauty of the exterior, and have no variety. They consist of wide round-arched openings divided by columnar mullions into three lights, each four feet wide, with a transom at the springing and one below: but the detail is singularly plain and artless. Nor are the doorways remarkable, being mere square openings with moulded jambs and lintel of marble. The prettiest entrance is the south-east porch which is not original, but is flanked by old Byzantine columns carrying a pointed arch moulded very like Gothic work.

The windows

The doorways

But if the outside inspires no strong feeling of admiration one has only to pass the threshold to realize the genius of the designers (Plate XIII). The outer, or exonarthex, is quite plain, but the splendour of the inner narthex is amazing. It is a vast hall about 200 ft. long, reaching all across the front of the church, with a width of 26 ft. and a height of 42 ft. It is cross vaulted and ceiled with mosaic, and the walls are lined with beautiful marbles in panels and bands, often split and opened to form a pattern. At each end is a porch, and adjoining it a winding inclined plane by which ladies were carried in sedans to the gynaeconitis or gallery above. Whether these are original, or subsequent additions by the Emperor Basil I, is a point still debated: but it is clear some such access must have existed from the first; Theodora, in robe, crown, and jewels, as we see her in the mosaic at Ravenna, could not have mounted by the narrow corkscrew stair of dusty brick in the buttresses. There was in all probability originally an ascent by an inclined plane where the present south-east porch has been formed, which would have landed near the Empress' seat in the south-east exedra.

The narthex

Each of the nine bays of the narthex has its door into the church, the royal gate in the middle being the largest. Above it, though now hidden, is the mosaic seen by Salzenberg and illustrated in his book, representing an emperor at the feet of Christ.

The interior

The first impression made by the interior view is that of a vast extent of floor area, and an enormous void above. To some extent the same feeling is aroused on first entering S. Peter's at Rome. But the effect here is still more surprising; for the simplicity of the plan allows the eye to take in the whole interior at once including the dome, which at S. Peter's and still more in our S. Paul's, is not fully revealed till you advance towards it. In this, S. Sophia contrasts strongly with the Gothic churches of Northern Europe, where all is mystery, and where the whole is only gradually discovered. At S. Sophia there is no mystery; the whole design is obvious at a glance, and strikes one at once with its majestic simplicity. Not that there is any lack of variety; the views in the aisles, with the ever varying grouping of the pillars, the semicircular sweep of the columns of the exedrae, ranged "like dancers in a chorus," the brilliant lights, and the deep shadows that throw them into relief, conspire to give one constantly fresh delight; but the memory always goes back to that vast central nave, over 100 ft. wide and 250 ft. long; and the great dome suspended above, with its ring of forty lights around the springing, and rising to the height of 180 ft. from the floor.

Construction of the dome

The dome is constructed with ribs of brick converging on a ring in the centre, and springing from forty piers set on radiating lines (Fig. 25), the panels between rib and rib being also of brick. The outside is covered with lead. It is not evident how thick this brickwork is[1], but

---

[1] Salzenberg says the thickness at the crown where pierced for the lamp chain is 24 inches.

CH. VI]   S. SOPHIA, CONSTANTINOPLE   97

it obviously amounts only to a frail shell in comparison with the massive domes of old Rome, cast as it were in solid concrete, almost making them monolithic. That it has more than once[1] had to be repaired is not wonderful, and its present condition is again causing alarm.

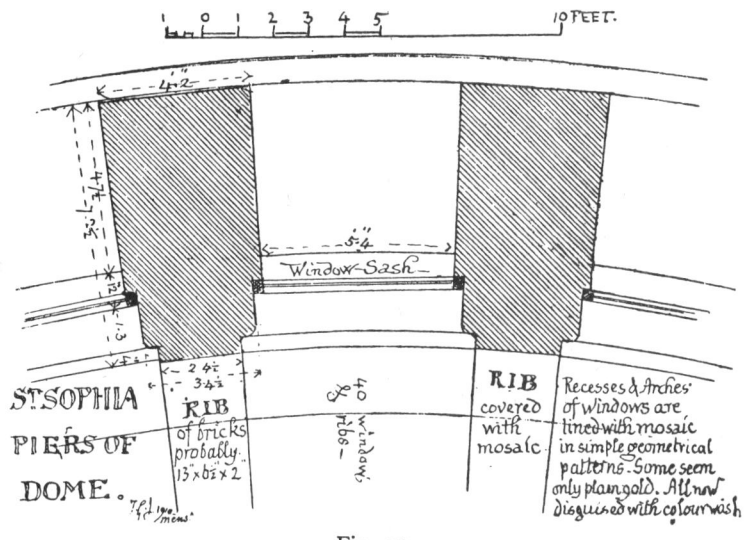

Fig. 25.

On reaching the dome one finds the ribs and panels and also the recesses of the windows that surround the base to be still covered to a great extent with the original mosaic, a good deal patched with painted plaster, and daubed over with colour wash. In the central circle the figure mosaic probably still remains behind the modern

The Mosaics

[1] It was extensively repaired by Basil I in the 9th century, and the western semi-dome and arch were thrown down by an earthquake in 975 and rebuilt in six years by Basil II. Antoniades gives a list of thirty-six earthquakes at Constantinople between 366 and 1894, and an account of numerous repairs. The Eastern arch with part of the dome and the adjoining semi-dome fell in 1346, and were rebuilt before 1356. The Eastern half-dome was rebuilt in 1575. In 1847 Fossati was employed in extensive repairs, and the dome was girdled with iron. (Antoniades, Ἔκφρασις &c., vol. I.)

J.A.   7

mask: but for the rest of the dome the ribs and narrow spaces between only allowed of diaper work in colour on a gold ground. This kind of decoration was applied also very generally throughout the church. Salzenberg saw several figures uncovered and has illustrated them, though very conventionally, in his book: but figure work seems to have been very sparingly used in the decoration. At present, though a good deal of mosaic is still exposed to view, the greater part is covered with plaster or distemper, which is coloured like gold and has patterns painted on it probably often, if not generally, reproducing the mosaic pattern behind. The six winged seraphs in the pendentives of the dome are left uncovered, but their faces are either concealed or picked out and replaced by a pattern in plain gold.

The colonnades A very happy effect is produced by varying the numbers of columns and arches in the two storeys of the screens that fill the north and south arches of the central square (Plate XIV). There are four great columns on the ground, carrying five arches, and six smaller columns above with seven arches. This feature in the design has the true artistic touch. The same variety occurs in the exedrae, where two columns in the lower storey carry six in that over it.

The least satisfactory part of the design is the great lunette wall that rests on the upper arcade in the north and south arches of the dome. These arches, as has been explained above, are in fact barrel vaults with a soffit of over 15 ft. The lunette wall is three feet thick, and contains 12 small round-headed windows. Mosaic decoration may have relieved the baldness of this composition to some extent, but it can never have been entirely pleasing. It has been suggested on the strength

Plate XIV

S. SOPHIA—CONSTANTINOPLE

S. SOPHIA—CONSTANTINOPLE

The West Gallery

CH. VI] S. SOPHIA, CONSTANTINOPLE 99

of a very obscure passage in Agathias that originally the closing wall was flush with the *outside* of the 15 foot vault, somewhat as it is at S. Irene, and rested on the inner range of columns in the gallery, so that the 12 foot soffit would have been inside the church instead of outside. This view has much to commend it, but as the weight of this great wall would have been taken by the arches of the gallery vault and the two marble columns of the inner arcade on ground and gallery floors, I doubt whether they would have been sufficient, even had the lunette been relieved by so great a window as that at the west end[1]. Moreover the substantial inner arcade which now carries the wall would have carried nothing.

The sculpture of the capitals is remarkable. There is no pulvino: it was never fashionable at Constantinople, and is, after all, rather a clumsy expedient: but the capital itself is shaped like a pulvino so as to give solid support to the impost of the arch; it is enriched with surface carving of the Byzantine acanthus, and there is an Ionic volute preserving distantly the memory of Roman Composite. The execution of these capitals, and of the surface carving in the spandrils is unlike and superior to that of any similar work in Constantinople, and they form a type by themselves. M. Diehl observes the resemblance of this surface carving to that by Syro-Greek artists in the palace of Mashita in Moab[2]. The other sculptural ornaments of the interior are not inferior to them; and in particular there is a lovely string course in the narthex intricately wreathed and undercut which seems to antici-

The sculpture

[1] Agathias, *Hist.* v. 9. See the discussion of this point by Messrs Lethaby and Swainson, ch. x. Also Antoniades, vol. III. p. 43. Probably if the younger Isidore really moved the lunette wall from the outer to the inner side of the 15 foot arch it would have been because it was too heavy for the supports on its first position.   [2] *Manual*, p. 49.

pate the flamboyant splendours of Albi. Unlike those of many Byzantine and Romanesque churches the capitals at S. Sophia are original works, made for the place, not the spoils of other buildings, though the columns themselves are said to have been brought from various abandoned temples at Baalbec and Ephesus. The splendour of these great shafts of porphyry and verd' antico, which are more than three feet in diameter, is very remarkable, and together with the slabs of coloured marbles that line the whole of the walls, they give the building an air of refinement, rich and rare, that contrasts strongly with the rude magnificence of our Northern Romanesque (Plates XIV and XV).

Adverse criticisms

In spite of Procopius S. Sophia has not always commanded the admiration of critics. Cockerell, the architect to whom the study of Greek art owes so much, writes in his journal, "I will tell you in confidence that I regret very little the impossibility of drawing in them," (i.e. the mosques of Stamboul) "they seem to me to be ill-built and barbarous[1]." Eliot Warburton, in his brilliant book of Eastern travel, says, "The mosque of St Sophia, with all its spoils, and the remains of such magnificence as led Justinian to exclaim 'Thank God, I have been enabled to outdo Solomon,' scarce repays the trouble of procuring a special firmân, and the troop of guards that must accompany you[2]." Others who have seen it complain that the proportions are too wide and low, and that the dome seems to come down upon you. This criticism is probably provoked mainly by the photographs of the interior, which are always taken from the gallery in order to embrace as much as possible in the field; and seen thus the height no doubt does seem insufficient: but from

---

[1] Extracts from Journal of C. R. Cockerell, R.A. Longmans, 1902.
[2] *The Crescent and the Cross*, vol. II. p. 375.

CH. VI] S. SOPHIA, CONSTANTINOPLE 101

the floor I, for one, felt no want of elevation, and the proportions seemed to me satisfactory.

With one exception S. Sophia is the only great building in Europe which has endured and been in constant use for nearly 14 centuries. The Pantheon is older, but it has no associations; while S. Sophia is a part of all that has made Constantinople memorable in the world's history. Wandering, as I did alone one evening, in the gathering dusk, through the vast deserted galleries, when the Arab chant below had ceased, and the worshippers had departed, it seemed a strange haunted place. It was as still as death: only a single figure down below moved with noiseless tread on the carpet, lighting a few lamps. One could not but think of all these walls had witnessed: of all the splendour and havoc of the past: of Justinian's exultant cry: of Theodora, actress, courtesan, and empress: of the long line of emperors,—Isaurian, Macedonian, Comneni, and Angeli: of the strange Latin conquest, when Crusaders wrecked the church and wrought worse havoc than the Turks; of the return of the Palaeologi to an enfeebled Empire; of the final catastrophe of May 29, 1453, when the church was crowded with trembling citizens, vainly praying for a saving miracle; of the bursting in of the Turks and capture of the multitude who were tied in batches and carried into slavery; and of Mahomet the conqueror riding up, gazing in amazement at the splendour of his prize, and smiting the soldier who was breaking up the marble floor in his zeal for the faith. Surely there is no building in the world with associations so vivid, so well known, so overpoweringly connected with the rise and fall of empires and the varying fate of mankind.

Historical associations of S. Sophia

APPENDIX

Reference has been made above to the dangerous state of S. Sophia. It has attracted the attention of the Turkish Government, who have taken professional advice in the matter. As I happened to be at Constantinople in the autumn of 1910, I was asked by the Ministry of the Efkaf to examine and report upon the building. The following extracts from my report will explain what has happened.

REPORT ON THE CONDITION
OF THE
MOSQUE OF ST SOPHIA, CONSTANTINOPLE.

A M. L'Architecte,
    Kemaleddin Bey,
        Ministère de l'Efkaf, Constantinople.

Sir,
    At the request of the Ministry of the Efkaf conveyed to me through Signor Mongeri a few days before I left Constantinople I made a careful examination of the structure of St Sophia, and of the defects which have created alarm, so far as I could without more preparation and better appliances.

I now have the honour to report to you the result of my observation.

There is an inclination outwards in both the side walls on the North and South, together with the columns on each floor next to them. In the galleries the last columns Eastward lean not only outwards but also to the East, in a diagonal direction. This inclination is common to both storeys, the ground floor and the gallery above it. I found by plumbing the walls about the centre of their length that the inclination was as much as 1 in 43 in the gallery and 1 in 58 in the ground floor storey.

This settlement of the walls is of course accompanied by a dislocation of the arches and vaulting which rest upon them. The cross arches in the great buttress-piers North and South have lost their semi-circular shape, and are much deformed. Some of the vaulting has sunk badly, that over the western part of the North gallery so much as to have lost its arch construction and to be in danger of falling.

* * * * * *

From the floor of the church an alarming bulging of the North-East pendentive is very noticeable: but it is only when seen from the gallery surrounding the dome at its springing that the full amount of the disturbance can be detected. From that level it will be seen that three of the great arches carrying the dome—those to North and South, and in a less degree that to the West—are much deformed by settlement; all four pendentives have suffered and lost their shape, so that the base of the dome no longer forms a true circle, while that to the North-East is so seriously dislocated as to seem dangerous; the crown of the dome seems to have sunk, and many of the ribs especially on the East, South, North-East and South-West sides have sunk so badly that they have lost their arch construction, being either straight or convex on the underside where they should be concave.

It remains to discover the cause or causes of this mischief.

One theory is that the whole centre of the building, namely the dome, the four great arches, and the four great piers they rest upon, has settled and sunk downwards.

In considering this suggestion it will be well to review briefly the principles of the construction.

The weight of the dome is taken by the four great arches and the pendentives between them, with a resultant bearing on the four massive piers at the angles of the central square of the nave.

On the East and West sides these arches are supported by the great semi-domes, which are fitted against them, and form in fact continuations of their soffits.

On the North and South sides the support is less continuous between the great buttresses, which are placed in the line of the East and West arches. The architect has trusted to the thickness of the arch which has a soffit of nearly 5 metres, and to the squinch arches across the angles near the top, to resist the thrust of the dome towards North and South; and as there seems no bulging of the construction between the buttresses his confidence is justified.

The great buttresses consist each of two parallel walls with an average thickness of 2 metres, standing about 3 metres asunder. They are pierced by wide arches on the ground and first storeys, over which are two chambers between the two walls, the intermediate space being vaulted across four times in the height. In the outer part is a staircase between the two walls leading from the ground floor to the level of the gallery round the dome.

In consequence of the arches which pierce them these great buttresses are in fact flying buttresses, and their strength depends on their abutment, which is the stair-turret and the short length of wall between it and the arch. Strange to say the removal of plaster in the South gallery reveals a clear joint between the stair-turret and the rest of the buttress wall, to which it is not bonded. It is important to ascertain whether the same separation exists in all the buttresses. Should it be so it reveals a structural weakness that might be repaired.

The lateral thrusts of the vaults of aisle and gallery are met by barrel vaults forming arches parallel to the side walls. They relieve the outside walls on one hand and the arcades of the great screens on the other from all pressure.

The stability therefore of the whole structure depends on that of the four great piers, and that of the four piers on the great double buttresses; and in searching for the cause of disturbance it is to them we must look.

Taking first the theory that the four great piers have sunk, drawing the centre of the church with them, I should expect in that case to find a fracture between them and the arcaded screens which fill the North and South arches; or possibly an arched line in their cornices descending towards their extremities, these screens having much less load on them than the piers. I should expect also some signs of subsidence in the floor of the church at the foot of the piers. I was however unable to detect any of these symptoms.

In the course of fourteen centuries the four piers must long ago have found their ultimate settlement, and I am informed they rest on an excellent bed of schist or gravel. I enquired whether any deep drain had lately been made near the foundations which might have disturbed them, but I was told that nothing of the kind had occurred. It is true that some of the gallery floors seem to slope towards the nave, but when tried with a level this inclination proved very slight; and the whole floor is very uneven, actually sloping the reverse way in some places, and in others sinking towards the middle.

Again, it is not apparent how any sinking of the piers would have pushed the walls of the church outwards as we see them. I imagine that in that case the rupture of the vaults and distortion of the arches would have taken a different form from that we see.

On the other hand, if it is supposed that the four piers have yielded to thrust Northward and Southward, and that the buttresses have given way to that extent I think all the disturbance of the fabric which we notice would be accounted for.

Without better facilities for testing the piers for any inclination than I had at my disposal, it is difficult to feel certain about it; but from the imperfect observations I was able to make I believe there is such an inclination, especially in the South-East pier, and I observe that Fossati's buttresses are placed just where they would be wanted if my supposition were correct, as if he had held the same opinion.

I recommend therefore as a first step that careful plumbings of all four piers be made from top to bottom, observing whether the rate of inclination, if any, is regular or not.

In my opinion the damage the building has suffered is due to the constant and violent shaking by earthquakes it has sustained, by which the resistance of the great buttresses on North and South has been weakened. It is to them I think that attention should mainly be given. The original design and construction of Anthemius and Isidorus was scientific and sufficient, and the greatest testimony to its merit is that it has survived so many disasters, and is still standing after a lapse of nearly fourteen centuries. That the dome, in spite of its distortion, has not fallen is due to the peculiar stability of that form of construction.

Being built with ribs, its repair, bit by bit, would be comparatively simple: but care would have to be taken to preserve and refix without taking them to pieces the mosaics with which the surfaces are covered. A great deal might also be done by injecting liquid cement into the cracked walls with the Greathead grouting machine, of which I have had very favourable experience. By its means a dislocated wall may be converted practically into a monolith.

The deformation of the dome is nothing new, and is noticed in Salzenberg's volume published fifty-six years ago. It is no doubt the result of a long series of catastrophes, but of course the time must come when the structure can bear no more, and ought to be set to rights.

I do not however go further with suggestions relating to repair, your present object being to discover the causes and nature of the mischief that has taken place, as the first step towards taking the necessary measures to arrest it.

* * * * * * *

I am, Sir,
Your most obedient servant,
T. G. JACKSON.

CHAPTER VII

JUSTINIAN'S OTHER CHURCHES

PROCOPIUS, in his book *de aedificiis* gives a long list and a more or less detailed description of various churches founded or rebuilt by Justinian, within the walls of Constantinople or in the neighbourhood, either in the reign of his uncle Justin or after his own accession[1]. That of SS. Sergius and Bacchus has been described already[2].

S. Irene, Constantinople

The only other one that has survived to our time is S. IRENE, which was rebuilt after the burning of Constantine's church in the tumult of the Nika sedition. Procopius says that after S. Sophia this church was second to none. It stands near the "Great Church," as S. Sophia was generally called, and was originally enclosed with it in one *enceinte*. It is said to have been injured, if not thrown down, by an earthquake in 740, and to have been restored or rebuilt shortly afterwards, but we probably have in the present building the original plan and scheme of construction of Justinian's time (Fig. 26). Mr W. S. George in his valuable monograph on the church, says that Justinian's walls remain up to the springing of the aisle vaults.

It is in its form a mixture of the basilican and the domed church. The nave consists of two large bays covered by cupolas, prolonged eastwards by an extra

---

[1] He says in one place, αὐτῷ γὰρ λογιστέον καὶ τὰ Ἰουστίνῳ εἰργάσμενα τῷ θείῳ, ἐπεὶ καὶ αὐτοῦ τὴν βασιλείαν κατ' ἐξουσίαν αὐτὸς διῳκεῖτο. *De Aedif.*, Lib. I. cap. 3.

[2] Chap. V. p. 78 *supra*.

CH. VII] JUSTINIAN'S CHURCHES 107

bay for the bema in front of the apse, and surrounded S. Irene
by two lateral aisles, and a third at the west forming a
narthex. But the colonnades of the aisles only rise high

■ = After fire A.D. 532.
▨ = After fire A.D. 564.
▧ = After Earthquake. 740.

S·IRENE.

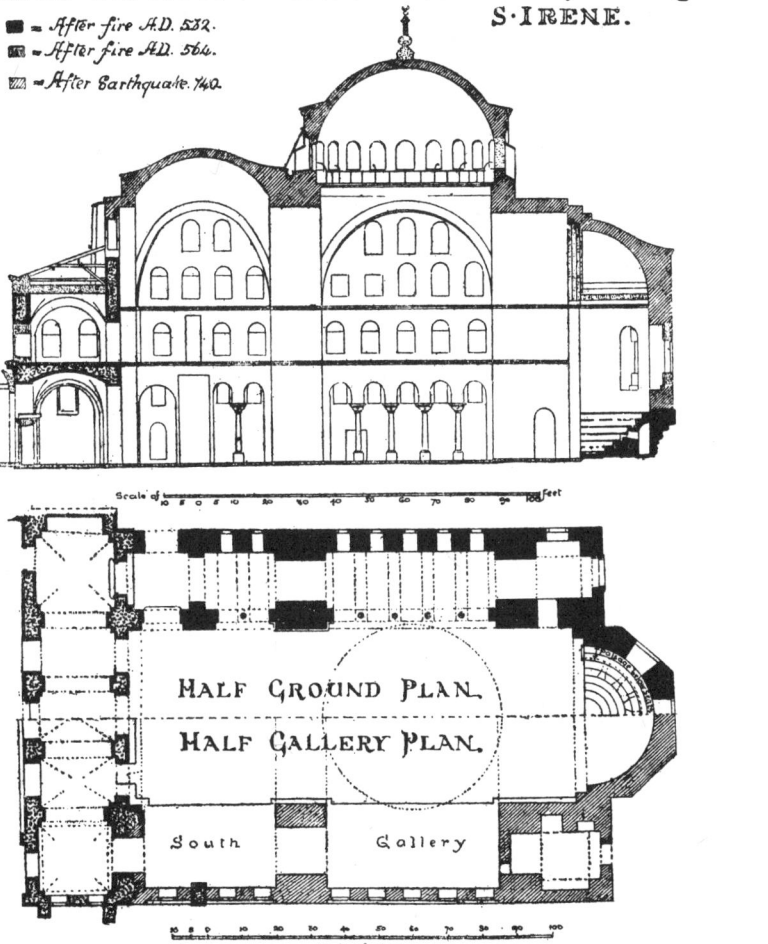

Fig. 26 (Van Millingen).

enough to carry a gallery, and the arches above which
carry the dome are open, and continued as barrel vaults
to reach the outer wall of the church, where they are closed
by a wall full of windows, thus forming sufficient abutment

for the domes. The result is that on the ground floor we have the plan of a basilican church with nave and aisles, but on the upper floor a transeptal plan, foreshadowing the Greek cross of the later churches, complicated, it is true, by the second dome and its side barrel vaults.

The dome over the principal bay is raised on a drum pierced with windows, a feature unknown to early Byzantine work, and one that may perhaps be referred to the later rebuilding. The second dome has no windows, is very flat and hardly shows above the roof, and like that at S. Sophia, Salonica, it is not circular but an imperfect square with the corners rounded off. The aisles (Plate XVI) are vaulted by a cross rib in brick from each pier and column to the wall, with a vault turned from rib to rib; this is formed with a bonnet at each end to fit the arcade and the window respectively, and closed in the middle with a sort of square dome, a curious device which occurs elsewhere in the brick vaults of Constantinople. The arcades have no charming Byzantine capitals, but only a pulvino with a monogram set on the top of the shaft which has nothing but a moulding forming a shallow Ionic capital to receive it (Plate XVI). All this is very inconsistent with an early date, and points to much subsequent alteration. The apse has a large simple cross on a gold ground, perhaps significant of the rebuilding under the Iconoclastic Emperors, and round the arch is the Greek inscription alluded to above in the account of S. Sophia at Salonica[1]. At the east end is a hemicycle of seats, tier above tier, for the clergy, with a semicircular passage below.

[1] In Salzenberg's time S. Irene was used as a military magazine as it had been ever since the conquest, and he says he was only allowed to see the narthex and the nave, and that his plans are mainly conjectural. In my Fig. 26 I have followed Mr George's plan and section as published in Prof.

S. IRENE—CONSTANTINOPLE
View in Aisle

The church is preceded by an atrium now surrounded S. Irene
by a double-aisled cloister of plain round arches, which
do not seem part of the original building and are partly
of Turkish work. Here are several huge porphyry sarcophagi, said to have been brought from the destroyed
church of the Apostles and to have contained the bodies
of Constantine and some of his successors. Another, much
broken, was lately dug up near the site of that church,
and was being slowly dragged through the streets on
rollers when I was there in 1910. There are also other
relics: notably a "stele" or pedestal commemorating a
charioteer, with sculptures of the hippodrome. Under the
four horses of one quadriga are their names ΑΡΙΣΤΙΔΗΣ,
ΠΥΡΡΟΣ, etc.

Of the 25 churches with which Justinian adorned his Church
capital, one of the most remarkable was that just men- of the
tioned of the Apostles, which was destroyed to make Apostles
room for the mosque of Mahomet II in 1464. As he
was not generally destructive, but on the contrary took
pains to save S. Sophia from injury, we may perhaps
assume that the church had become ruinous before
the conquest. Some of the fine marble columns in the
Mohammadieh and its atrium probably belonged to the
vanished building. The church was built originally by
Constantine for the burial place of himself and his successors, but in the 6th century it had become ruinous and
unsafe. Procopius describes Justinian's rebuilding as
a transeptal church with aisles and triforium[1]. The
sanctuary (ἱερατεῖον) was at the crossing under a central
dome which had windows[2] in it, and was constructed like

Van Millingen's *Churches of Constantinople*. The church is now used as a
military museum, and could be visited with a permit from the Seraskiat at
the time of my visit.

[1] κίοσιν ἄνωτε καὶ κάτω ἑστῶσι.   [2] θυρίδες.

Church of the Apostles

that of S. Sophia, on four arches (ἀψῖδες) with pendentives, but was not so large. This dome was surrounded by four other domes equal to it in point of size but without windows, one over each arm of the cross. The western limb, or nave, was longer than the others so as to give the figure of a cross. This vanished church has a special interest, as it is said to have given the plan for S. Mark's at Venice, with its five domes and lengthened western arm.

St Mary of Blachernae

No traces now remain of the great church and monastery of S. Mary at Blachernae except a modest chapel over the holy well, which is still owned by the Greek Church. Procopius praises its double storey of Parian columns and says the visitor would be delighted by its hugeness without any sign of failure, and its splendour free from vulgarity.

Church of the Pege—and others

The church of the Pege (Baloukli) in the suburb on the Marmora, is described by him as exceeding most of the other churches both in beauty and size. S. Michael's was surpassingly beautiful, and square in plan, from which one conjectures it was domical, like SS. Sergius and Bacchus. Words fail the writer to describe the church of S. Agathonius, or that of the martyr Irene at the mouth of the gulf (κόλπος). These and many more, of which he sings the praises, were built, Procopius says, by Justinian during the reign of his uncle Justin; and his pious enterprizes were shared with him by his consort Theodora.

Odon de Deuil's account

Odon de Deuil, a monk of S. Denis, who accompanied the French king Louis VII (Le Jeune) to the Crusade in 1146, and wrote an admirable history of their adventures, says, "one sees at Constantinople a vast number of churches less great but not less beautiful than S. Sophia, which besides their admirable beauty are also respectable

from the numerous relics of saints which they possess."
The imperial palace of Blachernae astonishes him. He says, "Its exterior beauty is almost incomparable; and that of the interior surpassed anything I could say of it. In all parts one sees nothing but gildings and paintings of various colours. The court is paved with marble of exquisite design, and I know not which contributes most to its value, whether it be the great beauty of this palace and the marvellous art it displays, or the precious materials one finds in it[1]." <small>Palace of Blachernae</small>

Ruy de Clavijo, the Spanish ambassador to Timour (1433–6) who passed through Constantinople, describes a church of S. John Baptist preceded by an atrium, and having a circular body surrounded by three great naves (sc. aisles). These aisles had an upper storey, with 24 columns of green jasper below, and 24 more above, and the church was decorated by mosaic on the walls and ceiling. There is no trace of any such church of S. John at Constantinople, and as the description fits roughly the church of SS. Sergius and Bacchus, one suspects Clavijo may have mistaken the dedication. And yet, though he was no architect, he could hardly mistake 14 columns for 24. His account is only the loose description of an unprofessional visitor and must not be taken as very exact. Among other things, he says there were seven altars in the church, but the Greek Church only allows one. <small>Church described by Ruy de Clavijo</small>

"The edifices of Justinian," says Gibbon, "were cemented with the blood and treasure of his people." The money for them, according to the Anecdota or

---

[1] Odonis de Deogilo, de Ludovici VII, Francorum regis, cognomento junioris, profectione in orientem cui ipse interfuit opus septem libris distinctum.

secret history attributed to Procopius, which he says it would have cost him his life to publish while Justinian or Theodora were alive, was procured by extortion and injustice, and the misery entailed on the people was incalculable[1]. It is a sad reflexion that so many of the masterpieces of architecture which excite the admiration of the world are based on tyranny and oppression. History and the monuments tell us that the great works of the Pharaohs were carried out under the lash of the taskmaster. "And the children of Israel sighed by reason of the bondage, and they cried, and their cry came up unto God by reason of the bondage." The temple of Solomon and his palace of the Forest of Lebanon, taxed severely the resources of a small country as we know from the complaints made to his son, and the gold and silver with which they were overlaid must have been wrung with difficulty from a comparatively slender agricultural population. The edifices of Justinian were on a much more splendid scale than those of Palestine, and much more numerous, and to his boast on their completion "I have vanquished thee, O Solomon!" it might be added that as Solomon chastised the people

---

[1] In the *Historia Arcana* the abuse is probably as exaggerated as the flattery in the larger history. "Nature," says the writer, "seems to have collected every evil quality from mankind and bestowed them on this man."

ἠλίθιός τε γὰρ ὑπερφυῶς ἦν, καὶ νωθεῖ ὄνῳ ἐμφερὴς μάλιστα, καὶ οἷος τῷ τὸν χαλινὸν ἕλκοντι ἕπεσθαι συχνὰ οἱ σειομένων τῶν ὤτων. Anecd. cap. 8.

He takes a malicious pleasure in Justinian's resemblance to the only portrait bust of Domitian that had survived the rage of the Roman people. As to the authorship of the Anecdota see Bury, *History of the Later Roman Empire*.

Evagrius writing about 593 confirms the story of Justinian's extortions. He says he was χρημάτων ἄπληστος, sold magistracies and collectorships and shared in illegal gains. He was extravagant in spending and built many splendid churches, "pious works and acceptable to God when done by men with their own means." Evag. *Hist. Eccl.* cap. xxx.

with whips, Justinian chastised them with scorpions. One turns with relief to the treasures of art with which a free people delighted to adorn their fatherland: to the Acropolis of Athens, the churches and public palaces of the great free commonwealths of Lombardy, Venetia, and Central Italy, and the town halls of the wealthy and industrious trading municipalities of the Netherlands.

CHAPTER VIII

ICONOCLASM

THE Iconoclastic movement convulsed the Greek Church for 120 years, and caused the final separation of Italy from the Empire and the Latin Christians from the Eastern communion. It did not affect ecclesiastical architecture, except so far as it depended on the association of the decorative arts of painting, and to a certain extent sculpture. It was not directed against art or religion, for some of the iconoclastic emperors were great builders not only of palaces but of churches; especially Theophilus, the last of them, who also composed hymns, which were sung in the services, the Emperor himself acting as conductor.

Milman[1] says the movement was doomed to fail because it was the attempt of an emperor to change by his own arbitrary command the religion of his subjects. But had it been merely that, it would hardly have had such vitality, or commanded the unanimous sanction of the 348 bishops who met at the third council of Constantinople in 746. There had been from time to time protests by ecclesiastics both in east and west against the growth of idolatrous tendencies in the Church. The absence of any figure sculpture in the remains of Syrian churches has been noticed already, and even in Justinian's

_{Third Council of Constantinople 746}

---

[1] *Latin Christianity*, chap. VII.

time representation of the Saviour, the Virgin Mary, and other saints seems to have been avoided. Procopius in his account of the decoration of S. Sophia says the whole roof was of pure gold, and that it was surpassed by the splendour of the stones which flashed it back; but there is not a word of any representation of figures. From the Poem of the Silentiary it appears that the reconstructed dome, which was so bright with gold that the eye could scarcely bear its brilliancy, had in the centre the cross, the guardian of the city[1], but neither is there here any mention of figures. As the poet describes the angels, and the figure of the Virgin and the Apostles depicted on the iconostasis, he would not have omitted the figures on walls and vaults had there been any. There does not even seem to have been any figure of Christ on the iconostasis, but only a symbol, though his picture was woven in the hangings between "Paul full of divine wisdom and the mighty doorkeeper of the gates of Heaven." The great cross in the centre of the dome corresponds with that still existing in the apse of S. Irene, and that of which traces remain in the apse of S. Sophia at Salonica, where it has been effaced by the later figure of the Madonna with the infant Saviour. The ribs of the dome at Constantinople still retain their original mosaic, which consists of a diaper pattern on a gold ground, and the panels between the ribs afford little space for figures. Enough remains of the original mosaic in the galleries and the narthex to show that the decoration there was by conventional patterns and diapers on a ground of gold, which indeed seem to be reproduced

<small>Original decoration of S. Sophia</small>

<small>Absence of figures in decoration</small>

---

[1] . . ἀκροτάτης δὲ
σταυρὸν ὑπὲρ κορυφῆς ἐρυσίπτολιν ἔγραφε τέχνη.
Paul. Silent. line 491–2.

in the distemper and painted plaster with which so much of the surface has been covered by the Turks. Even in the great apse the position of the small windows in the semi-dome leave no room for the large figure of Christ or the Madonna which forms the central object in the mosaics at Ravenna, and in the later work at Salonica. On the walls there was no opportunity for any figure-work, for they are all lined with marble incrustation from the floor to the springing of the vault. It is probable that, allowing for the difference between mosaic and painted plaster made to look like it, the appearance of S. Sophia in its prime was not very different from what we now see so far as regards the main structure, and that its superior splendour depended on the silver iconostasis with its paintings and chisellings, the magnificent ambo that stood under the dome, and the silver lamps over which the Silentiary expatiates.

Introduction of figures in decoration

In the course of two centuries, however, images were multiplied, chiefly in painting and mosaic, for even then sculpture seems to have been scarcely employed at all in representation of the figure. To depict the first person of the Trinity was agreed on all sides to be impious even had it been possible to conceive any image of him. It was left for a future age to disregard this scruple. The Saviour was at first represented by a symbol; by the figure of a lamb, or as at the Mausoleum of Galla Placidia by that of a youthful shepherd seated among his flock. But this had in time given way to a more direct representation. It was argued that as Christ had taken a human form, it was possible to represent him, as well as his mother, and his apostles, and all the saints of the Christian calendar. To these icons the credulity of the vulgar, and the superstition and interest of the

Symbolic representation of the Saviour

monks soon attributed miraculous powers; and from being *Superstitious reverence of images* historical pictures reminding the faithful of the holy personages they represented, they became fetishes, possessed of inherent supernatural virtues, and were themselves the objects of idolatrous worship.

Against this there must always have been an undercurrent of protest in the east, which finally found expression in the iconoclastic movement of the 8th century. Professor Bury observes that the objection of the iconoclasts to the representation of Christ in art, and also to Mariolatry was an outcome of the doctrine of the Monophysites. The influence of the Jews, and still more of the Mohammedans, who sternly forbad images, had no doubt something to do with the movement. Possibly the Paulicians, those early Protestants, had also a part in turning men's minds in the same direction. "Leo III and Constantine V," says Professor Bury, "and their party were animated by a spirit of rationalism in the same sense as Luther. They were opponents not only of iconolatry but also of Mariolatry. They did not believe in the intercession of saints, they abhorred relics which were supposed to possess magic potency. They were, moreover, especially Constantine V, the sworn foes of monks, whom they justly regarded as the mainstays of superstition and mental degradation[1]."

The monks were throughout the struggle the champions of iconolatry. Their religion and their interest were equally imperilled, for a wonder-working image was too valuable an asset in a convent to be lightly surrendered. The Emperor Constantine V consequently resolved to extirpate monachism as well as image worship and resorted to stronger measures than his father Leo.

Monks the supporters of iconolatry

Reforms of Constantine V

[1] Bury, *History of the Later Roman Empire*, vol. II. p. 428.

Convents were broken up; monks and nuns were exposed to public ridicule in the hippodrome and forced to marry, and a clean sweep seems to have been made of all images. By the unanimous voice of 348 bishops assembled in Council at Constantinople in 746, it was proclaimed that images are idols, inventions of the devil, that painting is an unlawful and blasphemous art, and an anathema was pronounced against all who pourtrayed the Incarnate Word, the Virgin and the Saints, instead of painting the living likeness of their virtues in their own hearts. Forty-one years later, in 787, a council of an equal number of prelates, among whom however were many monks, was assembled at Constantinople under the infamous Empress Irene to reverse this ruling and to restore image worship. The capital, however, seems to have become attached to the tenets of iconoclasm, for the soldiery broke in and dispersed the assembly. Meeting again at Nicaea in greater safety, they condemned the decrees of 746 and cursed all who obeyed them. "We who adore the Trinity worship images. Whoever does not the like anathema on him. Anathema on all who call images idols. Anathema on all who communicate with them who do not worship images[1]."

The XXI Article of the English Church says General Councils may err, and have erred. It is plain that they sometimes may and do disagree.

In Constantinople therefore we need not look for any mosaic or other decoration containing sacred figures older than the middle of the 8th century. All carved images had been thrown down and broken, mosaics were picked out, paintings were smoked or obliterated when on walls,

Third Council of Constantinople 746

Second Council of Nicaea 787

---

[1] Milman, *Latin Christianity*.

when on wood they were burned, and books containing sacred pictures were destroyed.

It is not to be believed that any religious pictures in the capital could have escaped destruction. S. Sophia in particular would be the first to be purged of what had been pronounced idolatrous imagery. The figure subjects which Salzenberg has illustrated, and which no doubt still exist behind the plaster and distemper of the Moslem, must, at the earliest, date only from the end of the 8th century, or more probably from the later half of the 9th. Those at S. Sophia, Salonica, seem to be proved of that date, but it would appear that the destruction of images was less complete in the provinces than at Constantinople; for those at S. George, and the fragments lately discovered at S. Demetrius go back to the 5th and 6th centuries: and in Italy, where the Pope put himself at the head of the image worshippers, the edicts of the emperors had no effect. *Destruction of images in Constantinople*

It must not however be supposed that the iconoclastic emperors were enemies of art. The churches were decorated afresh with paintings that had no religious significance, resembling those in the earlier Christian churches, and in some of the catacombs. In mosaics of the 4th century at S. Costanza in Rome[1] are depicted rural scenes, festoons of vines and flowers; and the decorations of the iconoclastic period seem to have returned to the same kind of subject. With the animals and birds amid wreaths of foliage which Constantine V had introduced on the walls of S. Mary at Blachernae, he was accused of having converted the church into an orchard or an aviary. Theophilus adorned with similar designs the splendid palace he added to the enormous *Natural decoration by iconoclastic emperors*

[1] v. Plates XLV and XLVI in chapter XIII.

group of imperial buildings of his predecessors. There was, as M. Diehl observes, a reversion from monumental art to nature and realism[1].

Conclusion of the struggle   Iconoclasm was not at once extinguished by the second council of Nicaea. Leo the Armenian and Theophilus renewed the struggle; but the Reformation was eight centuries before its time. On the death of Theophilus in 842 his widow, the gentle Theodora, deposed the iconoclastic patriarch and appointed a worshipper of images in his place; and after a conflict of a hundred and twenty years the Greek Church finally made the worship of images part of its system though sculpture has never been admitted to an equal footing with painting in its churches. Indeed all the efforts of Byzantine art in figure sculpture are on a small scale, and often barbarous; and statuary on a grand scale seems never to have been attempted after the 6th century.

The restoration of the images is recorded by an iambic distich in the Anthology, which M. Antoniades believes appeared in mosaic round the triumphal arch in S. Sophia[1]. The last nine and a half letters are still there, and were read by Salzenberg though not correctly:

Ἃς οἱ πλάνοι καθεῖλον ἐνθάδ' εἰκόνας
ἄνακτες ἐστήλωσαν εὐσεβεῖς πάλιν.
The saintly pictures vagabonds defaced
Once more by pious princes were replaced.

If the Emperor who kneels to Christ in the mosaic over the Royal door is correctly identified with Basil I (867–886) the present mosaics may be referred to his time.

[1] *Manuel de l'art Byzantin*, p. 340.
[2] Antoniades, Ἔκφρασις &c., vol. II. p. 30.

CHAPTER IX

LATER BYZANTINE ARCHITECTURE

CONSTANTINOPLE still abounds in ancient churches, though they have to be searched for and are not, all of them, easy to find. But as one tramps about the narrow, hilly, rough-paved streets of Stamboul one often comes by accident on time-worn relics of the Christian period, unmistakeable in spite of the white and yellow wash with which they have been daubed over. Otherwise they have been very little altered, though in some cases the marble columns have been taken away to decorate a new mosque of the conqueror, and their place has been supplied with meaner material. They are all, with one small exception, turned into mosques, and one cannot but feel that to this we owe their preservation and freedom from alteration, for the only little church that has been spared to the Christians has been altered out of all knowledge. The Turks call them Kilisse (ecclesiae) and though nearly all traces of the original decoration in painting and mosaic have been obliterated, except in the case of the Kahriyeh Djami or church of the Chora, and one other, the fabric has generally been well cared for. They are none of them on the scale of the buildings we have been considering at Salonica or Constantinople, though some are good big parish churches, and others are spread out by additions which convert the original building into a group of two

<small>Kilisse</small>

contiguous churches joined together, as at S. Maria, Panachrantos (Fenari Isa Mesjidi), or three as at S. Saviour Pantocrator (Zeirek Kilisse Djamisi). They are all domed, and on the outside square or nearly so in plan, while on the inside they gradually assumed the plan of a Greek cross. This resulted naturally from the necessary supports of the dome; its four piers formed an interior square, of the diameter of the dome, which rested on the four great arches turned from pier to pier. The arches, prolonged as barrel vaults to the outer walls, formed the abutment for the dome and its pendentives, and the four small squares left at the corners of the main square, were covered with domes or domical vaults. Thus the dome with its four barrel vaults formed a cruciform plan, and this was expressed externally by the greater elevation of the four main arms—nave, chancel, and transepts,—which showed the rounded back of the barrel vault, while the four small squares in the corners were roofed at a lower level. The eastern arm was lengthened by a short bay and an apse for the bema, and the western arm was generally prolonged by a bay before meeting the narthex. The fully developed cruciform plan is well shown in the church of S. THEODORE THE TIRO (Kilisse Mesjidi) (Fig. 27) which though in its present form it is mainly of the 11th or 12th century represents an older church of the 6th. The four mean columns that form the interior square and carry the dome have no doubt taken the place of fine shafts of marble appropriated by the Turks for use elsewhere. In the GUL DJAMI, or Rose mosque (S. Theodosia), which is variously attributed to the end of the 9th and to the 10th or 11th century, the later date probably relating to a remodelling of the exterior apses, the cruciform plan is less obvious. The two

CH. IX] LATER BYZANTINE BUILDINGS 123

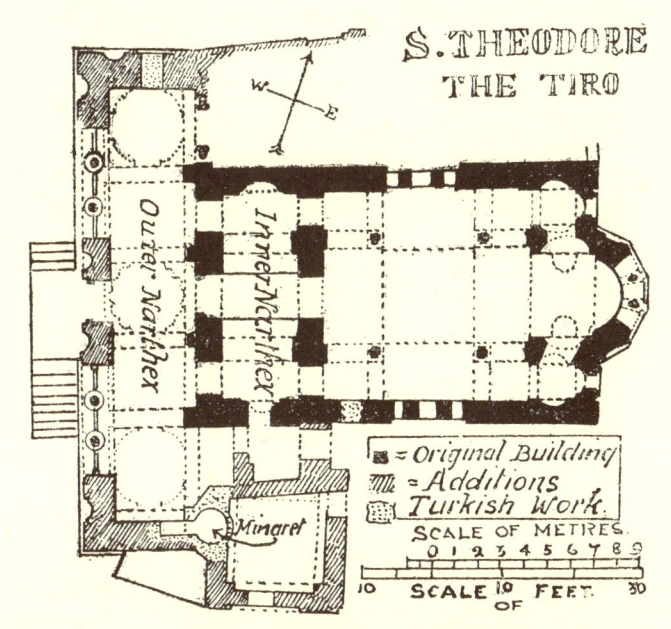

Fig. 27.

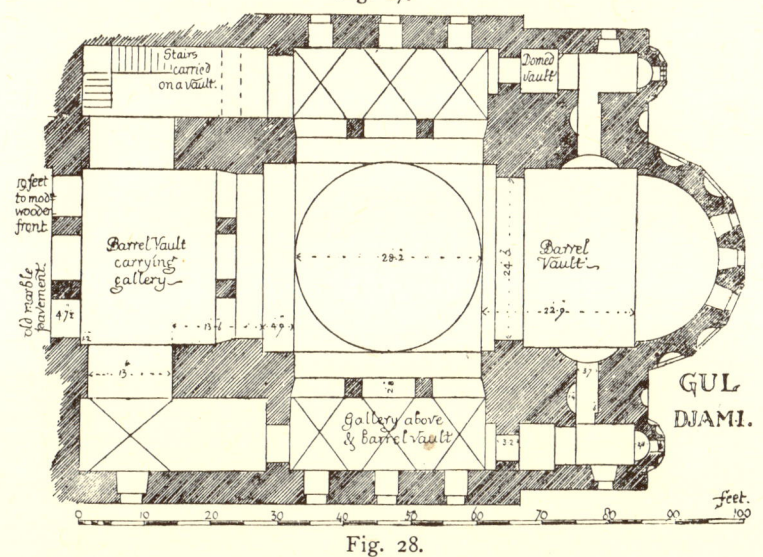

Fig. 28.

There are small chambers in the N.E. and S.E. piers; in one of which tradition has it that the last Byzantine Emperor lies. v. Van Millingen, *Churches of Constantinople*, p. 164 &c.

eastern piers (Fig. 28) are not isolated but are joined to the walls of the sanctuary, and the north, south, and west arms of the cross are filled with galleries carried on arcades and vaulting as at S. Irene. Above them, however, the cruciform plan is perfect. In the earlier KALENDER HANÉ DJAMI (S. Maria Diaconissa) the same attachment of the two eastern piers of the dome occurs, though the apse itself has disappeared. In the triple church of S. SAVIOUR PANTOCRATOR (Zeirek Kilisse Djamisi) the dome piers are isolated, and the cruciform plan is complete (Fig. 29). Here too the columns of the dome are obviously of Turkish workmanship, which at first sight is somewhat surprising. From Gyllius, however, we learn that the dome in his time rested on columns of fine granite, which are no doubt now doing duty in one of the great post-conquest mosques.

As a rule the rounded surfaces of all domes, subsidiary as well as principal, and of all vaults, were allowed to show on the exterior, rising into curves and swellings which were covered with lead. Anyone who has clambered over the roofs of S. Sophia will remember the difficulties these miniature hills and valleys occasionally present. This plan avoided the wooden exterior roofs which protect our northern vaults, and which, being combustible, have often caused the destruction of the fabric. There is so little in the Byzantine churches to catch fire that they have escaped the frequent conflagrations to which Stamboul, being mainly built of wood, is liable[1].

The double narthex is a constant feature in these churches, and a noble example of it is afforded at the

[1] I am glad to hear from friends in Constantinople that no building of interest suffered from the great conflagrations of 1911.

Plate XVII

S. SAVIOUR PANTOCRATOR—CONSTANTINOPLE
The Narthex

Plate XVIII

S. SAVIOUR PANTOCRATOR—CONSTANTINOPLE

CH. IX] LATER BYZANTINE BUILDINGS 125

church of S. Saviour Pantocrator (Zeirek Kilisse Djami), where the doorway between the exo- and eso-narthex (Plate XVII) is formed with three fine stones of red marble, on each side of which is a window opening lined with pieces of verd' antico, cut from a large column and still showing part of the round face of the shaft. Both nartheces are cross-vaulted, Roman fashion. The

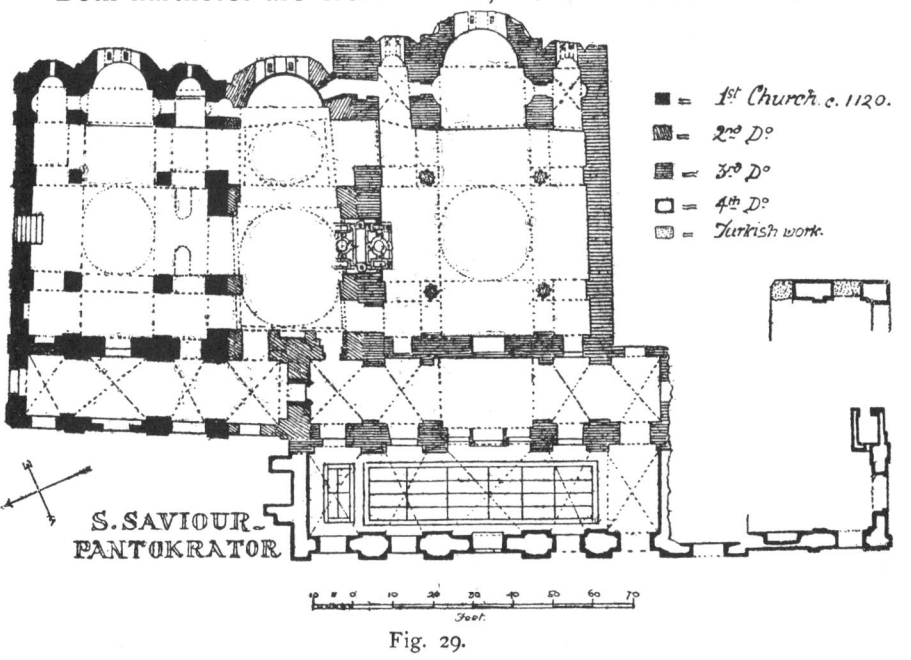

The Panto-crator

Fig. 29.

church itself is made up of three distinct churches joined together (Fig. 29). They are domed and cruciform, the four columns that carry the dome being Turkish insertions as has been mentioned already. The southern church has retained some marble linings in the apse, but they do not seem to be in their original state. Between this part and the central nave is a marble pavement of large slabs enclosed in interlacing borders, resembling in plan the

Opus Alexandrinum of Lucca and Rome; but here the borders are not of mosaic, but mere bands of red and yellow marble, and the effect is very poor. Some of the small spandrils have mosaics of scrolls and animals, now very much defaced, but of some interest.

The church is said to have been founded in 1124 by the Empress Irene, wife of John Comnenus, whose successor, the great Manuel, was buried in the central nave of the three. It shows a distinct decline in the arts from the palmy days of S. Sophia by the details which are much coarser, as may be seen by the windows of the small apses (Plate XVIII). Similar windows occur at S. Mary Panachrantos, but the cap and base there are decorated with surface carving. Still the general effect of the Pantocrator is fine, and there is much to admire in this and the other churches of the same period. The walls retain traces of fresco painting, with which the whole interior was no doubt once adorned.

S. Mary Panachrantos

The Pantocrator is one of the largest of the later churches, and the span of the widest of the naves and domes is about 22 ft. But in general the scale is smaller: at S. THEODORE THE TIRO (Kilisse Mesjidi) (Fig. 27) the span is only about 14 ft. The latter is externally the prettiest church in Constantinople with its arcaded and colonnaded front, and its four dome-towers (Plate XIX). The interior is small, and has lost its four columns on which the dome rested, as has been already explained; but the narthex is on a scale of importance quite disproportionate to the church behind it, and is a singularly graceful composition. It consists of five bays vaulted domically, of which the middle one contained the door, and that on each side of it had a triple arcade to the street, once open above a low

S. Theodore the Tiro

Plate XIX

S. THEODORE THE TIRO, CONSTANTINOPLE

CH. IX] LATER BYZANTINE BUILDINGS 127

parapet, though now enclosed by sashes. The parapet is of thin stone carved in panel-work on both sides, and

Fig. 30. GUL DJAMI—S. Theodosia.

the columns have fine bold capitals carrying round arches.

This charming building marks a new departure in Byzantine architecture. The inattention to exterior effect Attention to exterior design which we have noticed in the churches of the 5th, 6th, and 7th centuries, including S. Sophia itself no longer prevails, and in the buildings of the 10th, 11th, and 12th centuries the outside is as carefully designed as the inside. Brick still forms the material of the walls, but here at S. Theodore it is banded with stone, and in the arches the successive rings are recessed behind one another in the manner of the Gothic orders. Cornices of dentils appear, and the blank walls are recessed between the windows and doors with niches, or gigantic flutings which are closed at top with conch-shaped stoppings. These occur at S. Theodore (Plate XIX) and most of its contemporaries; at the Pantocrator; in the great apses of the Gul Djami (Fig. 30); and at the little church of S. Thecla near the site of the vanished S. Mary of Blachernae. New cornices were devised in brickwork such as the vandyked example in the Gul Djami apses and at S. Elias (Eski Serai Djami) at Salonica which dates probably from the 12th century: an ornament which occurs also in the Church of the Apostles (Souk-Su Djami) in the same city.

<small>Byzantine cornices</small>

But the greatest change was in the dome, which had from the 5th century downwards been accepted as the principal feature of a Byzantine church. In the Gul Djami at Constantinople, which is a large church with a span in the nave and dome of 28 ft., the dome still shows outside as in the earlier churches[1]. But at S. Theodore, the Pantocrator, S. Saviour Pantepoptes (Fig. 31), and the later churches at Constantinople and Salonica, the dome is enclosed in a lofty drum which from the small-

<small>The tower dome</small>

---

[1] The dome and the pointed arches and pilasters which carry it seems to be Turkish reconstructions. Van Millingen, *Churches of Constantinople*, p. 169. The form of the dome however is probably original.

CH. IX] LATER BYZANTINE BUILDINGS 129

S Saviour Pantepoptes
Constantinople
Eski Imaret Mesjid
Sept. 26. 1910.

Fig. 31.

J. A.   9

ness of the span becomes a tower and is carried up and closed with a pyramidal roof. The drum is brought into a polygon and panelled on each side with arcading, divided by shafts worked in brick, and with brick capitals, carrying arches which break into the pyramidal roof; and instead of being levelled above the back of the arch as we northerners should have done, the round extrados is left, and the roof fitted to it on each face of the tower, which gives it a fluted form like the outside of a melon. This drum-tower design prevailed through all subsequent Byzantine architecture to the last, and is found at Athens and throughout Greece, as well as in the Asiatic provinces of the Empire.

The church of the Chora Mone tes Choras

The KAHRIYEH DJAMI, the Church of the CHORA,—S. Saviour's in the Fields as we should say,—so called because it stood outside Constantine's wall, is said to have been founded by Justinian and rebuilt by Maria Ducaina, mother-in-law of Alexius Comnenus in the 11th or early in the 12th century. It is a very complicated structure (Fig. 32); the main body of the church is small, cruciform in plan with an apse, and a dome which has been very lately rebuilt after damage by an earthquake. The walls are lined with marble slabs as at S. Sophia in bands and panels, finished above at the springing of the arches and dome with a small cornice of acanthus leaves, below which is a band of marble mosaic. The arms of the cross are very shallow and formed not by detached piers standing within the square of the dome, but by solid projections from the main wall at the four angles[1].

---

[1] M. Schmitt has published a splendid monograph on this church and its mosaics, with full illustrations. Unfortunately the text exists only in Russian.

CH. IX] **LATER BYZANTINE BUILDINGS** 131

The south chapel contains two finely carved arched Church of
slabs, now fixed on the walls facing one another, but the Chora
evidently not in their original place. At first sight one
imagines them part of a ciborium, such as those at Arbe
in Dalmatia, S. Apollinare in Classe or Cividale in Friuli,
but they seem too large. One of them is surmounted by

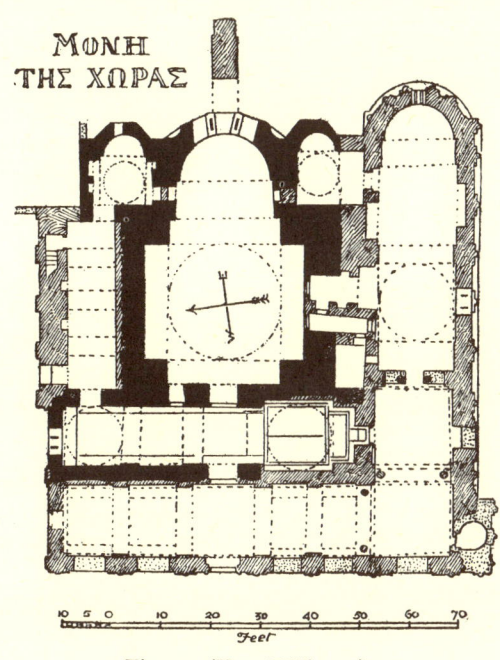

Fig. 32 (Van Millingen).

a panel with a long epitaph for the General Michael
Tornikes, which dates from the beginning of the 14th
century. If the panels are as late as that they show a
curious archaism, for they have preserved the character
of Byzantine carving very exactly. As they contain
sculptured figures, they so far break with Byzantine tradition; which may be the effect of contact with western

132 LATER BYZANTINE BUILDINGS [CH. IX

Church of the Chora

art resulting from the half century of the Latin occupation of Constantinople. But the question of western influence is raised more imperatively when we turn to the decorations of the narthex.

The narthex

The usual double narthex here assumes unusual proportions, and quite predominates over the church to which it forms the vestibule. The outer narthex is six bays long, each bay being covered with a domical vault, and the entrance door has a red marble frame of a usual Byzantine section. On the outside the bays are divided by half columns which now carry nothing, but may once have carried arches of brick like those in the front of the Pantocrator (Plate XX). The whole structure seems of brick, the elevation is not great, and the façade generally is very inferior to that of S. Theodore the Tiro. A door with a similar frame of red marble leads to the inner narthex where two of the bays have real domes on pendentives. The central door thence to the church has on the inside a cornice prettily carved with birds and foliage. A side doorway has one marble jamb lining made out of an earlier fragment representing a door with deeply sunk panels and in the centre of each panel was once some carving, now defaced. This resembles, and is probably coeval with a marble screen panelled in the same way, that crosses the south gallery at S. Sophia.

Mosaics

But the most remarkable thing in this church is the mosaic decoration of the two nartheces, which very fortunately is dated, and so fills an important place in the history of pictorial art. It is extremely like the work of the Italian primitive painters, Cimabue, Giotto, and Memmi. The faces are modelled a good deal, and there are attempts at foreshortening and expression very unlike the character of the older mosaics of the 5th or 8th centuries. There is no name or monogram of the artist,— for there seem to have been more than one, as the work is unequal,—but the donor is depicted kneeling with an enormous balloon-like bonnet on his head, and offering a church, intended no doubt for this one, to the Saviour. This mosaic is over the inner door leading to the church and bears an inscription :— *Church of the Chora*

ὁ κτήτωρ λογοθέτης τοῦ γενικοῦ Θεόδωρος ὁ Μετοχίτης. *Mosaic dated 1303*

Theodorus Metochites the Logothete or Treasurer repaired and decorated the narthex under the Palaeologi after the explusion of the Latins and restoration of the Greek Empire. It is recorded that the work did not extend to the interior of the church.

Over the door between the outer and inner narthex is the date 6811, which deducting 5508, the assumed age of the world at the birth of Christ, gives us 1303 as the date of this mosaic[1].

This has given rise to a lively dispute as to the relative preponderance of Greek or Latin elements in the art of those days. Is the character of these mosaics due to influences from Italy, or is the development of art in Italy derived from Byzantium? *Their relation to Italian art*

What was the state of art in Italy at the opening of the 14th century? In sculpture it had nothing to learn from the Byzantines, with whom sculpture, owing to religious restrictions, had always taken a lower place than painting. In Italy Niccola Pisano, who gave the greatest impulse to the art of any mediaeval master, had been dead a quarter of a century, his son Giovanni was sixty years old and Andrea Pisano was rising already *Italian art in 14th century*

[1] This date was I believe first observed by Sir Edwin Pears of Constantinople.

134 LATER BYZANTINE BUILDINGS [CH. IX

Church of the Chora

into fame. In architecture the cathedrals of Siena and Orvieto were approaching completion, works in comparison with which Constantinople has nothing to show but the one great church. Arnolfo was at work on the Duomo and S. Croce at Florence, and great buildings both civil and ecclesiastical were rising up in all the great towns of Lombardy and Central Italy. But if in these two arts Constantinople in the 14th century was immeasurably behind the schools of Italy, in painting she had for long taken the lead, and had held it up to that time. There can be no doubt that it is to Greek artists that we must attribute the mosaics at Ravenna and those in the early churches in Rome; and the influence of the Byzantine school on the earliest works of Italian painters is unmistakeable. Vasari tells us how in the latter part of the 13th century certain Greek painters were invited to Florence to restore the art of painting "which was not so much debased as actually lost[1]"; and how young Giovanni Cimabue used to play truant from school, and stand all day watching them at work in S. Maria Novella, which led to his apprenticeship to the art, in which he soon surpassed his Greek instructors. As Cimabue was born in 1240 this must have happened while the Latin Empire at Constantinople was still in being, and it is natural to suppose that the conquest of the Capital of the East by Franks and Venetians would have brought the two parts of the old Roman Empire into closer touch with one another. But Italian painting, like Cimabue himself, soon surpassed its instructors; and though Tafi, Gaddi, and Margaritone worked in the "maniera Greca," Giotto broke away

Greek artists in Italy

Cimabue

[1] Chiamati .. per rimettere in Firenze la pittura, più tosto perduta che smarrita. Vasari, *Vita di Cimabue.*

CHURCH OF THE CHORA—CONSTANTINOPLE

Plate XXI

S. ELIAS—SALONICA

CH. IX] LATER BYZANTINE BUILDINGS 135

from the sombre stiffness and conventionality of Byzantine art, and became more natural and realistic[1]. Born in 1276 Giotto would have been 27 years old when these mosaics were put up by Theodorus Metochites, and his fame and his example had begun to influence the current of art and to revolutionize its methods. It must have been soon after 1300 that his friend Dante wrote:

Giotto breaks with Greek art

> Credette Cimabue nella pintura
> Tener lo campo, ed ora ha Giotto il grido,
> Sì che la fama di colui oscura[2].

There was no doubt a concurrent movement among the Greek painters in the direction of a more natural and historical manner; but whether it was due to closer intimacy with the western schools which might be one result of the fourth Crusade, or whether on the other hand the two schools of the east and west moved independently of one another in the same direction is a question that will probably always be debated. The solution may perhaps be found in that curious magnetic communication of new ideas which explains the simultaneous, or almost simultaneous, appearance of changes in style in different districts and different countries, both in architecture, painting, and sculpture. But it must be observed as bearing on this question, that while Italian art rapidly progressed from Giotto to Raffaelle, Byzantine painting left to itself sank gradually into mere repetition and stagnation.

Mutual influence of Greek and Latin schools

The tendency to decorate the outside of their churches went further at Salonica than at the Capital. The church of S. ELIAS (Eski Serai Djami) is in the upper part of

---

[1] Divenne cosi buon imitatore della natura che sbandì affatto quella goffa maniera Greca. Vasari, *Vita di Giotto*.

[2] Dante, *Purg.* XI. 94.

136 LATER BYZANTINE BUILDINGS [CH. IX

S. Elias, Salonica

the former town, for as the Westerns dedicated their churches on the hill-tops to S. Michael, the Greeks dedicated theirs to S. Elias, the saint of Mount Carmel, perhaps with some allusion to the resemblance of the word ἥλιος. This church (Fig. 33) is cruciform and trifoliate, with apses to the transepts as well as the chancel, and a short square nave of which the western part is much lower than the rest; forming a sort of ante-

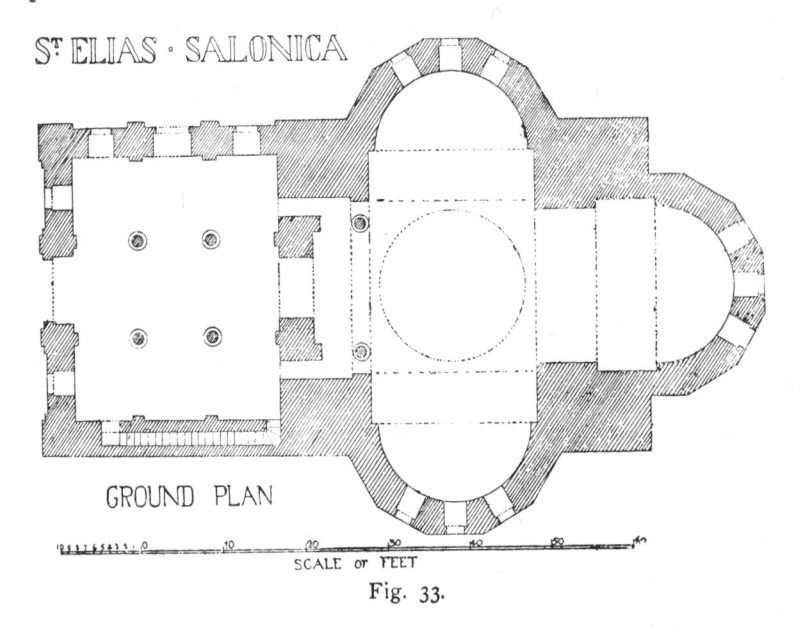

St ELIAS · SALONICA

GROUND PLAN

SCALE OF FEET

Fig. 33.

Decorative brickwork

church, not the usual narthex. The exterior (Plate XXI) is now much disfigured with colour and whitewash, but this does not conceal the elaborate patterns in brickwork with which it is decorated, formed by setting the large thin bricks with their edges outwards in zigzags, trellis work, diamonds, and guilloches, while above is the cornice of vandyked brickwork which has been noticed already at the Gul Djami.

In this church the drum-tower, which is 18 ft. in diameter internally, is unusually lofty and is domed at the summit. It is carried by four deep arches springing not from detached piers but from solid angles of the outside walls. In spite of this massive construction the church, owing no doubt to its precipitous site, has given way and is held up by enormous buttresses.

The two columns that break the span of the western arch have Corinthianizing capitals of the Byzantine type. M. Texier says the date 6562 is found on a piece of stone belonging to the building. This would be the year 1054 of our era[1], a date which seems too early for the existing fabric.

Very like this church is that of the Holy Apostles at Salonica, now the SOUK-SU DJAMI, or cold water mosque. Here the exterior decoration, especially at the east end, is still more remarkable (Plate XXII) and has a very charming effect. The ground plan (Fig. 34) is curious, and slightly recalls that of S. Sophia in the same city (Fig. 17 *supra*). It is cruciform with a central drum-tower, domed, and only 13 ft. in diameter, supported on four detached columns, and buttressed by barrel vaults on all sides: but outside the square which encloses the cruciform structure is an aisle to N. W. and S. which is vaulted, and carries at each of the four corners a drum-tower like the central one but smaller. All five towers are panelled with arches in brickwork, which break up through the eaves as has been described above, and all are open from the floor up to the dome which crowns the summit except that at the S.E., which is not open to the church. Being so small, they are

The Church of the Apostles Salonica

---

[1] I do not understand how M. Texier makes it 1012. The difference between the two eras is 5508.

138 LATER BYZANTINE BUILDINGS [CH. IX

Church of the Apostles Salonica

extravagantly high for interior effect, and are lanterns rather than domes.

Some of the capitals resemble that of the Porta Aurea at Constantinople (Plate IV) with a double coronal or

CHURCH OF THE HOLY APOSTLES SALONICA (Texier)

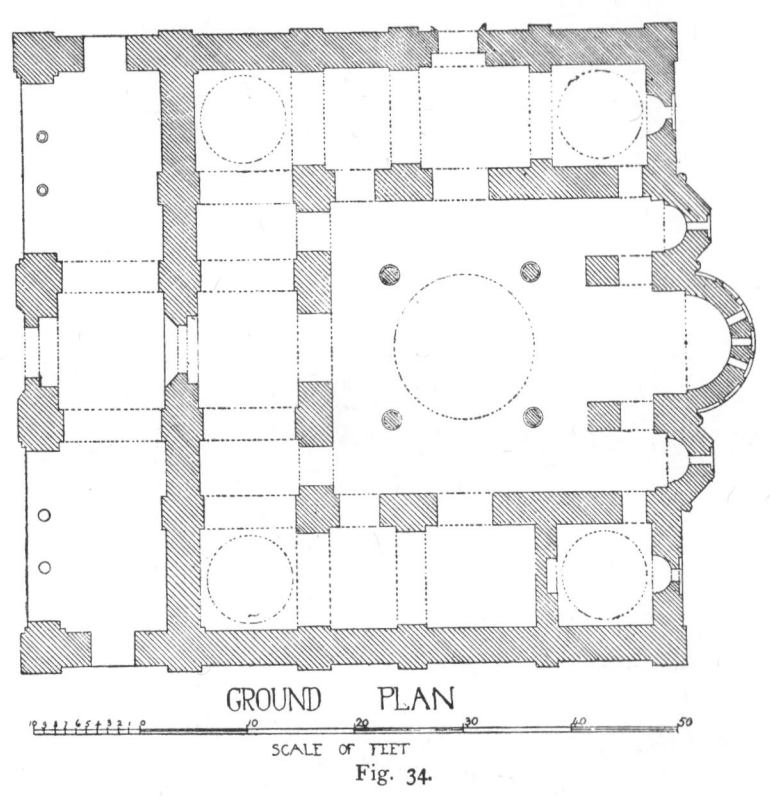

GROUND PLAN
SCALE OF FEET
Fig. 34.

frill of leaves erect, and the others are of the Corinthianizing Byzantine type and not very remarkable.

Here and there in the church are traces of mosaic, which the Hodja in charge implied would be found to a great extent still existing behind the plaster. In another place a figure very well done in fresco has been exposed.

Plate XXII

THE TWELVE APOSTLES—SALONICA

Plate XXII A

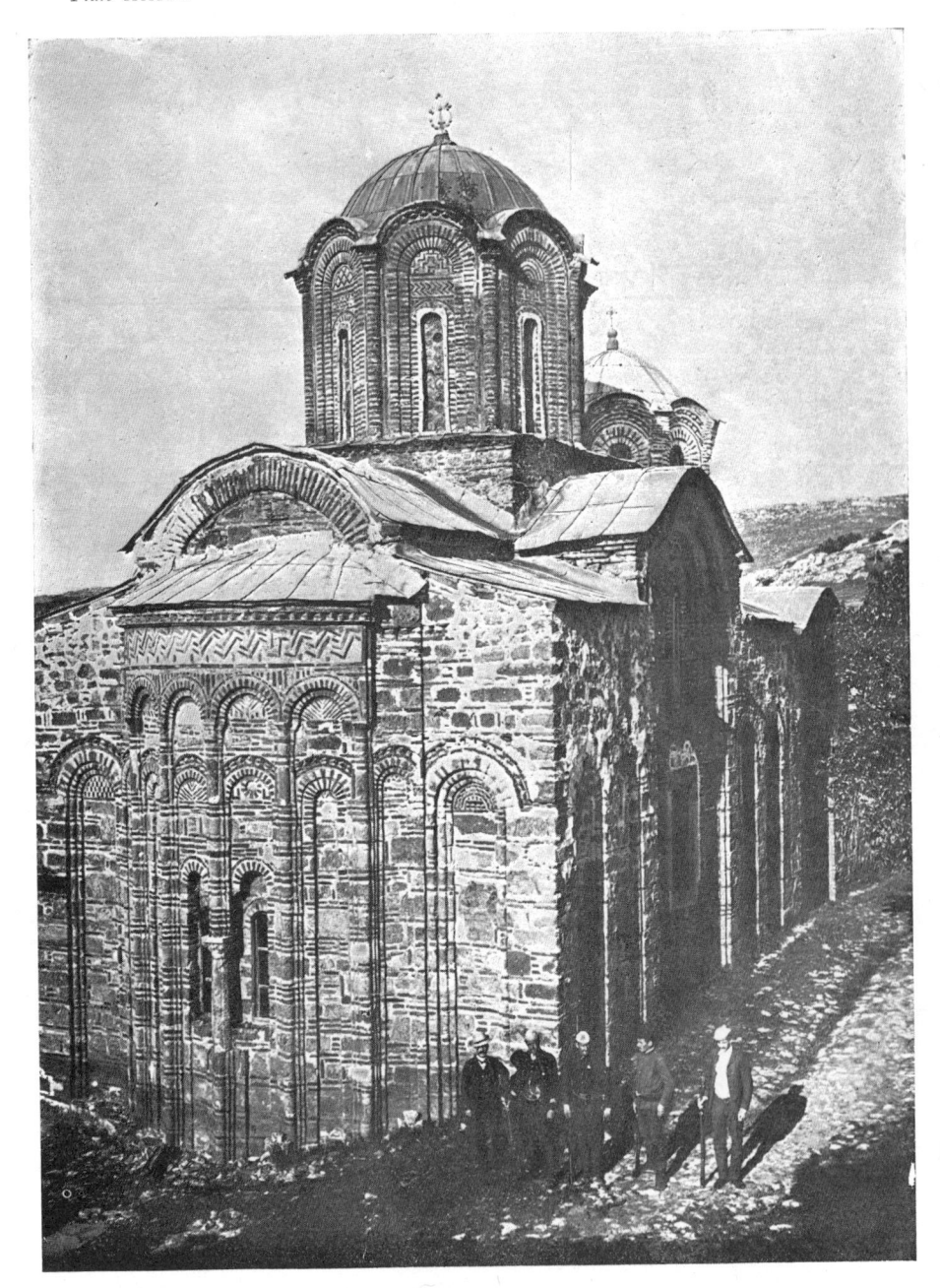

LESNOVO—Serbia

CH. IX] LATER BYZANTINE BUILDINGS 139

The date of the Souk-Su Djami is variously estimated. M. Texier sees in it characteristics of the 7th century, but that seems out of the question. Signor Rivoira places it in the 11th century, but M. Diehl dates it in the 14th, and even gives the precise years of its construction between 1312–1315[1], though he does not give his authority. The capitals in the nave certainly belong to a much earlier time, though of course they may have been used again from an older structure. But the exterior brickwork is identical with that of S. Elias which he dates in the 11th century, and has details like those of the Gul Djami apses which he believes to have been remodelled in the time of the Comneni. No documentary evidence can avail against that of the stones and bricks themselves; and the dates of the Apostles' church and that of S. Elias must rise or fall together. I am disposed to think that they both belong to the end of the 12th century and the time of the Comneni, but contain details used again from older buildings[2]. *Church of the Apostles Salonica*

It is, however, very difficult to be sure of a date in the buildings of these countries, where the style changed so slowly that there is little difference between those of the 5th or 6th centuries and others four or five hundred years later. There is a pretty chapel attached to the church of S. Mary Pammakaristos at Constantinople which is ascertained to have been built in the 14th century, but might from its style be many centuries older. There are in the interior two capitals which look like 6th century work, and if the date given for the building is correct they must have belonged to an older church. *Difficulty of dating Byzantine work*

S. Mary Pammakaristos

[1] *Manuel de l'art Byzantine*, pp. 705–724.
[2] Since the Greeks have recovered Salonica, the narthex of this Church of the Apostles has been ridded of various Turkish encumbrances, and the original brickwork of the arches is exposed. It is very like the work at Hilendar in Mt Athos which was built or at least founded by Stefan Nemagna of Serbia, who died in 1200.

Serbian churches

Decoration by patterns in brickwork, as in the churches just described, was carried to still greater lengths in the churches of Serbia. The architecture of that country, borrowed at first from the Romanesque of Dalmatia, finally, under the Nemanja dynasty, settled down into a Byzantine style which even survived the ruin of Serbian independence.

Lesnovo

The church at LESNOVO (Plate XXIIA), built about 1340 has the late Byzantine tower-dome, the banded stone and brickwork, and the sunk panels of S. Theodore the Tiro, and the fancy brick patterns of the Apostles Church at Salonica[1] (Plate XXII). There are many other churches where this mode of decoration is

Lazaritsa

used effectively; that at LAZARITSA in KRUSCHEVATZ is a brilliant example (Plate XXIIB), where we find also the great flutings or niches finished with a half-domed top, that have been noticed at Constantinople. The tracery of the rose window is also remarkable.

Byzantine domestic work

Very little domestic work of the Byzantine period remains, though careful search among the by-streets of Stamboul might result in discovery of more than is supposed to exist. The most remarkable example is

Tekfur Serai

the TEKFUR SERAI, which has been variously known as the Palace of Belisarius, and that of Constantine Porphyrogenitus. It stands with one end on the great wall between the Egri Kapu or Porta Caligaria, and the Adrianople gate, Edirne Kapu; and seems to have been a pavilion or annexe to the great Palace of Blachernae, of which nothing now remains but some curious vaulted substructures near the tower which contains the supposed prison of Anemas.

The Tekfur Serai (Plate XXIII) is a rectangular building originally three storeys high, which has lost its

---

[1] v. my Introduction to the *Churches of Serbia*, Murray, 1917.

*Plate XXII*B

LAZARITSA—Serbia

Plate XXIII

TEKFUR SERAI—CONSTANTINOPLE

CH. IX] LATER BYZANTINE BUILDINGS 141

floors, and is remarkable for the decoration of the façade towards what was once an interior court of the palace. The spandrils of the windows are filled with geometrical patterns made of squares and strips of white marble, and thin bricks placed edgeways, or cut into triangles and squares (Fig. 35). A band of the same divides the two upper storeys, and the arches have light and dark voussoirs of stone and brick alternately. Bands of brickwork through the masonry elsewhere complete a very effective polychromatic design. The windows were partly filled in with

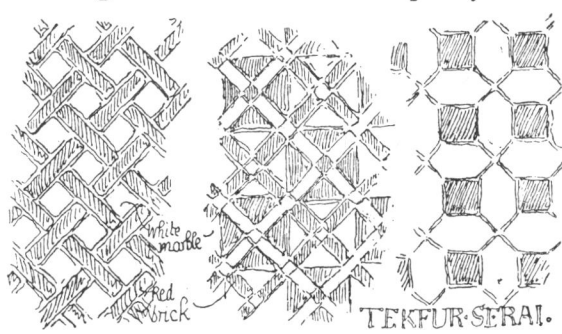

Polychrome decoration

Fig. 35. TEKFUR·SERAI. (white marble, red brick)

a marble tympanum, which remains in a few cases only. From its style the building might be assigned to any date from the 10th to the 12th century, and the tradition which assigns it to Constantine VII Porphyrogenitus (912–958) may possibly be correct, though I should be disposed to date it rather later. It is not likely at all events that such a building would have been erected after the desolating conquest of the Empire by the Crusaders in 1204.

Constantinople never recovered the blow given by the Latin conquest, and during the 200 years that elapsed between the return of the Palaeologi and the taking of the city by the Moslems, the boundaries of the Empire gradually

The Latin conquest in the 4th Crusade

shrank till little remained but the town itself, which safe behind its mighty walls defied all attacks till the advent of Mahomet's cannon.

Decay of later Empire

But before then Constantinople had evidently sunk much below the splendour of the days of Justinian or even those of the Isaurian and Macedonian dynasties. The condition of any mediaeval city would have been disgusting to modern ideas. One reads that the clerks at Oxford frequently complained of the unwholesomeness of the town. Beasts were slaughtered at Carfax and other public places, and chandlers polluted the air by melting tallow in the streets. The thoroughfares were deep in mire and filth and the water used for baking and brewing was drawn from streams into which the town poured its sewage. Constantinople would have been no better than Oxford and other European cities of the period and may even have added some of the squalor of an Oriental town. Foulques de Chartres at the end of the 11th century

Accounts of mediaeval travellers

speaks with wonder of the stately buildings, monasteries, and palaces, the great squares and forums decorated with treasures of art: and there still remained the triumphal arches, the great hippodrome, and the numerous imperial palaces; but all these were the work of ages long gone by. Odon de Deuil some 50 years later is loud in praise of the palaces and churches, but continues "the town nevertheless is stinking and filthy, and condemned in many places to perpetual shade. In fact the rich cover the public ways with their constructions and leave the sewers and dark places to the poor and strangers. There are committed murders, robberies, and all crimes which haunt obscurity[1]." Even the dogs which only disappeared

[1] Quoniam autem in hac urbe vivitur sine jure, quae tot quasi dominos habet quot divites, et pene tot fures quot pauperes, ibi sceleratus quisque

Plate XXIV

HOUSES AT THE PHANAR—CONSTANTINOPLE

Plate XXV

MOSQUE OF MAHOMET II—CONSTANTINOPLE

CH. IX] LATER BYZANTINE BUILDINGS 143

a few years ago are said to have been there, wandering about in the rubbish, and filling the town with their howls and barking.

The type of house in the later days of the Empire seems to have lasted for some time even after the conquest if we may judge from such examples as those in the district of the Phanar (Plate XXIV), which though the windows of the upper storey are evidently inspired by Turkish taste, show by the massive corbelling of the projecting first floor that the traditions of Byzantine art were not forgotten. This was natural. The Turks were not builders or architects themselves, and had to employ the Greeks to build for them, who had traditions of their own. Instances of this kind of work, always with the overhanging upper storeys, are still to be met with in all parts of Stamboul, in many cases perhaps older than the Moslem advent, none of them probably much later, for the art would gradually expire under the numbing influence of a foreign despotism, and a fatalist religion.

<small>Byzantine houses</small>

The Moslem, however, did not fail to fill the Capital with splendid mosques to celebrate the faith of Islam. The earliest is that built by the conqueror Mahomet II, who made room for it by pulling down the Church of the Apostles which Constantine had built and Justinian rebuilt as an Imperial Westminster or S. Denys, to be the burial place of themselves and their successors (Plate XXV). The architect of his new mosque was a Christian, Christodoulos, and as a reward the Sultan is said to have given him the little church of S. Maria Mouchliotissa, which of all the churches in Stamboul has alone remained Christian

<small>The mosques</small>

---

nec metum habet nec verecundiam. * * * in omnibus modum excedit: nam sicut divitiis urbes alias superat, sic etiam vitiis. Odo de Deogilo, Lib. IV. *op. cit.*

since the conquest. The new mosque, which has been much repaired and altered since it was built, is imitated from S. Sophia; and that church indeed gave the pattern for all succeeding mosques, those of Suleyman, Achmet, Bayazid, the Validé, and the rest. These great buildings are all much alike, and after a time become monotonous, and a great part of their charm arises from the beautiful faience which lines the walls. They are many of them designed by Sinan, who is said to have been an Armenian, or an Albanian, and it is not known that any Turk has been distinguished as an architect. It is, however, to these great marble mosques, with their swelling domes piled up in succession one above another, till the mighty central cupola is reached, soaring above the rest, that Constantinople is indebted for the magnificent and perhaps unrivalled picture she presents; and not the least of her beauties is the forest of graceful minarets that contrast so successfully with the domes,—surely one of the happiest conceptions of architecture. Those who have approached Constantinople by sea, or watched day by day from the heights of Pera the sun set in glory behind the seven hills and the countless domes and spirelets of Stamboul will not easily lose the impression made by the spectacle.

CHAPTER X

ITALO-BYZANTINE ARCHITECTURE. FIRST PERIOD. UNDER THE EMPIRE

THE history of the Eastern Empire during the 4th and 5th centuries is not one of undisturbed repose, and the citizens of Constantinople had beheld from their walls the armies of victorious Goths and Alans. But the western half, which fell to Honorius the younger son of Theodosius, had a history during that period of more serious disaster which not only in the end extinguished the latest remains of the Roman Empire, but largely affected the character of the population. Disastrous state of Italy in 5th century

The maritime situation and the mighty walls of Constantinople forbade any serious attack on that capital by the hordes of Goths, Alans, and Huns that swept over the provinces: but within 45 years, from 410 to 455, Rome, that had seen no enemy within its walls since Brennus and his Gauls, was sacked twice by Goths and Vandals, and barely escaped destruction by Attila. The fairest provinces of Gaul were overrun by German tribes, Suevi, Vandals, Goths, Franks, and Burgundians, who never returned but settled down as permanent colonists in the conquered territory. Rome had long ceased to be the capital, which was fixed at Milan; but on the approach of Alaric in 403 the trembling Honorius fled to Asti, where he was besieged till relieved by Stilicho and the victory of Pollentia. In the following year he retired to feed his poultry in safety behind the impassable marshes and lagoons of Ravenna which became the capital of Capital removed to Milan Capital removed to Ravenna

J. A.   10

the Western Empire till its final extinction by Odoacer in 476.

<small>Survival of paganism at Rome</small>
The old Roman religion made a more vigorous struggle for existence in the west than in the east. At Rome it was still professed by the majority of the Senate more than 80 years after the Edict of Milan in 313. The Vestals still survived, the feasts of the Magna Mater were celebrated, the Pontifical College met, and the Christian emperors till the time of Gratian continued like their Pagan predecessors to assume the title and wear the robes of the Pontifex Maximus. The bloody games of the amphitheatre were continued under the Christian emperors as under their Pagan predecessors, and were not repressed finally till the self-sacrifice of the monk Telemachus in the time of Honorius[1].

During the reign of Julian, and the brief usurpation of Eugenius, the adherents of the older religion might have thought their cause not yet hopeless. The edicts of successive emperors against Paganism were not enforced, and when Gratian removed the statue of Victory which had stood in the Senate House since the time of Augustus, a deputation of the Fathers, headed by the illustrious Symmachus, was only prevented by the influence of Ambrose and Damasus from getting a hearing. Under Valentinian they were more fortunate in obtaining an audience, but the Church still prevailed[2] and the statue was not restored.

[1] Gibbon observes that no church has been dedicated, no altar has been erected to the only monk who died a martyr in the cause of humanity. *Decline and Fall*, ch. XXX.
[2] Symmachus pleaded for toleration of the religion under which Rome had prospered and become great. He adds "uno itinere non potest pervenire ad tam grande secretum," v. Gibbon, ch. XXVIII, and Dill, *Roman Society in the last century of the Roman Empire*, ch. II; to the latter work let me once for all express my acknowledgements.

CH. X] RAVENNA, ROMAN PERIOD 147

Sterner edicts were issued by Theodosius, not only against paganism but against Christian sectaries. In 390 he proposed in a full meeting of the senate the question whether Jupiter or Christ was to be the object of Roman worship, and the obedient Fathers, warned by the exile of Symmachus, decided according to the emperor's wishes. By the edict of 392 sacrifices to idols and acts of divination were made high treason and punishable with death: the temples were closed, and it was made a crime to resort to them. Yet we are told that in that very year the rite of Taurobolium, which was supposed by the votaries of Mithra to bestow a new birth to eternal life, was celebrated in Rome itself, and more than 30 years later it was thought necessary to repeat enactments against the relapse of Christians into idolatry. It is true no penalty was incurred by remaining a pagan: yet with the proscription not only of outward and public worship, but even of the private domestic rites of the household gods, the pagan cults declined. A younger generation brought up under these conditions conformed to the state creed, and though in some quarters it may still have been cultivated in secret, paganism practically disappeared from outward observation within 28 years of the death of Theodosius in 395[1].

Theodosius proscribes paganism

Disappearance of paganism

With the country in this state of confusion, the capital divided between paganism and Christianity, and the land overrun and ravaged by German invasion, it is not to be

[1] It is difficult to trace the occult survival of old superstitions. In the 19th century Pagan idols were still worshipped in southern Dalmatia probably under the name of Catholic saints. According to Mr Leland divination is still practised and the old Etruscan deities Tinia, Teramo, and Fufluns are worshipped secretly among the peasantry of the Tuscan Romagna. I was told on a recent visit to that country that it is usual for one of a family to be taught the *Vecchia Religione*, to secure protection from all quarters.

expected that architecture should have prospered in Italy during the 4th century of the Christian era.

Revival of art at Ravenna

It is not till the 5th century that we have any signs of progress in Christian art to consider; and then it is to be studied not at Rome or Milan, but at Ravenna. Here we find ourselves at once in the presence of a phase of architecture new to Italy, which has broken away completely from the art of Vitruvius, and become a thoroughly developed style with precepts and traditions of its own. It was no doubt influenced by the schools of the east, with which the situation of Ravenna made communication easy. But it had also an independent character, and contained the seed of future development which was wanting in purely Byzantine art.

Three periods of Italo-Byzantine art

Ravennate art falls into three periods: the first during the later Empire till its extinction in 476, which may be called the Imperial or Roman period: the second under the Gothic kingdom till the conquest by Justinian in 539; the third under the Byzantine exarchate till the Lombard conquest.

Ravenna had no doubt attracted many of the scattered artists who fled from Rome and Milan at the approach of Alaric and his Goths, and with the arrival of Honorius, and the choice of the city for the seat of empire an era of building evidently set in. The bishop at that time was

The Ursian basilica

Ursus (400–412) "chaste in body, holy in his work, intent and handsome in face, slightly bald, who first began to build God's Temple, to gather in one fold from their separate hovels the wandering Christian flock." "He built," continues his biographer, "the church we call Ursiana, surrounding the walls with precious stones, and the whole roof of the church with diverse figures in varied tessellated work[1] ***. Cuserius

---

[1] This is inexplicable. The colonnades could never have carried a vault to receive mosaic.

THE URSIAN BAPTISTERY—RAVENNA

Plate XXVII

THE URSIAN BAPTISTERY—RAVENNA

and Paulus adorned one wall on the women's side, next the altar of S. Anastasia, which Agatho made. Another wall, on the men's side, Janus and Stephanus adorned, as far as the aforesaid door, and on this side and that incised in alabaster slabs[1] divers riddles of men, animals and quadrupeds, and composed them excellently well[2]." The Basilica Ursiana was unhappily destroyed in 1734 to make way for the modern cathedral, but from plans left us by Buonamici, the architect of the new building, it appears to have been a five-aisled basilican church, with a single apse, semi-circular inside and polygonal out. There were fifteen round arches on each side carried on columns bearing pulvini, marked with a cross, both on the main and intermediate colonnades. The body had a wooden roof and the apse a semi-dome with mosaic like the other churches in Ravenna[3].

The baptistery of Ursus however remains (Plate XXVI); a domed octagonal building now sunk deep in the ground, built, some say, on the foundations of a bath in the Roman Thermae, with four semi-circular apses on alternate sides. It is lined with precious marbles and mosaic which were added by Bishop Neon, and are as fine as anything in that art which has come down to us. "He painted round the vault in mosaic and golden tesserae the images and names of Apostles, and girt the walls with various stones[4]." According to

The Ursian baptistery

---

[1] Gypsaeis metallis.

[2] Agnellus, *Vita S. Ursi*. Agnellus was an Abbot at Ravenna about the middle of the 9th century. He tells us his genealogy in the *Vita S. Felicis*.

[3] *La Metropolitana di Ravenna*, Fol. 1748-9. Buonamici illustrates the mosaics on the apse and on the arch, which are dated in 1112. The inscriptions are in Latin. See also Agincourt, Plate LXXIII, Fig. 21. Also Rivoira, I. 26.

[4] Agnellus gives the boastful inscription which Neon placed on his work:—his episcopate dates from 425-430.

    Cede vetus nomen, novitati cede vetustas,
    Pulchrius ecce nitet renovati gloria Fontis.
    Magnanimus hunc namque Neon, summusque Sacerdos,
    Exsolvit pulchro componens omnia cultu.

150 RAVENNA, ROMAN PERIOD [CH. X

Sign. Rivoira the dome is constructed with earthenware jars or amphorae, laid horizontally, and probably in an ascending spiral, with the tail end of one in the mouth of another; and Buonamici, who destroyed it, says the apse of the Ursian basilica was vaulted in the same way. The dome of the later church of S. Vitale is known to be similarly constructed. One object was no doubt lightness, but I should imagine also this construction admitted of being put together without centering or with very little[1].

Architecture of baptistery

The architecture of this baptistery is rude and inartificial. The outside is of plain brickwork, with simple arcading slightly sunk and a flattish pointed roof over the dome. Inside, two tiers of arcading surround it, of which the lower is pierced in the oblique sides of the octagon with the apses already mentioned. All the capitals but two in this stage seem to be antiques, the other two are Byzantine. One of the six was once an angle capital, and one of the shafts is an old cornice or handrail set on end. They all have a pulvino or super-abacus, but the archivolts are clumsily managed and do not sit nicely on the abacus. Many of these irregularities, however, are due to subsequent alterations.

Original level of floor

The original level of the floor was some six or seven feet lower than the present, which has been raised above the water level. Even now it is I believe below the high water mark of the feeble Adriatic tides. The columns have been raised, for the capitals would have been originally more than a foot lower; they are now above the springing line of the lunettes, but a good part of

[1] Experiment alone could prove this. The difficulty would be with the thick beds of mortar necessary to fill in between the amphorae. One wonders it did not occur to the builders to make them square.

the shafts and the bases is still buried below the floor. The proportions of the interior have of course suffered seriously by these alterations.

The lunettes under the lower arches are now lined with a dado of porphyry and marble, which has been added within the last few years.

The next stage contains in each bay a large window between two small blank arches. The columns between these arches and in the angles of the building carry Ionic capitals, and the three arches of each bay are included under a wide arch springing from a corbel on the top of the angle column. The dome springs from the same level, so that these eight arches cut up into it somewhat awkwardly, with a soffit that widens as it rises and the dome comes forward.

The mosaics which cover wall and ceiling are excessively beautiful: they are carried round the edges of the arches and under their soffit without any stone architrave, in the way formerly described. The glass tesserae are set edgeways, showing the fracture, the only way of getting full value for the colour, and for different whites Sicilian marble and the warmer toned Coccola are used as well as glass. For the figures black lines are very sparingly introduced, and only on the shaded side (Plate XXVII). The gigantic figures of the Apostles that fill the dome are placed on a sky-blue ground, and divided by gold candelabra. They have their names in gold letters and stand on green grass, on which they cast a shadow. Each figure has the latus clavus and they wear alternately a white toga with a gold tunic and the reverse. They have no nimbus. At the crown of the dome, within a circle of brilliant white and red, is the Baptism of our Lord, the figures in flesh colour and

The mosaics

white on a gold ground. The river god, with his name IORDANN, forms part of the group.

Mausoleum of Galla Placidia

Almost contemporary with this baptistery is the tomb of the Empress GALLA PLACIDIA, daughter of the great Theodosius and sister of Arcadius and Honorius, who ended her tempestuous life at Ravenna in 450. Her mausoleum (Plate XXVIII) is a small cruciform building, the plan itself being a novelty, for the usual form of such a building was circular. The four arms of the cross are barrel-vaulted, and the central crossing is carried up into a low tower with a pyramidal roof of wood and tile, within which is a brick vault or quasi-dome of the form shown above (Fig. 10, No. 2, p. 39). The outside is plain,—even somewhat mean,—constructed simply of brick, with sunk arcaded panels and pedimented ends with brick dentils. The interior has lost the original marble lining of the lower part of the wall[1], but the whole of the upper part and the ceiling above is covered with mosaic of the best kind, in which we still find traces of good classic art (Plate XXIX). Our Lord as the Pastor bonus is seated among his sheep, a graceful youthful figure that might have served for Orpheus or Apollo. In so small a building as this the system of carrying the mosaic round all angles of arches and openings has a less satisfactory effect than when employed on a large scale. There the want of a firm line is not felt and the softened edge is not disagreeable but rather the reverse. But on a small scale the rounded and uneven forms of the arched lines have a somewhat barbarous effect and this interior seems rather as if hewn out of a rock, than regularly built.

[1] Revisiting it in 1911 I found the wall had been lined with yellow Siena marble about 12 years before.

Plate XXVIII

TOMB-HOUSE OF GALLA PLACIDIA—RAVENNA

Plate XXIX

TOMB-HOUSE OF GALLA PLACIDIA—RAVENNA

Under the dome is an altar with sides of transparent alabaster carved in low relief with two sheep regarding a central cross. Behind is the huge sarcophagus of Placidia, so high that she was placed in it seated on a throne[1]. Honorius lies in another sarcophagus, and a third contains the bodies of Constantius, Placidia's second husband, and her son, the unworthy Valentinian III, the murderer of his great general Aetius.

Like the baptistery and other buildings in Ravenna this mausoleum had sunk and the floor has been raised nearly six feet, which has ruined its interior proportions. Even now the water sometimes rises from below and invades the floor.

The church of S. GIOVANNI EVANGELISTA at Ravenna, sadly stuccoed and disfigured some 300 years ago, was built by Galla Placidia about 425 in performance of a vow made during a storm at sea. Like several other buildings in the city it had sunk, and has had to be raised above the level of the invading water. In this case the floor has not been filled in as was done in the Ursian baptistery, but the whole of the nave has been taken down and reconstructed at a higher level. Though the authenticity of the church has suffered by this re-building we have the original plan, and the old arcades have been set up again. The apse also, which is round inside and polygonal out, seems to have been left as it was, with the addition of a plain wall above to raise it to the new height.

S. Giovanni Evangelista

It is a basilican church with antique columns of marble,

---

[1] It is said she was destroyed by the curiosity of someone who introduced a candle through a hole for a better view, and set her alight.

Revisiting the building in 1911 I found the altar had been removed. It is now in S. Vitale. Signor Ricci (*Italia artistica*) says the sarcophagi now contain only a few bones.

S. Giovanni Evangelista

and capitals of a Corinthian type some of which are too small for the shafts, and others are much defaced and repaired with stucco. Their raffling is Roman rather than Greek but that of the carving on the pulvino, which they all have, is more Byzantine in character. The

Fig. 36.

capital of which an illustration is given (Fig. 36) preserves all the four characteristic features of volute, caulicolus, rosette, and acanthus leaves in two tiers, as well as a tolerable classic proportion. The execution however is very rough and unlike real classic work.

CH. X] RAVENNA, ROMAN PERIOD 155

The apse is adorned outside with marble colonnettes carrying brick arches. S. Giovanni Evangelista

The lofty campanile, which is square with a brick spire, is not of the date of the foundation, and Sign. Rivoira assigns it to the 11th century. It occupies the last bay of the south nave aisle, and the N.E. corner is propped by a column which is of granite and antique, and has a capital of purely Byzantine work. As the columns of the nave belong to the 6th century, and the tower to the 11th, it is obvious that the nave arcades, of which the bases are now some seven feet above the pavement of the 11th century, must have been taken down and re-built. This re-building also affects of course the authenticity of the blank arcading in brick of the exterior walls[1].

In the crypt which is not ancient, and of no interest, is an old altar with four marble legs surmounted by early capitals and grooved to receive alabaster panels half an inch thick, of which only one remains. The top is a marble slab, slightly sunk within a raised edge all round, like another at S. Vitale. There is an episcopal chair inscribed

A·D·M·CC·LXVII
ABBs BEVEDTV·F·F
D·OPVS·

The front of the church was preceded by an atrium of which the present garden preserves the form. It is entered by a doorway of 14th century Gothic, but the two jamb posts seem to me Byzantine.

[1] The re-building took place I believe in the 13th century. Sig. Gaetono Nave, the architect in charge of the ancient monuments at Ravenna, told me he found decoration of that date in the roof during recent repairs.

S. Giovanni Evangelista

In a chapel at the west end are preserved on the wall many pieces of the mosaic pavement in small tesserae with which the original floor was covered. More of it is preserved in the museum. There are animals in small panels, often very well drawn, and some figure subjects which are very barbarous. The ship also appears, referring to the Imperial Foundress's terrors and escape.

The dimensions of the church are considerable, the nave being about 40 ft. wide from centre to centre of the columns, and the aisles about 20 ft. The bays are 11 ft. 6 ins. long and there are eleven of them.

S. Agata

The coeval church of S. AGATA would seem to have shared the same fate, and to have been re-built at a higher level; for though the bases of the nave arcades are all exposed above the present floor and carry the ancient columns, the responds which are original are only 8 ft. above the floor, and from one may be seen the springing of a brick arch of the original arcade. One of these responds is a bit of a Roman modillion cornice, the other three are Byzantine. The capitals are rough, some unfinished; one column is lengthened by a short piece below the apophyge and torus, which are 3 ft. up, and it rests on a base much too large for it. All this shows that the building has been much and clumsily altered.

The apse outside is of rough brick, and is polygonal without, semi-circular within. There is no triforium, but a small round-headed clerestory high up. All the roofs are of wood. Measuring to the centres of columns, the nave is c. 33 ft. wide, the aisle 19 ft. 6 ins. and the bay c. 12 ft. There are eleven bays. This makes the proportion of length to width in the nave exactly four to one, a usual basilican proportion.

CH. X] RAVENNA, ROMAN PERIOD 157

The clerestory walls outside are richly arcaded in brickwork which looks original, as if the lower part of the walls only had been re-built. We shall see that this was the case elsewhere in Ravenna. S. Agata

The frontal of the high altar is a fine Byzantine slab or pluteus of the 6th century, measuring 6 ft. by 3 ft., which was dug up some two years ago from below the floor. The ambo seems to have been fashioned out of the top drum of an enormous fluted column. The stoppings of the flutes are carved into a little arcade, and the fillets that divide them have bases and capitals worked on them. The column, if it were a column, would have had a bottom diameter of 5 ft. 6 ins. and been about 44 ft. high.

The church of S. SPIRITO seems to belong to the same period as the two just described. It is basilican with a single apse, antique columns, and capitals various and rather rude, mostly with no Byzantine feeling, carrying pulvini adorned with a cross between two acanthus leaves which have more of the Byzantine character. The four columns next the east however have capitals of a better type, and more akin to Byzantine art. S. Spirito

There is a fine pulpit or ambo of pronounced Byzantine work very like that in S. Apollinare Nuovo, which was moved to a side chapel in 1736, as an inscription records.

The CHAPEL OF S. PIERO CHRYSOLOGO in the archbishop's palace has wall linings of white veined marble, and very interesting mosaics a good deal patched with plaster[1]. The central bay is cross-vaulted and on each Chapel in Arcivescovado

---

[1] At a subsequent visit in 1911 I found the plaster was being removed, and some interesting discoveries had been made, which raise doubts as to the work dating from Archbishop Chrysologus.

arris of the vault is an angel doubled back right and left of the diagonal line, like those in the chapel of S. Zenone in S. Prassede at Rome. This bay is preceded by another with a barrel vault covered with mosaics consisting of a diaper of birds and lilies, a fancy much in vogue at Ravenna at this time. The remains of the marble ambo of the Ursian basilica and another in the church of SS. Giovanni and Paolo are decorated by panel-work with a little bird or beast in each compartment[1]. They may be the work of Janus and Stephanus whom Agnellus has immortalized. I have noticed above a similar motive in the mosaic of S. George at Salonica, and we shall find it at S. Costanza in Rome.

The ivory throne of Maximian In the archbishop's palace is now preserved the famous ivory throne (Plate XXX) generally said on the strength of a monogram to have been that of S. Maximian, the archbishop in Justinian's reign. Later discovery seem to identify it with "a chair superbly carved in panels of ivory" sent by Doge Pietro Orseolo II from Venice as a present to the Emperor Otto III in 1001, which the emperor left to be preserved at Ravenna[2]. The monogram of Maximian on it, if it really spells Maximian, which I doubt, might in that case belong to some other bishop of that name in the 5th century and in the Eastern Empire.

The havoc of barbarian inroads have destroyed many famous churches of which mention is made by Agnellus. The port of Classis, and the suburb of Caesarea which connected it with Ravenna, have disappeared leaving

---

[1] They are illustrated by Rivoira, Vol. I, Figs. 66, 67.

[2] Ricci, *Italia artistica*, pp. 35, 36. Dalton, *Byzantine art and archaeology*, p. 203. Its provenance is variously attributed by archaeologists to Alexandria or Antioch. The monogram however is in Roman letters.

hardly a stone behind them. With them has gone the Ecclesia Petriana, begun by Archbishop Peter, and finished by his successor Neon, which Agnellus tells us excelled all the other churches in Ravenna in length and height and splendour of marble and mosaic. Here was a marvellous portrait of our Lord which seems to have disappeared before Agnellus wrote in the 9th century[1]. The legend connected with it is pretty, and superior I think to the ordinary dull level of mediaeval wonder and miracle.

The Ecclesia Petriana

> "There was a holy Father in the desert who besought the Lord daily to show him the form of his incarnation. And when he was weary of praying a man in white robes, in angel garb, stood beside him at night, and said 'Thy prayer is heard, and I have looked on thy labour. Rise, go to the city called Classis, and enquire for the Ecclesia Petriana, and having entered look above the door[2], and there shalt thou see me depicted on the plaster of the wall.'"

The hermit accordingly goes to Classis, accompanied by two friendly lions, to whom neither Bosphorus nor Hellespont seems to have offered any impediment, and he finds the picture.

> "Seeing it he fell prone on the ground, and worshipped with tears, giving thanks for having seen it just as was revealed in his sleep....'Now I am satisfied with thy holy riches, now I am endowed with heavenly treasure. Take my soul in thy holy court, that bidden to the supper of the Lamb, I may win entrance to thy kingdom, and sit at thy table.' With these words, praying a long while, and rejoicing between the lions who roared around him, he yielded up his spirit."

The wondering people rushed to the scene, and buried him while the lions licked his hands and feet.

---

[1] Hic asserunt aftuisse imaginem Salvatoris depictam. Agn. *Vit. S. Petri*.
[2] Aspice super valvas ejusdem Ecclesiae infra Ardicam, ibi me videbis depictum, &c. v. Ducange as to Ardica.

"Then one lion prostrated itself at his head and another at the feet, roaring loudly, running hither and thither, desirous of bowing their necks to his tomb; and while the people wept loudly in concert with the lions, they both died. And the people buried them on each side of the holy man's body in the same grave."

With this tale we may take leave of the Pre-Gothic or Roman period of the architecture of Ravenna in which, though the influence of Byzantium is not unfelt, the art clings to the West rather than to the East.

Plate XXX

IVORY THRONE—RAVENNA

Plate XXXI

S. APOLLINARE NUOVO—RAVENNA

CHAPTER XI

ITALO-BYZANTINE ARCHITECTURE. THE SECOND OR GOTHIC PERIOD

THE Western Roman Empire was brought to an end by the Herulian Odoacer in 476 : and he in his turn was conquered and afterwards murdered by Theodoric, who founded the Ostrogothic kingdom of Italy in 493. *End of the Western Roman Empire, 476*

The fall of the Western Empire was not as has often been supposed the result of any violent cataclysm; the last five or six emperors had been mere puppets in the hands of German chieftains who were nominally in their service, and the imperial office when it came to an end was but the shadow of a great name. Nor were the Germans who overthrew it new comers. Invasions by vast armies of these strangers had been chronic, ever since the days of the Republic, though till the time of Stilicho they had been steadily repulsed by inferior numbers of disciplined troops under the Roman banner. Nor was it the object of their ambition to destroy the Empire. On the contrary, Visigoths, Franks, Saxons and Burgundians fought under Aetius at the battle of Chalons, and the barbarians often wanted nothing better than a settlement and an engagement under Roman rule. Stilicho himself was a Vandal. Alaric had fought in the service of the great Theodosius, and his successor Astaulfus has left in a memorable speech his view that *Influx of German settlers* the preservation of the Empire[1] was necessary to the maintenance of law and order, for which he saw the fierce temper of the Goths to be unsuited. Germans had risen to the consulship. Many of them were men of cultivation and social charm. The Emperor Arcadius chose the fair Eudoxia, daughter of the Gothic general Bauto, in preference to the Byzantine bride destined for him. German fashions became the rage, and the wearing of trousers, long hair, and fur coats had to be forbidden by three edicts of Honorius[2]. Vast numbers of Germans either as slaves or coloni were to be found on estates all over the provinces. The character of the population must have been largely affected by the steady infiltration of northern blood from beyond the Alps even before the fall of the Empire; and after his conquest of Italy, Theodoric divided one-third of the territory among two hundred thousand of his followers. It is to this wholesome infusion of energy from a youthful freedom-loving people, uncorrupted by the vices of an effete and selfish civilization, that we must attribute the vigorous life of the provinces of the old Western Empire, which displayed itself in the growth of a new and living art, while that of Byzantium, under a semi-oriental despotism, sank into stagnation and immobility in spite of its splendid beginning.

Influence of German fashions

Invigorating effect of German infusion

The Gothic kingdom

Under the firm rule of Theodoric, Italy recovered her prosperity. Though illiterate himself, for he used a stencil to sign his name, he respected the arts and literature. He peremptorily forbad the spoliation and destruction of the monuments of ancient Rome, and appointed an architect to take care of them[3]; and he

---
[1] Gibbon, ch. XXXI.   [2] Dill, II., ch. I.
[3] Formula ad Praefectum urbis de Architecto Publicorum. Cassiod., *Var.* VII. 15.

CH. XI] RAVENNA, GOTHIC PERIOD 163

adorned his capital at Ravenna with new buildings, palaces, and churches[1]. Ruins in various parts of his kingdom supplied him with materials. He writes to the authorities at Aestunae that he hears columns and stones are lying uselessly in their municipality, and that they are to send them to Ravenna, for it were better to use them than to let them lie out of mere sentiment[2]. There are similar letters about the transport of old material addressed to the Count Suna, and the authorities of Faenza and Catania.

Of his palace at Ravenna perhaps nothing is left. The building that goes by that name is of doubtful origin, and even if it be part of the palace it is uncertain to what part of the establishment it belonged. It is ornamented, though in a more barbarous fashion, with the miniature colonnading which first appeared at the Porta Aurea of Diocletian at Spalato. *Theodoric's palace*

But the finest monument which Theodoric has left at Ravenna is the basilica of S. Apollinare Nuovo[3] which was his Arian cathedral, and was "reconciled" to Catholic use by Archbishop Agnellus nearly half a century later (Plate XXXI). This noble basilican church shows in its capitals distinct traces of Byzantine influence. They are of Corinthianizing type, rudely cut, but with the sharp *S. Apollinare Nuovo*

---

[1] Propositi quidem nostri est nova construere sed amplius vetusta servare. *Ibid.* III. Ep. 9. Symmachus is directed to repair Pompey's theatre at Rome, and the architect Aloisius is sent to do the same for the buildings at Fons Aponus (Abano). *Ibid.* IV. 51 and II. 39.

[2] Et quia indecore jacentia servare nil proficit ad ornatum debent surgere redivivum, antequam dolorem monstrare ex memoria precedentium seculorum. Cassiod., Ep. III. 9.

[3] Its old dedication was to S. Martin. Ecclesiam S. Martini Confessoris, quam Theodoricus Rex fundavit, quae vocatur Coelum aureum. Agnellus, *Vita S. Agnelli.* It was dedicated afresh to S. Apollinaris when the relics of that saint were transported thither in the 9th century from S. Apollinare in Classe, to be safe from the Saracens.

raffling of the acanthus leaves that the Greeks loved. They all carry pulvini decorated with a simple cross. Above the arcade, occupying the position of a triforium, is a lofty frieze or wall-space, over which is another lofty stage pierced with clerestory windows. The frieze was evidently intended for decoration, and is occupied by a magnificent mosaic on each side, from end to end of the church. The clerestory has between each pair of windows the figure of a saint in white with the latus clavus, standing on a green ground with a cast shadow. Above is a sort of tabernacle in which hangs a crown, and on the top of the tent are two birds facing a cross. In little panels over the windows are scenes from Scripture history. The figures in this storey are admirably drawn and executed in the best style of the mosaicist. They have an excellent variety of face, and would seem to be portraits.

In the storey below, occupying the place of a triforium, processions of saints, men on the south side, women on the north, corresponding to the division of the sexes of the congregation below, occupy the whole length of the nave above the arcade. The figures are relieved on a gold ground with dresses chiefly of white in which mother of pearl is introduced, and are divided by palm trees with green leaves and brown stems bearing red fruit. Each figure carries a crown, and is named, and has a nimbus, defined by a line forming a circle some way from the head. In the draperies gold is shaded with brown, and white with grey, and the white is defined against the gold on the shaded side by a black or dark brown line. The ground on which they stand is green. The 22 female saints (Plate XXXII) on the north of the nave proceed eastward from the city of Classis towards the Virgin and Child who are enthroned at the far end. Their procession is headed by the three kings, who in extravagant attitudes are hastening to offer their gifts. They are dressed in strange barbarian garb, with flowing mantles and embroidered trousers, the forbidden garments of the Goths. In their arrangement and attitudes they resemble a little Roman sculpture in relief now fixed on the wall of the church of S. Giovanni Battista, by which, or some similar antique, they may have been suggested. On the opposite side the 25 male saints proceed from the town of Ravenna, where is a representation, probably quite conventional, of the "Palatium" of Theodoric, towards a figure of our Lord seated between four angels. The procession is headed by S. Martin to whom the church was dedicated, and who is distinguished by a purple dress instead of the usual white.

S. Apollinare Nuovo

Procession of male saints

The figures in these processions are conventional and have no variety, and are distinctly inferior both in design and execution to those above them; and they belong evidently to a different period. The church, it will be remembered, was built by Arians for their cathedral, and was not converted to Catholic use till after the Byzantine conquest. Theodoric no doubt covered his walls with mosaic, and to his artists I think there can be no doubt the fine mosaics of the upper storey must be credited. To them also should be attributed the figure of our Lord and his attendant angels on the south side, which are as fine as those above them. I am not so sure of the group of the Virgin Mary and her satellite angels opposite, for her figure is distinctly inferior. But the town of Classis at the end of one procession and the palace of Theodoric at that of the other are of the early and Arian period.

Superiority of Arian mosaics

What the Catholics found to object to in Theodoric's processions we cannot tell, but it is obvious that they destroyed them and substituted the monotonous figures we now see in their place. The division between the old and the newer part is quite visible. Further evidence is afforded by the mosaic of the Palatium. The arches are now filled with white festoons of drapery, but close observation will detect the faint outlines of figures; in the middle may have been Theodoric, whose heretic form would of course be obliterated; others occupied the side arches, and three hands may still be seen faintly relieved across the columns, though the figures they belonged to have vanished.

These are not the only alterations the church has undergone. The arches of the nave arcade with their Bramantesque architrave and coffered soffits have always puzzled me, but it was not till my last visit that I had the chance of examining them from a ladder and found them to be all of red terra cotta washed over with stone colour. The string course above which forms the base of the great saintly procession is of the same material.

It is obvious therefore that the whole of the arcades must have been rebuilt and lifted at some time in the early period of the Renaissance. This was no doubt occasioned by the invasion of water, just as was the case at S. Giovanni Evangelista and S. Agata. The raising of the arcade would have cut off part of the mosaic, and it was pointed out to me by Signor Gaetano Nave that the arches are less than a semicircle, the object being to avoid intruding too much on the processional frieze.

The nave has a fine coffered ceiling painted and gilt, dated 1611. The south aisle has a flat ceiling of

Plate XXXII

S. APOLLINARE NUOVO—RAVENNA

Plate XXXIII

TOMB OF THEODORIC—RAVENNA

wood, but the north aisle is vaulted and has chapels between buttresses, a construction designed to support the nave arcades which were leaning outwards.

In the mosaics at this church we see the Christian hagiology thoroughly organized. The nimbus was originally attributed to great personages without any regard for sanctity. Achilles had one when he stood by the ditch and thrice shouted to the dismay of Troy[1]. They occur frequently in pagan mosaics. Herod is adorned with one in the early mosaics of S. Maria Maggiore in Rome; Justinian and Theodora both have them in those of S. Vitale, Ravenna. The apostles and saints in the dome of the baptistery have none. At Salonica they are bestowed on the Virgin and angels but denied to the apostles. Here in S. Apollinare they are given to all the male and female saints in the two processions. From being the objects of tender and affectionate regard in the Church of the Catacombs, whose courage and devotion were gratefully treasured in the memory of their fellow-sufferers, the saints and martyrs were now become celestial powers, succeeding as it were to the daemons of paganism, by whose useful ministry the later philosophers imagined that God governed the world. The Council of Ephesus in 431 had confirmed the title of Θεοτόκος, Mother of God, on the Virgin Mary, and here we see her enthroned and receiving equal and parallel adoration with that accorded to her Son on the opposite wall.

Development of Christian hagiology

S. MARIA IN COSMEDIN, the Arian baptistery, reconsecrated afterwards to Catholic use, is decorated with good mosaics like those of the orthodox baptistery.

The Arian baptistery

---

[1] ὡς ἀπ' Ἀχιλλῆος κεφαλῆς σέλας αἰθέρ' ἵκανεν. *Il.* XVIII. 214.

The Rotunda

The last building at Ravenna of this age is the TOMB OF THEODORIC, built either by himself[1] or his daughter Amalasuntha, a polygonal two-storeyed structure, of which the upper storey seems to have been surrounded by a peristyle like Diocletian's temple at Spalato, but with radiating vaults. This peristyle has all disappeared, and it is not easy to imagine what it was. The building is crowned by a dome consisting of one vast piece of Istrian stone, with pierced handles or ears left in the solid for raising it (Plate XXXIII).

Byzantine conquest

Theodoric died in 526, and in 539 Ravenna was captured by Belisarius and attached to the Eastern Empire.

Ravennate art

If we review the architecture of Ravenna during the 122 years that had elapsed since Honorius transferred the seat of empire thither, we shall find that at first it was very little affected by Greek influence, though the mosaic decoration was probably by artists from Constantinople. But in the time of the Gothic kingdom the Roman element in the architecture became modified, and Greek influence began to make itself felt. This will be understood by a comparison of the capitals at S. Giov. Evangelista built by Galla Placidia, with those of S. Apollinare Nuovo which was built by Theodoric; and after the Byzantine Conquest Greek influence of course became supreme.

Native Ravennate artists

Signor Rivoira holds that sufficient credit has not been given to native artists and too much to the Greeks. He will not admit that from 404, when Honorius came to Ravenna, down to the fall of the Lombard kingdom in 774 Italy was obliged to the East for artists of every

[1] Quod ipse aedificare jussit...sed, ut mihi videtur esse, sepulcro projectus est et ipsa urna ubi jacuit, ex lapide porphyretico valde mirabilis, ante ipsius monasterii aditum posita est. Agnellus, *Vita S. Johannis.*

kind, whether painters, mosaicists, or architects. On the contrary, he thinks that the architecture of that period is due to native artists, and principally to the School of Ravenna, and the sculpture at first to Greek artists in the time of Theodoric and Justinian, and afterwards to native artists working in a Byzantinesque manner.

In this conclusion I think we may generally agree with him. Although at the Gothic invasion many of the trade guilds were broken up and dispersed, one cannot suppose that the craft of building among native Italians was suddenly extinguished. The skilled workmen must have found their way to any place where, as at Ravenna, there was some chance of security and employment. It would be unreasonable to suppose that when any work had to be undertaken, masons and carpenters had to be imported from Constantinople. At Rome certainly, the art of working marble was still understood, for Theodoric writes to Agapitus, prefect of the city, to send him skilled workmen, who would know how to put together wall linings of variegated marbles, for the Basilica Herculis which he was about to begin[1]. *Partial survival of arts in Italy*

But although the actual fabric may be the work of Italian hands, it is quite possible that the superior direction was given by architects from the east. It is recorded that in 814 the Emperor Leo V sent "excellent masters in architecture" to the service of the Doge of Venice. This is not inconsistent with the continuance of native tradition. In those days, and indeed throughout the middle ages, *Native tradition in the workmen under direction*

---

[1] Ut secundum brevem subter annexum, de urbe nobis marmorarios peritissimos destinetis, qui eximie divisa conjungant, et venis colludentibus illigata naturalem faciem laudabiliter mentiantur. De arte veniat, quod vincat naturam: discolorea crusta marmorum gratissima picturarum varietate texantur. Cassiodorus, *Var.* I. 6. Antoniades gives examples from S. Sophia where the natural markings of marbles thus split and opened form human faces—"Ἔκφρασις &c. vol. I. p. 347.

when buildings were not designed on paper but directed on the spot by the architect, or chief craftsman, the liberty of the workman was much greater; and though the touch of the master may be detected in the general design the bulk of the workmanship will be that of the craftsman working under him, who would be largely entrusted with the detail. A familiar illustration in comparatively modern times is found in the tomb of Henry VII at Westminster, where, though the figures and the general conception are due to Torrigiano, we can see the English workman in the details. The same may be said of the tomb of Henry III, the general design of which is most un-English, and probably was imagined by the Italian to whom the mosaic decoration is due, but the mouldings betray the English mason.

The sarcophagi at Ravenna

One sort of sculpture seems certainly to have been practised at Ravenna, that of making the marble sarcophagi of which so many still remain there. There is a letter of Theodoric to one Daniel, whose name, however, seems to proclaim a foreign origin, giving him it would seem a monopoly in Ravenna of these works, "by the benefit of which bodies are buried above ground, which is no little consolation to the mourners." He recommends him in conclusion to be moderate in his charges[1].

The Ravenna brick cornice

As special features of Italian and more particularly Ravennate origin Signor Rivoira claims the arcaded cornices in brickwork which are so constant a feature in North Italian work, and appear here for the first time; also the outer orders of brickwork round windows, forming a series of shallow arches along the wall, and

---

[1] .. artis tuae peritia delectati quam in excavandis atque ornandis marmoribus diligenter exerces, praesenti auctoritate concedimus, &c., &c. Cassiodorus, III. 19.

the polygonal exterior of the apse semicircular inside. The latter does not amount to an invention, but is a mere variety of design, with no constructional significance: one that probably arose independently in many places widely apart. It is an obvious improvement on the solid square ends of churches like those in Southern Palestine[1], which have apses hollowed out of an enormously thick wall, of which the material could thus be economised. According to Buonamici's plan[2] it occurred in the Ursian Duomo at Ravenna which seems to be the earliest recorded example; but it occurs also in Syria at Ezra (Fig. 7 *supra*) and at Bosra, and in the church at Tourmanin, now destroyed, where the influence of Ravenna cannot be supposed to have penetrated. It is unnecessary to suppose a foreign suggestion for so obvious a feature in S. Sophia at Salonica and S. Sophia and S. Irene at Constantinople.

The invention of the pulvino is a different matter, as it is a novel element in construction. It appears in the churches of S. Giov. Evangelista at Ravenna, and the Eski Djouma at Salonica, both of them dated in 425. But Buonamici's drawing of the Ursian basilica shows pulvini on the colonnades, each bearing a cross, and Sign. Rivoira therefore claims the invention of the pulvino for Ravenna. The date of Ursus is variously given. According to one authority he died in 412 in the reign of Honorius, according to another in 396. If the latter date is correct it would seem that the earliest known examples of the pulvino are to be found in Italy. The suggestion may have been given by the entablature block to be found above the columns in late Roman work, shown in Fig. 3, p. 23. Though no use of that member was made to increase the area of support.

[1] *E.g.*, those at Esbeita and Abda. v. *Palestine Exploration Annual*, 1914-1915. Several examples of the same kind are shown in De Voquè's *Syrie Centrale*.
[2] *La Metropolitana di Ravenna*.

CHAPTER XII

ITALO-BYZANTINE ARCHITECTURE. THIRD PERIOD UNDER THE EXARCHATE

By a fiction the Western Empire after the deposition of the last emperor was supposed to have reverted to the representative of Theodosius in the east. Odoacer was created Patrician by the Emperor Zeno, and Theodoric undertook to conquer Italy and govern it in the imperial name. The disorders of the Goths after the death of Theodoric gave Justinian the opportunity of converting this nominal suzerainty into a real dominion.

<small>The Exarchate</small>

In 539 Belisarius captured Ravenna, and Vitiges the Gothic king was sent into a splendid captivity in Asia. Though under Totila the Goths rebelled, and twice took Rome before they were finally subdued by Narses in 552, Ravenna remained under the government of the Exarchate for two centuries till taken by the Lombards.

The new masters of Ravenna at once conveyed to the Catholics the Arian churches of the Goths. Agnellus mentions four churches which were "reconciled" in the suburbs of Classis and Caesarea; and within the walls the Arian baptistery, now known as S. Maria in Cosmedin, and S. Martin, now S. Apollinare Nuovo[1].

---

[1] S. Eusebius, S. George, S. Sergius in Classis, S. Zeno in Caesarea. He is puzzled by the word "Cosmedin" and can only suggest "sine omni reprehensione *Cosmi*, id est ornata, unde et mundus apud Graecos *cosmos* appellatur." Agnellus, *Vita S. Agnelli*. It is supposed to refer to some place in Constantinople, probably the quarter of Eyoub, anciently dedicated to SS. Cosmas and Damianus.

Plate XXXIV

S. VITALE—RAVENNA

Plate XXXV

A

B

C

D

S. VITALE—RAVENNA

CH. XII] RAVENNA, BYZANTINE PERIOD 173

Under Byzantine rule architecture assumed a more decidedly Greek character, and the most remarkable building at this time in Ravenna was the domed church of S. Vitale. "There is no church in Italy like it in building and in constructive work," says the historian. It was founded by Bishop Ecclesius who held the see from 524 to 534. In 525 he had been to Constantinople together with Pope John I on a mission from Theodoric, who sent these Catholic prelates to treat with the Emperor Justin for toleration of the Arians in his dominions. On his return in 526 the Pope was thrown into prison at Ravenna as a traitor and died there, but Ecclesius seems to have fared better.

S. Sophia was not begun till eight years after the visit of Ecclesius to the capital, but we know there were other domed edifices there. The domed church of SS. Sergius and Bacchus, which Procopius says Justinian built during the reign of his uncle Justin, must have been nearly completed, and the plan has so much in common with that of S. Vitale that it seems tolerably certain Ecclesius followed it to a great extent in his new church at Ravenna. In no other way can we account for the novelty of the plan, which breaks away entirely from the basilican form of preceding churches. The inscriptions stated that at the command of the blessed Bishop Ecclesius, Julianus Argentarius[1] built, adorned, and dedicated it, and the Very Reverend Bishop Maximian consecrated it. Bishop Ecclesius died in 534, five years before the conquest of Ravenna by Belisarius, and probably the building did not progress very far under the Gothic kings, who were Arians. The completion at all events is due to Justinian and Theodora, who with

S. Vitale

Novelty of its plan

[1] *Argentarius* probably means steward, or treasurer of the church.

174 RAVENNA, BYZANTINE PERIOD [CH. XII

S. Vitale their attendant courtiers appear in the mosaics of the chancel bringing bowls in their hands containing offerings for the pious work. The consecration took place in 547.

The dome over octagon S. Vitale (Fig. 37) is a domed church, but it does not challenge the difficulties which make S. Sophia a masterpiece of construction. Within an octagonal aisle is an octagon 58 ft. in diameter, of which the angles are bridged out into a circle by a kind of squinch to receive the dome. The dome itself is constructed, as has been already said, with terra-cotta tubes laid horizontally in a spiral, every tube having its foot in the mouth of the one behind it. Seven sides of the octagon are broken out into an exedra or semi-circular recess with pillars in two storeys like those at Constantinople, though at SS. Sergius and Bacchus there are only four exedrae, the two sides facing north and south having colonnades, as was afterwards done at S. Sophia (*v. sup*. Fig. 19, p. 78). The eighth side at S. Vitale contains the triumphal arch which rises to the full height of both storeys. Beyond it is projected the chancel with an apse, which is kept low enough to allow of windows above it in the outer wall of the octagon.

The drum and roof The dome is not shown externally (Plate XXXIV), like those in the east, but is concealed within a drum covered with a pyramidal roof of timber, thus following the fashion of the temple at Spalato and the baptisteries at Ravenna. This plan allows large windows at the base of the dome, which is I think the best lighted dome I have ever seen.

The vaults The exedrae and the apse are covered with semi-domes: the choir, which interrupts the octagonal two-storeyed aisle surrounding the building, is cross vaulted, and ends square with three lights in the east wall above the apse (Plate XXXVI). The aisle is cross vaulted

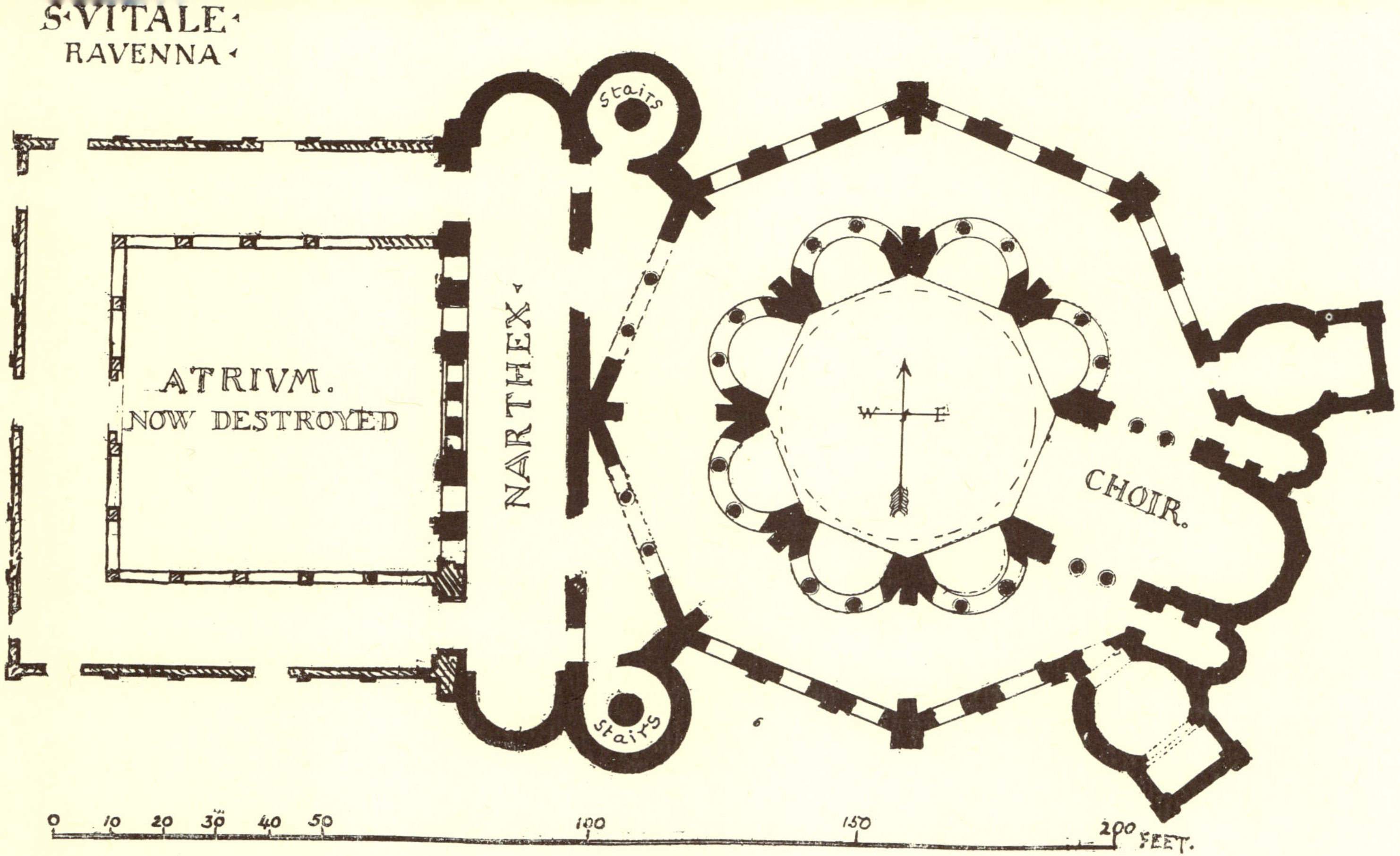

S. VITALE.
RAVENNA.

CHOIR.

NARTHEX.

ATRIUM.
NOW DESTROYED.

stairs

stairs

0 10 20 30 40 50   100   150   200 FEET.

Fig. 37.

176 RAVENNA, BYZANTINE PERIOD [CH. XII

S. Vitale at both levels, the plan of the groins being strangely affected by the intrusion of the exedrae which force them into many irregularities[1].

The marble linings

The lower part of the walls is lined with marble slabs, arranged in panels of strongly veined red and white plaques (red Cipollino) within borders of veined white: no doubt the "eximie divisa, et venis colludentibus illigata" of Cassiodorus[2]. There is a certain poorness in the way the exedrae meet under the dome without any architectural feature to mark the junction.

The capitals

The capitals (Plate XXXV), which all have the pulvino, are thoroughly Byzantine, and in all likelihood were imported from Constantinople. They are of several forms; some of the concave Corinthian outline with acanthus leaves and volutes; some of the plain basket shape either with an Egyptian-like lotus within borders of plaited work, or covered with a network of scrolls which are undercut so as to be detached from the bell; and others of the melon shape, fluted from the corners and from a projection in the middle of each face representing the Corinthian rosette.

The outer walls

The outside octagonal wall has a pier at each angle, and between these piers on each face of the octagon two flat buttresses running up to the eaves and interrupting the brick cornices. Arches across the gallery in the line of the angle buttresses support the central drum and vault, which is also steadied by the weight of the walls that are carried up and enclose the cupola. There is in this construction something approaching that by equilibrium of forces which prevailed in the middle ages,

[1] Rivoira, *Origini* etc., vol. I. p. 57, says recent discoveries show the gallery floor was originally of wood, and vaulted later.
[2] *V. sup.* p. 169 note.

Plate XXXVI

S. VITALE, RAVENNA

CH. XII] RAVENNA, THE EXARCHATE 177

but the construction seems to have required further support, S. Vitale
for at some time flying buttresses have been constructed
against two of the exterior angles of the octagon.

The exterior of the semi-circular apse is polygonal.

The original plan included a fine narthex, now much The
dilapidated, with a round turret and winding stair at each narthex
end to reach the women's gallery. One of these towers
was raised afterwards into a campanile.

The façade however was in later times masked, and
the narthex absorbed by the cloister court of the Benedictine monastery. This in its turn has been converted
into a barrack, and the narthex till lately has served as
a military storehouse, completely cut off from the church.
It is now being rescued from this condition; the arches
into the church are reopened, and the conventual buildings
above the narthex removed, leaving however the Benedictine cloister, which is a fine piece of Renaissance work,
standing in front.

Excavations have resulted in the discovery of the The
foundation of an atrium in front of the narthex, consisting atrium
of three cloistered walks, the narthex itself forming the
fourth[1]. This partly explains the curious position of the
narthex in relation to the octagonal plan of the church,
which it touches not on one of its sides but on one of its
angles. The object in this, which though at first it seems
an eccentricity is really an ingenious piece of planning,
was I imagine to get a narthex long enough to form one
side of the atrium, and yet to leave room between it and
the octagonal aisle for the two circular stair-turrets leading
to the matroneum or gynaeconitis. Had the narthex
been laid along one side of the octagon it is obvious that
there would have been no room in the angle for the

[1] See *Tempio di S. Vitale in Ravenna*. Maioli, *Faenza*, 1903.

J. A.

S. Vitale turrets, and they would have been pushed out so far as to blind the windows of the oblique faces of the octagon. As it is, the triangular spaces between narthex and aisle contain the turrets very well, and only two sides of the octagon lose their windows instead of three.

From the narthex a triple arch in each of the two bays leads into the aisle. The columns, capitals, and arches of the northern triplet were found intact on the removal of the blocking wall. Those in the other were missing and have been re-constructed with two marble columns from a demolished sagrestia, and two capitals which were dug up in the principal piazza of the city, and are supposed to have belonged to Justinian's vanished church of S. Pietro Grande. They are of good Byzantine work somewhat like the Theodosian capital at Constantinople (*v. sup.* Plate V, p. 55).

The narthex The narthex forms a fine Hall, re-calling on a smaller scale that of S. Sophia. It ended each way in an apse, and would no doubt have been handsomely decorated with marble and mosaic. It was originally only one storey in height like the three other sides of the atrium, and the back wall was carried up so as to enclose the two triangular spaces and hide the oblique sides of the octagon. The triangular chambers thus formed were vaulted and had a door to the stair turret, and a triple arch to the gallery or matroneum.

The stair-turrets The North turret has the base of a huge brick newel, and a few of the lowest steps still remaining. The other has the bottom of the newel, but the stairs are modern and of wood. This turret has been raised to form a campanile, but the other retains the brick dome above the entrance to the gallery beyond which originally neither of them rose.

Plate XXXVII

S. VITALE—RAVENNA
(Justinian)

Plate XXXVIII

S. VITALE—RAVENNA
(Theodora)

CH. XII] RAVENNA, THE EXARCHATE 179

The choir and apse, and their vaults, with the entrance arch from the central nave are all lined with glass mosaics (Plate XXXVI), of the greatest beauty and importance. It is true they have declined somewhat in excellence of drawing from the standard reached by those of Bishop Neon a century before, but they retain all their splendour of colour, and almost surpass them in interest. For here on the side walls are contemporary portraits of Justinian and Theodora with their attendant suites, advancing with gifts in their hands for the sacred fabric. On the north side of the apse (Plate XXXVII), is Justinian crowned, and with a nimbus, robed in purple and gold, followed by three courtiers and an armed guard, and preceded by Maximian the Bishop with two attendants one bearing a jewelled volume, and the other a censer. On the opposite wall is Theodora (Plate XXXVIII) crowned and with a nimbus, wearing pendants and collars of jewels or pearls, attended by her ladies and a courtier in white, and preceded by a priest who is pushing aside the curtain of a doorway. Embroidered on the border of her robe are three figures in gold advancing with much action and like herself carrying bowls, which re-call the figures of the three kings at S. Apollinare.

In the semi-dome of the apse is a youthful figure of Christ seated on a cærulean globe between four angels on a ground of gold. The chancel arch is lined with medallions containing busts of saints, scriptural subjects fill the tympana of the side arches, and the vault is covered with scroll-work round a medallion at the crown from which radiate four angelic figures.

The removal of a wooden lining round the apse has revealed two panels of an inlaid dado of marble and porphyry, one on each side, and they have lately been

*S. Vitale
The mosaics*

Justinian and Theodora

The apse

Marble dado

180   RAVENNA, THE EXARCHATE [CH. XII

S. Vitale — copied in the remaining spaces. They resemble those at Parenzo which will be described hereafter, but these are not so fine. Between panel and panel are fluted pilasters of green serpentine with rude capitals, and little if any projection. The marble bench round the apse and the episcopal throne are modern.

Coloured glass — During the late repairs some very remarkable pieces of coloured glass were found. A few pieces were cut and leaded together, but most of them are discs of about nine or ten inches in diameter.

Altered floor-levels — As elsewhere in Ravenna the floor has had to be raised more than once on account of the spongy soil into which the buildings are sinking. The present pavement of *opus Alexandrinum* has bits of Renaissance patterns in it and was raised and relaid in 1539. Justinian's pavement is partly exposed in the aisle some three feet down, and below that is a still older mosaic now under water which seems to show there was an earlier church here in the 5th century[1].

S. Apollinare in Classe — Coeval with S. Vitale, and inferior to it in originality though not in beauty is the great basilican church of S. APOLLINARIS AT CLASSIS, once the maritime suburb of Ravenna, but now deserted both by mankind and by the sea. (Plate XXXIX.)

We read that it was built by Julianus Argentarius at the bidding of Bishop Ursicinus (534—538) and it was consecrated by Bishop Maximian (546—552)[2]. As at the

---

[1] Agnellus records that 26,000 golden solidi were spent on this church. Dean Milman taking the golden solidus at 12s. 6d. makes the amount between £15,000 and £16,000, but that is quite insufficient. *Lat. Christianity*, Book III. Chap. III.

[2] Agnellus, *Vita S. Ursicini*, Cap. I.; *Vita S. Maximiani*, Cap. IV. He says of it "nulla ecclesia similis isti, eo quod in nocte ut in die pene scandefiat," a word, according to Ducange unknown elsewhere. The appendix to Agnellus, *ed.* 1708, reads "coruscat." The meaning is that the marble is so brilliant you can almost see it in the dark.

Plate XXXIX

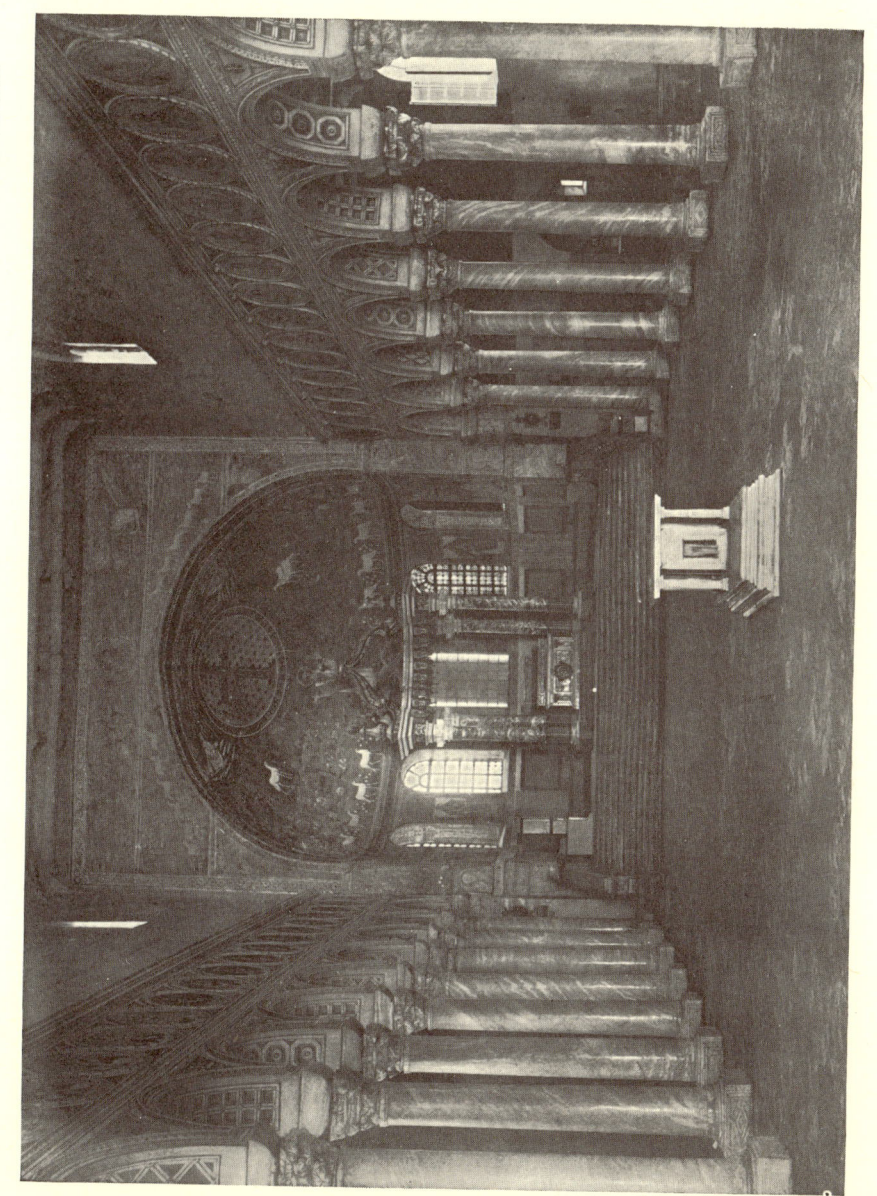

S. APOLLINARE IN CLASSE—RAVENNA

CH. XII] RAVENNA, THE EXARCHATE 181

earlier church of the same name within the city·the columns here are evidently made for the place and not stolen from some antique building. The capitals too are clearly original: they all have the pulvino, and their design is based on the Roman composite, with volutes at the angles, and acanthus leaves below; but they are treated in a thoroughly Byzantine manner, and are no doubt the work of Byzantine artists. The leaves are strangely curled and twisted, as if blown by the wind, a design occurring also at S. Sophia, Salonica, and at S. Demetrius in the same city. The splendid columns of polished grey and white veined marble rest on high marble plinths which might almost be called pedestals. The semi-dome of the apse and the wall above the arch are covered with extremely fine mosaics. Here also may be noticed the superiority of a curved surface to a flat one for this species of decoration. There is no example of a basilican church finer than this, except that of S. Paolo fuori le Mura at Rome, which excels it in scale only. *S. Apollinare in Classe*

At PARENZO in Istria is a church of the 6th century which has preserved its scheme of interior decoration even more completely than the churches on the opposite shore at Ravenna. It is a basilica with an atrium at the west end, and to the west of that an octagonal baptistery and a later campanile dating from the 15th century (Fig. 38). There are ten arches and nine columns on each side, and here it seems that they come from some classic building, and have been adapted. The capitals however are all worked originally for the building, and are of various types, one like a capital at S. Sophia, Constantinople, others like those at S. Vitale which they greatly resemble, and indeed they might have been cut by *Parenzo*

The capitals

the same Byzantine hand[1]. They carry a pulvino on which is the monogram of Euphrasius, the bishop in whose time the church was built, or rather re-built, and finished as is supposed in 543.

The apse   The apse is semi-circular inside and polygonal out, with four large windows, and the peculiarity of a pier in the middle instead of a window as we should have had it; showing that the architect looked to mural decoration for his effect rather than to painted glass as we northerns do. It has still the hemicycle of seats for the clergy with the bishop's throne in the middle, and finished at the ends with the dolphin which occurs in some of the details of S. Sophia, Constantinople.

The mosaics and dado   The walls and vault are lined with mosaic, beginning with a dado of porphyry, serpentine, opaque glass, onyx, burnt

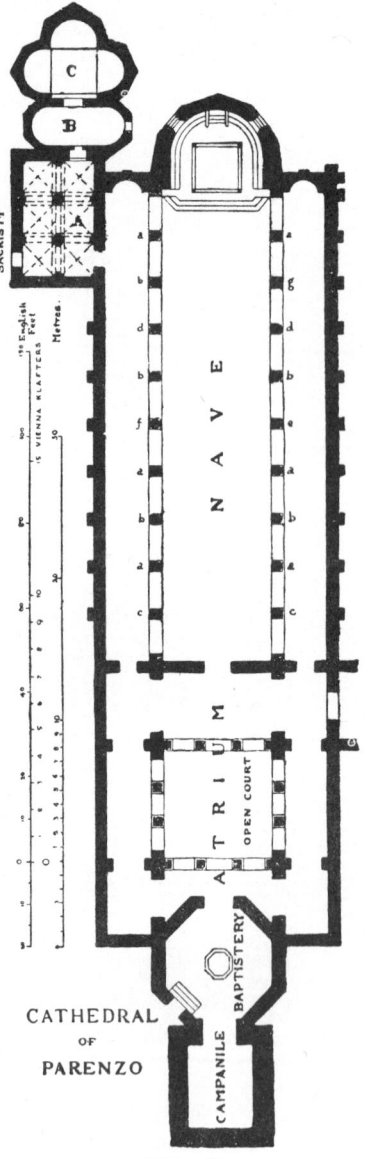

Fig. 38.

---

[1] They are illustrated in my *Dalmatia, &c.* Vol. III. Cap. XXXI.

PARENZO

clay, and mother of pearl which is finer than anything of the kind at Rome, Ravenna, or Milan (Plate XL). This is finished with a cornice of acanthus leaves modelled in stucco, and the whole of the wall and half dome above is lined with glass mosaic. In the dome is the Virgin Mary with the infant Saviour between saints and angels. These are large figures on a gold ground. Other saints occupy the spaces between the windows of the drum below, and on the walls beyond are the Salutation on one side and the Annunciation on the other. The whole finishes as at S. Vitale with a wide border on the soffit of the triumphal arch into the nave, on which are medallions with busts of saints.

In front of the apse is a marble baldacchino with mosaics bearing the date 1277.

Preceding the west front is an atrium, perfectly preserved and coeval with the church. The upper part of the façade which forms one side of it had external mosaics of which considerable traces remain.

The church at GRADO[1], in the lagunes north of Venice, was built by the Patriarch Elias, as the mosaic inscription in the floor records, between 571 and 586. It is a basilica with 11 arches and 10 columns on each side of the nave, and has a narthex, and an octagonal baptistery, which unlike Parenzo is at the side and not at the west end of the church. The columns are of marble, seven of them of magnificent *bianco e nero*, as splendid as any I have ever seen. Some of the capitals are antiques, too small for their shafts, but the majority are of fine Byzantine workmanship based on the Composite order but treated with

[1] The churches of Parenzo and Grado are fully described and illustrated in my *Dalmatia, the Quarnero and Istria*, Vol. III. I refrain therefore from long descriptions here.

originality. The arches spring from them directly without the pulvino. The windows, now modernized, were originally wide round-arched openings filled with interlacing tracery cast in concrete, of which one specimen was discovered built into a wall and is now preserved in the sacristy.

Mosaic pavements

The pavements, of which a great part remains, are unusually fine and interesting. They are all of small tesserae without any of the large plaques of the later pavements, and contain several inscriptions recording the names of donors and the number of feet in each gift. One of them is in Greek, showing the connexion of this part of North Italy with the Byzantine empire. They abound in misspellings and grammatical mistakes, and a Latin V has crept into the Greek inscription. One of the names seems that of a Goth.

At the east end remains the patriarchal throne made up from fragments of slabs covered with interlacing work, mixed with original ornament of later date. The pulpit owes its picturesqueness mainly to the Arab-like canopy of Venetian work which surmounts it, but the lower part is of marble sculptured with the Evangelistic emblems, and dating apparently from the 8th or 9th century.

S. Maria, Grado

The small church of S. MARIA close to the Duomo of Grado is of the same date, and has Byzantine capitals, some of which have the pulvino and others not.

Pomposa

The church of POMPOSA between Ravenna and Venice is known to me only by photographs. It appears to have capitals of a composite form with pulvini; the frieze on the side walls is painted with figures, where in S. APOLLINARE NUOVO the mosaic processions occur, and the apse and its semi-dome are decorated with figures in fresco. But the glory of Pomposa is the splendid campanile which eclipses everything of that sort at Ravenna. It is supposed to have been built in 1063.

One must not fail to notice the abundant use of stucco in these churches at Ravenna and Parenzo either in the soffits of arches, wall decorations in spandrils or lunettes as at S. Vitale, figures as at the Ursian baptistery, or in string courses at Parenzo. At Cividale in Friuli the little church of S. Maria in Valle has "stucchi" of the most elaborate and beautiful kind including figures as well as foliaged ornament. They however belong to a much later date. Cattaneo refers them to 1100, and to the hand of a Greek artist[1]. In all these examples stucco has proved as durable as any other material in Byzantine buildings.

Stucco decoration

[1] Cattaneo, pp. 110, 112.

CHAPTER XIII

ROME

<small>Constantine's churches</small>

AFTER the recognition of Christianity by the Edict of Milan in 313 the Imperial City was rapidly supplied with churches, and those of S. Paolo fuori le Mura, S. Clemente, S. Agnese, S. Giovanni Laterano, S. Maria in Trastevere, S. Maria Maggiore, S. Lorenzo fuori le Mura, among others claim Constantine as their founder, or at all events date their foundation in his time. His principal church of S. Peter at the Vatican, which was described in a former chapter, has made way for the great church of Bramante and Michael Angelo, and the rest have all been completely altered or re-built in later times. But considering the burst of church-building in the 4th century, and the vast size of the metropolitan cathedral, it is surprising to read that the "notitia Urbis," more recent than Constantine, does not find one Christian church worthy to be named among the edifices of the city, though in the time of Gratian it still contained 424 temples and chapels of the heathen deities[1]. It is possible that except S. Peter's, which one would think could hardly have been overlooked, the rest were small and unimportant, for they were all re-built with greater magnificence within a few hundred years.

[1] Gibbon, Ch. XXVIII.

Plate XLI

S. PAOLO FUORI LE MURA—ROME

The Church under the era of toleration rapidly grew   Wealth of Roman clergy
rich, and the clergy became idle and luxurious. Their
corruption is chastised by S. Jerome, and their avarice
had to be restrained by an edict of Valentinian. The
bishopric of Rome was the subject of a bloody fray
between the adherents of Damasus and Ursicinus in 366,
when 137 corpses were left on the floor of S. Maria
Maggiore. Ammianus says the prize was well worth
the struggle; "the successful candidate is sure he will be
enriched by the offerings of matrons: and that as soon as
his dress is composed with becoming care and elegance
he may proceed in his chariot through the streets of Rome,
and that the sumptuousness of the Imperial table will not
equal the profuse and delicate entertainments provided by
the taste and at the expense of the Roman Pontiff[1]."

The Pagan Praetextatus said jokingly to Pope Damasus, "make me bishop of Rome, and I will turn Christian at once."

The wealth of the Church was shown in the splendour   S. Paolo fuori le Mura
bestowed on its buildings. S. PAOLO FUORI LE MURA, which
had been founded by Constantine, was pulled down within
half a century and re-built on a magnificent scale by
Valentinian II, Theodosius, and his sons. Till destroyed
by fire in 1823 it remained perhaps the most untouched
by subsequent alterations of all the ancient churches of
Rome. It was re-built and re-dedicated in 1854 by Pius IX
and finished by the Italian Government after 1870 on the
old lines (Fig. 39), and is decidedly the finest basilican
church in existence (Plate XLI). It covers an area of
about 400 feet by 200, and is 100 feet high. The nave
has a span of 78 feet, and is 200 feet long, an Eastern
transept and the apse making up the rest of the long

[1] Ammianus Marcellinus, 27, 3, cited Gibbon, Ch. xxv., Dill, Bk. II. Ch. I.

188 ROME [CH. XIII

S. Paolo fuori le Mura

dimension. The triumphal arch with its mosaics given by Galla Placidia escaped the fire, as well as the apse with its mosaics of 1226.

The well-known lovely cloister with its coupled shafts and mosaic inlays was begun by Pietro da Capua in 1193 and finished before 1211. With its round arches, and its semi-classic capitals and bases it may with some justice be claimed as a Romanesque work, though its delicate

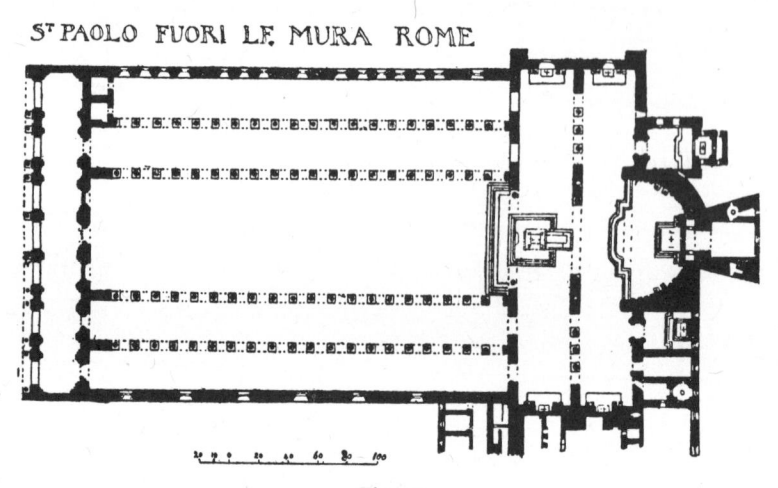

Fig. 39.

proportions and the Cosmatesque mosaics belong rather to the succeeding style.

S. Giovanni. Laterano

The cloister at S. JOHN LATERAN (Plate XLII) is so exactly like that of S. Paolo, that one might take it for work of the same hand; but according to an inscription now no longer existing it was built by one Vassaletto, who worked on it with his father[1]. In the centre of the

[1] Angeli, *Le chiese di Roma.*

CLOISTER: S. GIOVANNI LATERANO—ROME

Plate XLIII

S. GIOVANNI LATERANO—ROME

court is a 10th century *pozzo* or well-head (Plate XLIII). The church of the Lateran, built by Constantine to be "Omnium urbis et orbis Ecclesiarum mater et caput," has long disappeared, and after being ruined and re-built four times before 1362 it was turned into a classic church by Eugenius IV and has been altered by almost every succeeding Pope till it is now quite uninteresting. The last change it has suffered was the lengthening of the choir and removal of the apse eastward in 1884, together with the mosaics of 1290 by Jacopo Torriti, which have somewhat suffered in the transport.

S. Giovanni Laterano

The adjoining BAPTISTERY was founded by Constantine but has been much altered since. It is an octagon of considerable size with eight pillars of porphyry set within an aisle, and carrying an horizontal entablature. Eight more of white marble stand on this over the lower columns, and carry a lantern storey. The porphyry columns are said to have been put there by Sixtus III (432[1]—440). Four of them have Ionic capitals, which do not look ancient, two have Roman Corinthian and the other two Composite capitals. The form of the construction may be Constantine's, but the whole seems to have been largely re-built.

Baptistery of the Lateran

A mile and more beyond the Porta Pia is a round building now the church of S. COSTANZA, erected by Constantine as a mausoleum for his family, and especially his daughter Constantia, whose huge porphyry sarcophagus stood originally in the centre. In 1595 it was moved to one side, and in 1819 conveyed to the museum of the Vatican where it now is[2]. The building was not made a church till 1256.

S. Costanza

---

[1] Angeli, *Le chiese di Roma*.   [2] *Ibid.*

190   ROME   [CH. XIII

S. Costanza

It consists of a circular domed chamber (Fig. 40) 35 feet in diameter, surrounded by an aisle, the total diameter within the walls being 73 feet. The central drum on which the dome rests contains a clerestory and is carried up like those at Spalato and S. Vitale, so as to conceal the dome; and it is covered with a low pitched pyramidal roof. This central part is supported by a ring of coupled columns, each pair on a radiating line from the

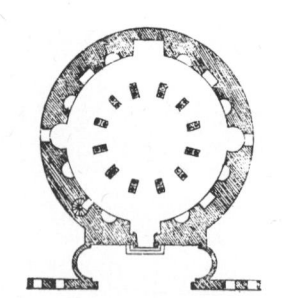

S COSTANZA
Fig. 40.

The arcades

centre, so that one column is behind the other; and each pair carries a section of the entablature of the order, with architrave, pulvinated frieze and cornice, returned on all four sides, so as to form as it were an elongated pulvino (Plate XLIV). From this spring the twelve round arches of the arcade. The capitals are ordinary Roman Composite. The surrounding aisle is also circular, and is covered by an annular barrel vault which is decorated

The mosaics

with mosaics coeval with the building. They are made with small tesserae chiefly black and white, resembling those in the baths of Caracalla, and there is no gold. The subjects are divided bay by bay (Plates XLV and XLVI). In some there is only a geometrical pattern: in others interlacing bands form circular compartments with irregular intervals, in each of which is a figure or a bird, designed with spirit: these slightly resemble some mosaics at S. George in Salonica that have been noticed above, and also others in the Archbishop's palace at Ravenna. Some compartments are filled with scroll-work of vines, amid which birds flutter and boys climb; below, under canopies, men are treading grapes, while others

Plate XLIV

S. COSTANZA—ROME

Plate XLV

MOSAICS AT S. COSTANZA—ROME

Phot. Alinari

bring the fruit in carts drawn by oxen. Elsewhere the surface is strewn with detached sprays of leafage among which are pheasants and partridges, and "things," such as vases, horns, mirrors, boxes, and shells. There is nothing to suggest mourning, but just as in the Etruscan paintings in the tombs of Tarquinii all is feasting, dancing, sport, and jollity, so here everything speaks of life and cheerfulness, and enjoyment of nature, contrasting strongly with the solemn conventionalities of the religious art that followed. It was to this natural school that it would seem Constantine V, Theophilus, and the other iconoclastic emperors in the 8th century reverted for the decoration of their churches and palaces after they had made a clean sweep of religious imagery.

The church was preceded by a narthex with an apse at each end like that at S. Vitale; but it is now in ruins.

The church of S. STEFANO ROTONDO (Fig. 41), has long been a puzzle to antiquaries. Some have supposed it to be a Pagan temple dedicated to Bacchus or Faunus. Others have taken it for a meat market of Nero's time. Cattaneo identifies it with the church on the Celian hill which Simplicius is said to have dedicated to S. Stephen between 468 and 472, while Rivoira thinks the inner part is Roman, and the outer the work of Pope Simplicius, when he converted the building into a church.

It is a circular building of large dimensions, and originally consisted of two concentric aisles round a central area. The inner ring of columns has granite shafts with Ionic capitals carrying a circular horizontal architrave, on which an inner drum rests. The capitals of the next ring are all surmounted by the pulvino and carry arches instead of lintels. On two sides five arches of this arcade are raised higher than the rest and their four

S. Stefano Rotondo columns have Corinthian capitals. The other capitals are of a rude Ionic type, clearly not antiques but work of the 4th or 5th century. With this ring the building now stops, for the third ring, the original outer wall, has been destroyed and with it of course the second or outer circular aisle; and the intervals of the second ring of columns were walled up to enclose the church by Pope

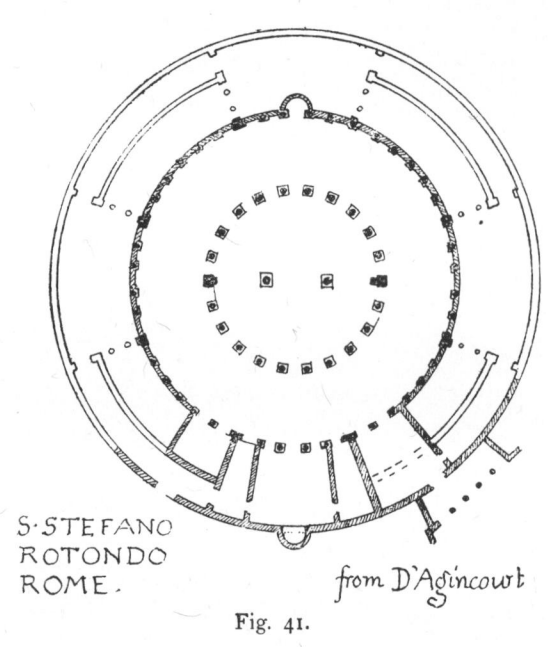

S. STEFANO ROTONDO ROME.   *from D'Agincourt*

Fig. 41.

Nicholas V in 1450, thus reducing the interior to its present dimensions (Fig. 41).

It is obvious from the slender construction of the inner ring, consisting of single columns instead of the double columns of S. Costanza, that no dome could have been intended over the central area, which must either have been left open to the sky, as was the case in the round church of S. Benigne at Dijon in 1002, or else been

Plate XLVI

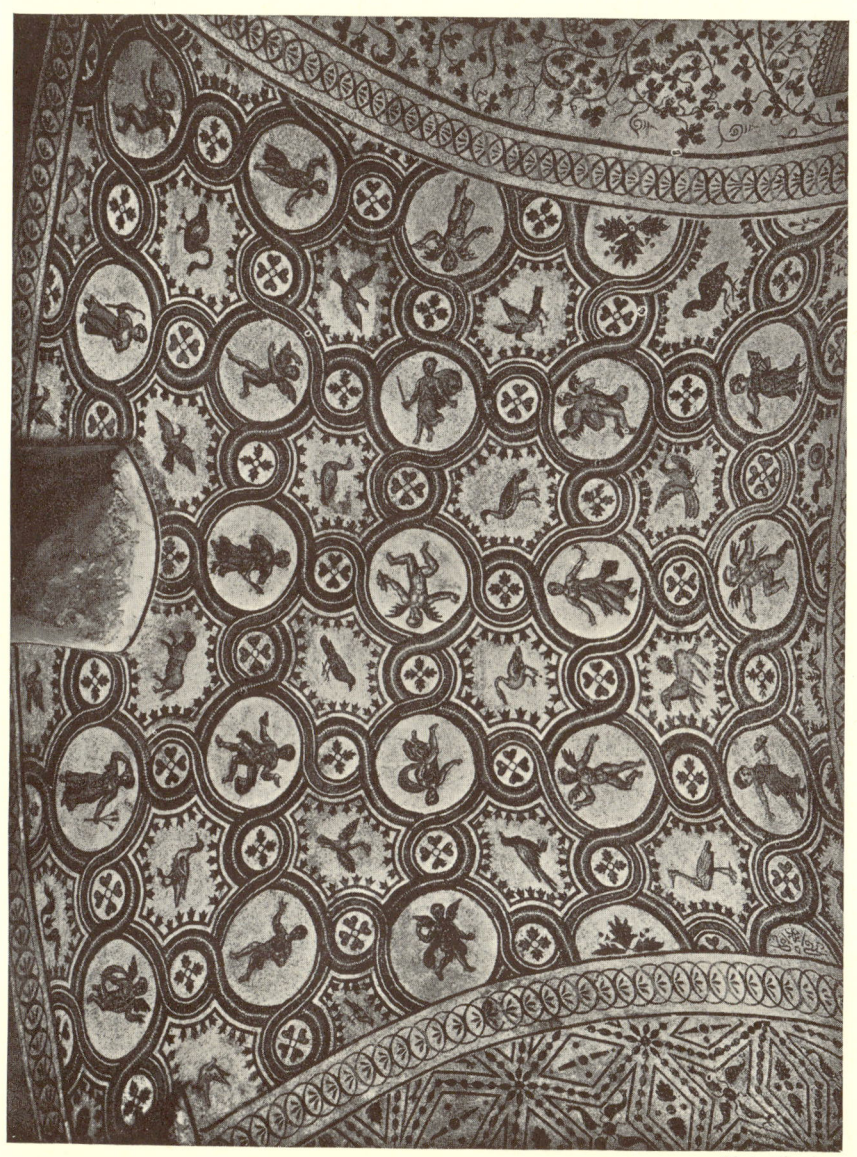

MOSAICS AT S. COSTANZA—ROME

Phot. Alinari

Plate XLVII

S. LORENZO FUORI LE MURA—ROME

closed with a wooden roof. The dimensions are not such as to make the latter plan difficult, and it is not easy to understand why in 772 Pope Adrian I built an arcade of three arches across the diameter of the circle. They are carried by two enormous granite columns with antique Corinthian capitals, and two massive piers which interrupt the first ring of columns, by displacing one on each side. This intrusive arcade destroys the whole scheme of the circular plan, and makes it unmeaning ; but it seems to strengthen the opinion that the central space was not originally covered in at all. Were this the case the elevated drum would not have existed till the time of Pope Simplicius, who we must suppose put a roof on when he turned the building into a church. *S. Stefano Rotondo*

The round church of S. ANGELO at Perugia dating from the 6th century, resembles S. Stefano Rotondo, but its single ring of columns has Corinthian capitals and pulvini and carries arches. The roofs are of wood. *S. Angelo, Perugia*

The church of S. LORENZO FUORI LE MURA is really composed of two apsidal churches, one orientated the other not, so that the apses met in the middle, till they were thrown together by Honorius III in 1216 (Fig. 42). The present choir (Plate XLVII) is the older church and was restored by Pelagius II in 588. It had the apse at the west end and the entrance at the east, which explains the square end of the existing choir. This church has the peculiarity of a gallery over the aisle, a matroneum or gynaeconitis like the churches of the Greek rite, which occurs elsewhere in Rome only at S. Agnese and at the S.S. Quattro. Angeli says the gallery here and at S. Agnese was made for dryness because the site was low and the floor damp, which is an explanation impossible to be accepted. It is more likely attributable to Byzantine influence which was *S. Lorenzo fuori le Mura*

J. A.

S. Lorenzo fuori le Mura

powerful in Italy during the 6th century. The two columns that carry the end gallery are quite Byzantine in style, and rest on pedestals of the same character. The side columns carrying the gallery are antiques and have capitals of the best period of Roman Corinthian, among which are two formed of trophies with Victories at the angles. They carry a horizontal entablature made up of classic fragments of all sorts and sizes put together in a strange medley, no one piece fitting its neighbour. The

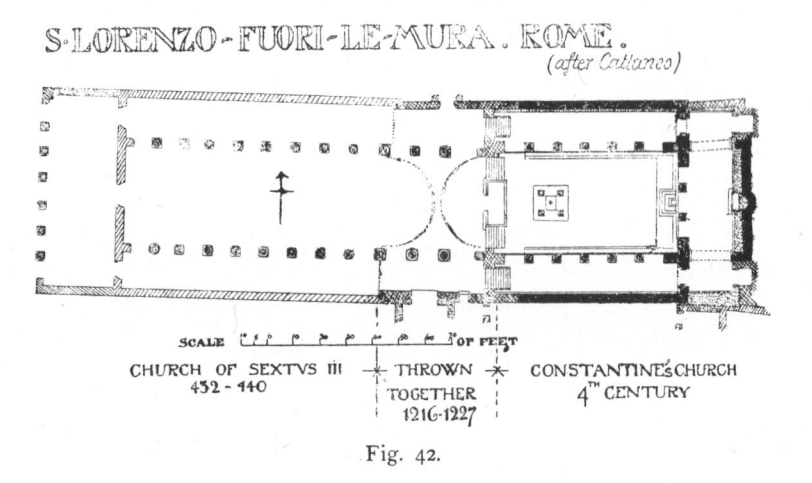

S·LORENZO-FUORI-LE-MURA. ROME.
(after Cattaneo)

SCALE [...] OF FEET
CHURCH OF SEXTVS III — THROWN — CONSTANTINE'S CHURCH
432-440   TOGETHER   4TH CENTURY
            1216-1227

Fig. 42.

columns of the upper storey are slighter and have Corinthian capitals that look like antiques, and they all have the pulvino and carry round arches, above which is a clerestory. The floor of the aisles remains at the original level, but that of the choir was raised in the 13th century over a crypt, so that the full length of the great columns can only be seen in the aisle.

The second church, with an orientation the reverse of the other, was built by Sixtus III (432—440). The columns are no doubt antiques for they are of various sizes,

Plate XLVIII

CLOISTER: S. LORENZO FUORI LE MURA—ROME

Plate XLIX

S. MARIA MAGGIORE—ROME

but their Ionic capitals fit them well though they are of unequal diameter: from which we may suppose they were made for the church[1].

S. Lorenzo has an interesting cloister of the 12th century (Plate XLVIII) on the walls of which are fixed many fragments of earlier work from the 5th century onwards.

The fine basilica of S. MARIA MAGGIORE (Plate XLIX), founded in 352, was re-built from the foundations by Sixtus III in 432, in honour of the promulgation of the dogma of the Θεοτόκος. *S. Maria Maggiore*

Like that of old S. Peter's, and that of S. Maria in Trastevere, which in its present form dates only from the 12th century, the colonnade carries a lintel instead of arches. Mosaics of the 5th century, representing Bible stories, fill compartments above the colonnade[2], and a splendid pavement of *opus Alexandrinum* laid by the Cosmati in the 12th century covers the floor.

In the mosaics, dating from the 5th to the 8th century which abound in Rome we see the influence of Byzantine art, and in many cases the handiwork of Greek artists. We may see it also in the mural decorations of the beautiful basilica of S. SABINA on the Aventine, which has inlaid patterns of porphyry and coloured marble in the spandrils of its arcades, recalling the Byzantine dados of Ravenna and Parenzo (Fig. 43). *S. Sabina*

---

[1] When the churches were thrown together by the removal of the two apses, which were *dos-à-dos*, the triumphal arch of the Pelagian church remained, but the mosaics that fronted the old nave are hidden from the present one, and can only be seen from what is now the back.

[2] Angeli says these mosaics were executed by Sixtus III, as the inscription states, and are mentioned in a letter of Hadrian I to Charlemagne. He says they were appealed to as an argument against the Iconoclasts.

S. SABINA.

Fig. 43.

S. Maria in Cosmedin

Many Greeks were driven from Constantinople by the iconoclastic movement in the 8th century, and a colony of them settled in Rome, near the Velabrum, where they were given the church of S. MARIA, which was called "in schola Graeca," or by the new settlers "in Cosmedin" after a region of their old home in Constantinople. The church was built in 772 by Hadrian I on the site of a temple to Ceres, Libera, and

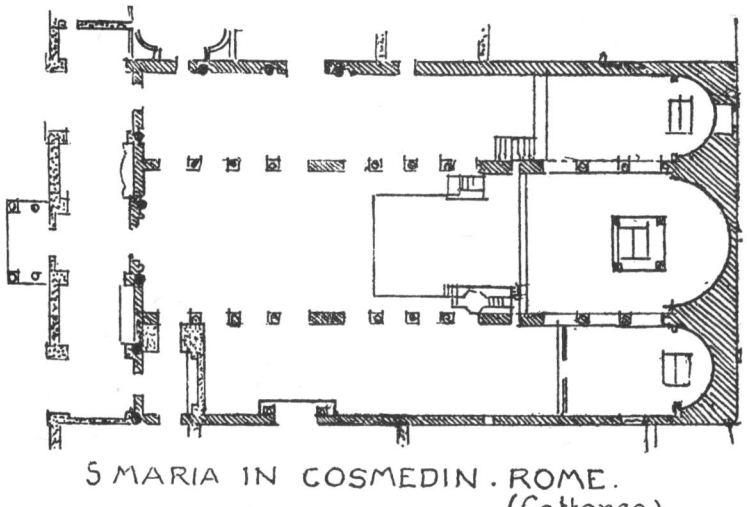

S MARIA IN COSMEDIN. ROME.
(Cattaneo.)

Fig. 44.

Libero (Proserpine and Bacchus) of which traces remain in the *opus quadratum* on one side of the crypt. The new church had and has three apses according to the Greek rite (Fig. 44), a novelty at Rome at that time, and it had a matroneum, or women's gallery, which later alterations destroyed. The twelve arches of the nave on each side are divided by wide piers into groups of four: the columns are of granite with antique capitals of various

S. Maria in Cosmedin

forms: a blank wall has replaced the triforium or matroneum; there is a clerestory of small windows above and except where blocked by later chapels the aisles are lit by similar small round-headed lights.

At the west end are three lofty blank arches partly cut into by the nave arcades, and therefore evidently belonging to an older edifice of wider span. This is believed to have been a "statio annonae" of Imperial times which had been formed out of the earlier temple. Its demolition by Hadrian I is said to have involved "great expense, and great labour of arms, with iron and with fire," and a whole year was occupied in reducing the site to a platform on which the church was built[1].

The singer's choir

The choir enclosure, or *schola Cantorum* with its ambos of Cosmatesque work, together with the marble screen east of it from side to side of the church, had been dismantled, but has lately been restored with the old materials, and now shows the ritual arrangement of early times[2]. Of the plutei that form the enclosure one has the Byzantine peacock with trees, now set upside down, and another a diaper of intersecting circles, which has also an Eastern look. The pavements of *opus Alexandrinum* are among the most beautiful in Rome.

In the lunettes of the side arches, and in the wall of the apse and in the narthex were found pierced window slabs, which are now exposed, and I think in some cases imitated.

S. Clemente

The well-known church of S. CLEMENTE on the Celian (Plate L) has preserved its ritual arrangements of choir and ambos with less alteration. The original church

---

[1] Angeli, *Le chiese di Roma*.
[2] Instauratis pluteis ac subsellis magnam partem excisis et eversis vetus schola cantorum ad pristinum decus renovata est anno domini M.D.CCCXCVIII.

was destroyed during the sack of Rome by Robert Guiscard in 1084. In 1108 Paschal II, instead of re-building or restoring it, built an entirely new church on the top of the ruins (Fig. 45), using again some of the old materials, among which were the *Coro*, or *schola Cantorum* with its ambos, the interesting Byzantine door of the atrium and various antique sculptures. The west side of the choir walls has Cosmatesque inlays, but the others are very Byzantine in style. They bear the

S. Clemente

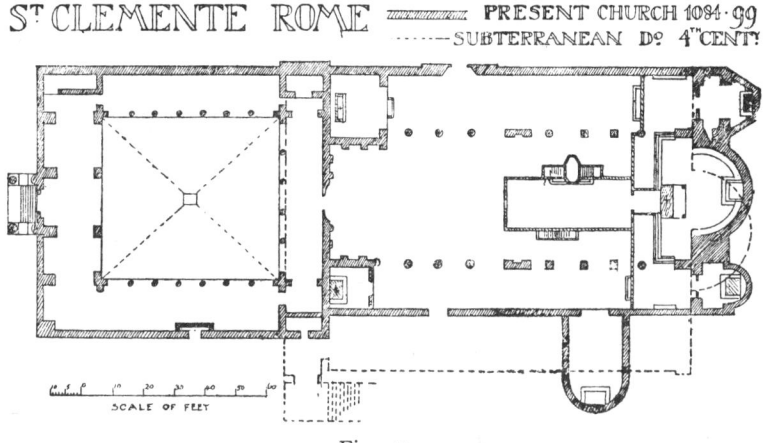

Fig. 45.

monogram of "Johannes," who afterwards became Pope Giovanni II, 532—5 (Fig. 46). The columns are of various sizes, brought from an older building. Two of them come from the lower church and bear the name of Johannes like the choir enclosure: but the nave has been much modernized and the Ionic capitals do not seem old. Below the present church is the older one, which was excavated in 1858, and is now quite accessible. It is so much wider than the church above, that the old nave is

S. Clemente

equal to the nave and south aisle of the upper building, and a wall had to be intruded to carry the south arcade above. On the north side the columns of the upper church stand over the old, and the north wall is over that of the lower building. The intervals of the lower columns were walled up for strength. The capitals of the old church can be seen: they are very simple, with leaves merely blocked out and not raffled. Worked into

Fig. 46.

the tomb of Cardinal Venerio (d. 1479) in the upper church are two elaborately carved shafts with Byzantine capitals belonging to the lower church, which are said to have carried the baldacchino over the altar, but seem too small for that office. The walls of the lower church are covered with interesting paintings[1].

Lower still are the remains of a Roman building with walls some of which go back to the time of the kings,

[1] They are illustrated in Fra Nolan's book, *The Basilica of S. Clemente in Rome*, 1910.

Plate L

S. CLEMENTE—ROME

Phot. Alinari

Plate LI

SS. GIOVANNI E PAOLO—ROME

forming part of a domestic building which is supposed to have been the dwelling of S. Clement himself, in which the original *ecclesia domestica* held its meetings. Beyond it is a subterranean temple of Mithras, whose statue, and a sculpture of the familiar slaying of the mystic bull, have been found there. Unluckily all these buildings of the lower stage are now full of water and inaccessible[1].

S. Clemente

Like S. Clemente the church of SS. Giovanni e Paolo, on the Celian, was built over the house of the saints to whom it is dedicated, which is fortunately quite accessible. The principal rooms have paintings, the most important one representing Ceres, Proserpine and Bacchus (Libera et Libero) with other figures. The Pagan pictures of the 2nd century are well done, but the Christian paintings on the other walls of the 3rd, 4th and 6th, are inferior. The body of the church above has been entirely modernized and gorgeously decorated: but the portico, pavement and apse of the 12th century remain, and the latter has a good exterior arcaded gallery, the only case, so far as I know, where this Pisan and Lombard feature appears in Rome (Plate LI). The east wall of the north aisle shows on the outside some *opus reticulatum*.

SS. Giovanni e Paolo

The church of S. Maria in Domnica on the Celian close to the Navicella, and near S. Stefano Rotondo, was re-built by Paschal I in 817. It is basilican with a wide nave and apse, antique columns and narrow aisles. The apse has a fine mosaic of the Madonna and Child between angels on a dark blue ground: the figures stand on a green field studded with red flowers. On the soffit

S. Maria in Domnica

[1] The Mithraic temple takes the usual form of a cave which it was necessary to imitate in the Mithraic cult, and could hardly have been a Christian shrine originally, afterwards appropriated to Mithraic worship. It is difficult to reconcile its presence with the Clementine theory. Fra Nolan does his best. He gives an illustration of the interior.

of the arch is a wreath starting from a pot on each side and in the centre is the cypher of Pope Paschalis in white on blue, whose re-building of a church "*confracta ruinis*" is recorded by six hexameter lines in the mosaic. The figures of the angels are attenuated and have small heads, but the little figure of the kneeling donor with a square nimbus is barbarous. One may conceive that the artists of the 9th century had stock patterns for saints and angels, and this kept them up to a certain standard, which they failed to reach when they had to introduce anything original.

Another interesting basilican church of the same period is that of S. GIORGIO IN VELABRO, which was re-built from its foundations by Gregory IV, 827—849. It adjoins the Roman arch of the goldsmiths, near that of Janus. The aisles end square and there is a single apse (Plate LII).

The church of S. PRASSEDE, of very early foundation, was re-built by Paschal I in 822. Like S. Maria Maggiore and other early Roman churches it has the apse at the west and the entrance at the east end. The aisles are divided from the nave by colonnades with horizontal architraves, which are made up of various incongruous fragments like those at S. Lorenzo. They are divided into three bays with two columns in each by great piers from which spring arches across the nave as at S. Miniato in Florence. But this would seem to be a later device, and the church has evidently been a good deal pulled about, the capitals of the columns being apparently of 15th or 16th century work, and only those of the responds are Romanesque. The little chapel of S. Zenone is lined with admirable mosaics, and is one of the best preserved

Plate LII

S. GIORGIO IN VELABRO—ROME

examples of Byzantine work in Italy. Its doorway has Romanesque Ionic capitals, carrying a cornice of late Roman work, and jambs covered with interlacing patterns. An inscription claims it for PASCHALIS PRAESVLIS OPVS, &c. &c., and bears his cypher as above. *S. Prassede*

The mosaics of the great apse are unusually fine. In the centre is Christ, bearded, above him is the divine hand with a wreath, and underneath him are sunset clouds. Three saints stand on either hand and the river Jordan, which is named, flows round the apse below. These all are on a dark blue ground. On a gold frieze below this is the Lamb in the centre, with nimbus, standing on a green ground whence flow the four rivers of Paradise, and right and left are six sheep approaching him. Round the springing of the semi-dome is an inscription of six hexameter lines recording the work of Pope Paschal[1].

EMICATAVLAPIAEVARIISDECORATAMETALLIS
PRAXEDISDÑOSVPERAETHRAPLACENTISHONORE
PONTIFICISSVMMISTVDIOPASCHALISALVMNI
SEDISAPOSTOLICAEPASSIMQVICORPORACONDENS
PLVRIMASCÕRVMSVBTERHAECMOENIAPONIT ✣
FRETVSVTHISLIMENMEREATVRADIREPOLORVM

Between the triumphal arch and the apse is a narrow shallow transept: both the wall over the apse and the triumphal arch are covered with mosaic pictures; the latter representing the Heavenly Jerusalem.

S. AGNESE FUORI LE MURA, near S. Costanza beyond the Porta Pia, is said to have been founded by Constantine at the desire of his daughter Constantia about 324, fourteen years after the martyrdom of S. Agnes. It was repaired and restored in 508 and again in 620 by Honorius I, to whose time the existing *S. Agnese fuori le Mura*

---

[1] This inscription is given incorrectly by Angeli.

S. Agnese fuori le Mura mosaic is attributed. To the same date it is probable the triforium gallery or matroneum belongs, which is peculiar in Rome to this Church, and those of S. Lorenzo, and S.S. Quattro, though it is said there once was one at S. Maria in Cosmedin. The columns are antiques from some pagan temple, and so appear to be most of their capitals. In the upper order there is a mixture of ancient and modern capitals; one is rather Byzantine in character. Some of the others are Corinthian and some Composite, and they all have the pulvino. In the apse mosaic the saint stands between Popes Symmachus and Honorius I. The latter holds in his hand a model of the church. He is recorded as donor of the church in an elegiac inscription.

Increase of Byzantine influences at Rome In this brief review of some of the principal churches typical of Rome, which might easily be extended, one may trace the gradual increase of Byzantine influence down to the final rupture between the eastern and western churches on account of the Iconoclastic controversy. It was felt even before the Byzantine conquest under Justinian; and after that event Rome was a dependency of Constantinople from the middle of the 6th till the 8th century. After the conquest numerous disused public buildings were converted into churches; the Templum Sacrae Urbis was altered into the church of SS. Cosmas and Damianus by Felix IV (526—530): the Pantheon was dedicated to Christian worship by Boniface IV (608—615). S. Adrianus was founded in the Curia by Honorius I (625—638), and it was probably at the same time that the *S. Maria Antiqua* interesting church of S. MARIA ANTIQUA, lately excavated at the foot of the Palatine, was formed out of an imperial building, whether a private dwelling or a civil structure is uncertain. The remarkable paintings on its walls are the work of Greek artists, or of men trained in the Greek school, and the inscriptions are mostly in that language. The floor slab which has been discovered of the ambo given by Pope John VII (705—707) has a bilingual inscription[1]:

S. Maria Antiqua

☦ ΙѠΑΝΝȢ ΔȢΛȢ ΤΗC ΘΕѠΤΟΚȢ
☦ IOANNESSERVVSSCAEMRIAE

Greek governors ruled in the Palatine, and Greeks had occupied the Papal chair. We see the impress of Greek tradition in the triforium or matroneum at S. Lorenzo, and S. Agnese, and S. Maria in Cosmedin; and in the mosaics which gradually pass from the semi-classic freedom of those at S. Maria Maggiore, and S. Pudenziana, through those of SS. Cosma e Damiano, which are the last of the Roman school, to the stiffness and conventionality of Byzantine art at S. Agnese, and S. Prassede. The Byzantine conquest was the end of Roman art.

Byzantine details at Rome

In spite of Byzantine influence however the dome obtained no footing at Rome; nor did the circular plan. S. Costanza was not built for a Christian church, and the origin of S. Stefano Rotondo is doubtful; there is the small rotunda of S. Theodore near the Palatine, but all the early churches with these exceptions are basilican, and had wooden roofs. There was nothing in the basilican style to suggest fresh departures in architecture, and we must not look to Rome for the seeds of further artistic development. This is an apt illustration of the part played by problems of construction in the growth of architecture. No great advance in the art was ever made without

Roman churches basilican

Constructive problems wanting

[1] *Papers of British School at Rome*, Vol. I. p. 90. Dr Ashby gives me the following inscription which apparently had not all been dicovered when the above was published. *Ibid.* p. 62.
THEODOTVS PRIMO (cerius) DEFENSORVM ET DISPENSATORE S(an)C(t)E D(e)I GENETRICIS SEMPERQVE VIRGO MARIA QVI APPELLATVR ANTIQ(u)A.
It shows the degradation of Latin in the 7th century, and also suggests the first beginning of Italian.

a reason outside the art itself; and this reason is generally to be found in some necessity of construction that arose, or some novelty in construction that recommended itself, or some facilities that presented themselves for doing things before impossible. It is to suggestions derived from construction that we must look for the origin of all great movements in the history of the art.

<small>Basilican type not progressive</small>

Now in the simple basilica, such as the two churches of S. Apollinare at Ravenna, and those we have been describing at Rome, and the Eski Djouma and S. Demetrius at Salonica, there were no constructional difficulties. Anybody could set up a row of substantial pillars with arches or lintels from one to another, and a wall with windows above, and could cover both nave and aisles with wooden roofs that had no thrust; and—given a solid foundation, and a weathertight covering—the building would stand as long as the materials lasted of which it was made. Consequently, one basilican church differs from another only in being larger or smaller, and more or less decorated; and though greater skill might be gained in carving capitals and designing mosaic or paintings, the architecture itself stood still. There was nothing to push it onwards so long as the basilican type was followed, and the nave of the duomo of Torcello, built early in the 11th century, is not one whit advanced in point of construction beyond those of Ravenna, Salonica, or Rome, which are earlier by five or six centuries.

<small>The vault provokes progress</small>

It is by the stone or brick vault, whether in simple groining or in the dome, that the inspiration came which led to most of the subsequent developments of architecture. It revolutionized the art at Constantinople and throughout the East generally, whence the basilica practically disappeared in the 6th century, and was succeeded by a new style based on a more ambitious and scientific form of construction. And though in western Europe, in spite of the example of S. Vitale and S. Mark, the basilican plan held its own, the wooden roof gradually gave way to vaulting, first over the aisles as at Pisa, and Peterborough, and finally over the whole church, both nave and aisles, as at S. Ambrogio at Milan, Vézelay, and Canterbury. Disappearance of basilica in the East

One characteristic and beautiful feature of the Roman churches is the brick campanile. One finds these towers in all parts of the city. They date from the 12th century for the most part. That of SS. GIOVANNI E PAOLO on the slope of the Celian hill is perhaps the most beautiful (Plate LIII), and from its setting it has a quaint picturesqueness. It stands on the top of a Roman building, of which a pier and the springers of an arch protrude from the lower storey. That of S. FRANCESCA ROMANA (Plate LIV), on the platform of Hadrian's great temple of Venus and Rome, is scarcely less beautiful, or that of S. MARIA IN COSMEDIN which was built in 1118, and there is another of more modest elevation at the church of S. GIORGIO IN VELABRO. Others will be found in various parts of the city. The Roman campanile

These campaniles are all built of dark brownish brick, divided into many storeys by cornices of brick into which are introduced little modillions or corbels of white marble with a dentil course below them. The windows have two lights grouped in pairs in the upper storeys, round arched, with brick strings at the springing decorated with dentils. Some of them have plaques of majolica let into the walls, or discs of porphyry or green serpentino, and now and then crosses of the same sunk in cruciform panels.

Roman campaniles.

They differ from the campaniles of Lombardy in having their divisions marked horizontally, storey by storey, instead of being panelled between vertical pilasters at the angles; and of the two varieties the Roman is undoubtedly the more beautiful.

Pavements of mosaic

One must not quit the ancient churches of Rome without mention of the lovely pavements of *opus Alexandrinum* with which most of them are floored, though they do not properly come within the period which forms our subject. They are designed with a limited palette, seldom going beyond white marble, red porphyry and green porphyry, or, as it is called, *serpentino*. The red and green must be fragments of Roman work, for in the middle ages the quarries of porphyry were unknown and have in fact only been re-discovered lately. But with these materials almost anything can be done, and without them the same effect is unattainable, as any one will know who has tried to make a pavement of the same kind with other materials. The soft white borders in which the geometrical figures are set are essential to the beauty of the design. At Westminster Abbey, the Italian Odericus, having no white marble, was obliged to use Purbeck for the setting of the porphyries and other marbles which Abbot Ware had brought with him from Rome[1], and the effect is very inferior to that of the similar pavements in Italy.

---

[1] When the inlaid brass lettering was perfect it read
  Tertius Henricus Rex Urbs Odericus et Abbas
  Hos compegere porphireos lapides.
The inscription on Abbot Ware's tomb was this:—
  Abbas Ricardus de Wara qui requiescit
  Hic portat lapides quos huc portavit ab Urbe.
    Gleanings, Westminster Abbey, G. G. Scott and others.

Plate LIII

SS. GIOVANNI E PAOLO—ROME

S. FRANCESCA ROMANA—ROME

Notice must also be taken of the baldacchini or canopies of tabernacle work of which there are examples at S. Lorenzo, S. Clemente, and S. Giorgio in Velabro. They consist of four columns carrying a four-square horizontal architrave, on which are raised octagonal receding stages, resting on colonnettes and finished with a pyramidal roof. They date probably from the 13th century, and the only instances of similar constructions of which I am aware elsewhere are in Dalmatia, at Traü, Curzola, and Cattaro.

Baldacchini in Rome

CHAPTER XIV

THE LOMBARDS. ARCHITECTURAL BATHOS AND RE-VIVAL. RUPTURE BETWEEN ROME AND BYZANTIUM

The Lombard kingdom

IN 568 Italy received the last great invasion and settlement of a German people. The Lombards under Alboin, whether at the invitation of Narses, whom the Empress Sophia had insulted and recalled from the scene of his victories, or not is uncertain, descended from Pannonia into the plain which has since borne their name. They met with little resistance, and established a kingdom over the whole of Lombardy, Venetia, Piedmont, Tuscany and the corresponding coasts of the Mediterranean and the Adriatic, excepting Ravenna which with Rome and S. Italy remained to the Exarchate. The Lombard capital was fixed in Ticinum or Pavia, where Theodoric had built himself a palace, and Ravenna did not yield to the Lombard arms till 727.

The Lombards or Long-beards at first showed the roughness and displayed the cruelty of barbarians. The story of Queen Rosamond's revenge and the murder of Alboin is well known: his son and successor Clepho also fell by the hand of an assassin, and it was only under Autharis the third Lombard king that anything like a settled government was established. Codes of law were enacted by Rotharis and Luitprand, and "the Italians enjoyed a milder and more equitable government than any of the kingdoms which had been founded on the ruins of the Western Empire[1]."

We read that Agilulf, who succeeded Autharis in 591, pursued a rebel duke of Bergamo to an island in the Lake of Como, from which he expelled him and his men; and carried off to Pavia the hidden treasures which had been deposited there[2] by the Romans. *Insula Comacina*

This was the *Insula Comacina*, which has been the centre of many ingenious theories relating to the early history of medieval art. According to some it had been the refuge of all the arts when Rome was sacked by Alaric in 410. There was then a great exodus from Rome of numerous corporations, which had to be brought back by an edict of the Emperor two years later. There is no doubt that the island was also the refuge of many Romans who fled there before the Lombards, who did not succeed in subduing it till 588. It was afterwards strongly fortified and had nine churches, though the island is barely a mile round, and it had a territory on the mainland. In the 12th century the Island Commune was strong enough to defy and attack Como, by which city however it was destroyed and depopulated in 1169[3]. But it cannot be supposed that all the building craft fled to this remote little islet in the Lake of Como and stayed there when, to say nothing of other places, Ravenna itself offered a more secure retreat, and a prospect of continued employment; for the monuments of Honorius's reign prove that there was no interruption of building in that city during this troubled period. *The Island Commune* *Destroyed 1169*

[1] Gibbon, Ch. XLV.
[2] Paulus Diaconus, *De gestis Longobardorum*, III. 3.
[3] *The Lombard Communes*, W. F. Butler.

The Magistri Comacini

The theory which makes this island the last refuge of the old and cradle of the new art rests on the name of the *Magistri Comacini*, who are mentioned in many old writers. They first appear in two edicts of King Rotharis, in 643, relating to the liability of the employers of *Magistri Comacini* for injury received by them on the works. Unlike modern legislation they provide that the employer is not to be held liable, because the builder has made his own terms for his own profit and should take the risk. But with some inconsistency it is decreed that if a pole or a stone should fall and kill a passer-by not engaged on the work, then the employer is to pay.

Guilds of artizans

From this we gather that there was a trade guild of builders in North Italy in the middle of the 7th century important enough to need legislation. But they were probably only one society of many. At Ravenna, as we have seen, architecture had had an uninterrupted history. At Rome there was a school of marble masons from which Theodoric drew workmen to Ravenna[1]. Whether these guilds were survivals of the old Roman Collegia Fabrorum or not, it is impossible to say, but we know that guilds of the kind existed through the middle ages; and from these edicts of the Lombard kings we may gather that they had already been in existence for some time before the middle of the 7th century.

The Magistri Comacini

As for the Comacini it has even been doubted whether their name has anything to do with Como[2]. But from the analogy of the Insula Comacina[3] there can be little doubt that it refers to that district or diocese. It is probable that the region of Como and the neighbouring

---

[1] *V. sup.* p. 169, note. [2] *V.* Mr Porter's *Lombard Architecture*.
[3] Ad insulam quae intra lacum Larium non longe a Como est, confugit, ibique fortiter se communivit. Paul. Diac. v. 39.
It seems to have been often used for the same purpose, *v. Ibid.* VI. 19.

country produced a race of skilled masons and carpenters who worked the quarries, and wrought the free-stone, and the timber, in which materials that district abounds; and that they supplied the great cities in the plain not only with stone and wood but with the skilled labour necessary for construction. That they should organise themselves into a guild was natural. They were not Lombards, but Romans under Lombard rule, and the trade-guilds were a regular institution of every craft[1]. The attempt to trace in these societies the origin of what is now known as freemasonry is absurd[2]. *The Magistri Comacini*

Although the Exarchy divided Italy with the Lombards till the fall of the Lombard kingdom the connexion with the Eastern Empire grew fainter and fainter, not only in Lombardy proper but even in the Exarchate. Italian architecture reflected this change and, ceasing to be influenced by the Greek school, took that independent national character which we call Lombard. In other words it ceased to be Byzantine and became Romanesque. *Decline of Byzantine influence*

It is not to be supposed, of course, that the Lombards themselves had much to do with it directly. They were for some generations a conquering aristocracy, rude in manners and caring for war alone, for whom the subject provincials had to work. The Magistri Comacini were at all events at first Romans, though in the 8th century we hear of artists named Rodpertus and Auripertus who *The Lombards*

---

[1] Among the corporations that fled from Rome in 410 at the capture by Alaric are mentioned those of the bakers, carriers, swineherds, cowherds, bath men. Dill, *Rom. Soc.* p. 307.

[2] There is an ambiguity in the word Free-mason. It occurs constantly in old building accounts, where it means the mason who works *free-stone*, that is stone fit for traceries, mouldings, and other wrought work, as distinct from the layer, who set it, or the waller, who built the plain rubble masonry, and who is also called mason though not freemason.

Queen Theodelinda

would seem German, and may have been Lombards. For the Lombards, as they became settled, became civilised. The story of king Autharis, and how he wooed his bride Theodelinda in disguise, breathes the spirit of chivalry and romance: and not less graceful is the way in which the widowed Theodelinda bestowed her hand and the crown of Lombardy on Agilulf his successor[1]. But even under the gentle Theodelinda the Lombard warriors retained something of barbarism. Their historian, writing 200 years later, saw painted on the walls of the Palace, which Theodelinda built in Monza, pictures of the Lombards of her day; and he describes with amused curiosity their hair hanging down to the mouth in front and parted on the forehead, but shaven at the back of the head, their loose linen dress like that of the Anglo-Saxons with stripes of various hues, and their sandals with leathern laces[2].

Early Lombard buildings

Besides the Palace Theodelinda built a Cathedral at Monza which she dedicated to S. John the Baptist in the year 595. It is described as Byzantine in plan, an equilateral cross with a dome, from which it may be conjectured that the design is due to a Greek architect from the Exarchate, if not from Constantinople. This church was destroyed at the end of the 13th century to make way for the present building, but the treasury still contains the pious queen's *Chioccia*, her hen and chickens,

---

[1] Paulus Diac. III. 29, 34. Is cum reginae accepto poculo manum honorabiliter osculatus esset, regina cum rubore, subridens, non debere sibi manum osculari ait, quem osculum sibi ad os jungere oporteret.

[2] Paulus Diac. IV. 23. Vestimenta vero eis erant laxa, et maxime linea, qualia Anglo-Saxones habere solent ornata institis latioribus vario colore contextis. Cunibert, who reigned from 688—700, married Hermelinda an Anglo-Saxon. Paulus mentions a visit from Ceodaldus (Caedwalla) king of the Anglo-Saxons (*sic*) to Cunibert on his way to Rome. Lib. v. 38 and VI. 15. See Bede, *Eccl. Hist. ann.* 689.

and in the Cathedral is still preserved the iron crown of the Lombard kings.

The influence of Theodelinda in softening the rudeness of the times is gratefully recorded by Paulus[1]. She converted her husband Agilulf to orthodoxy, and the bishops who had been in a state of abject repression were restored to dignity. Under her and her successors architecture began to revive, and churches and nunneries were built and endowed in Pavia, Beneventum and elsewhere. The interesting bapistery of Callixtus at Cividale, the ancient Forum Julii, where Paulus Diaconus was born, dates from the middle of the 8th century or rather later. A dwarf wall carries eight columns which are tied with iron on the top of the capitals, and support eight arches shaped out of the thin slabs common to the time, and covered with interlacing patterns of knots and figures of birds and animals. The capitals are versions of Corinthian fairly carved though rude, and the knotted ornaments are well done, but the animals are grossly barbarous, the angelic emblem of S. Matthew being ludicrously childish. There is little or no attempt at modelling, the ground being sunk square, leaving the figure in flat relief, on which the detail is given by superficial lines. There are other sculptured slabs, altar frontals, and "plutei," at Cividale like these, in which the ornament is excellent, even beautiful, but the attempts at figures of men and animals are beneath criticism. Dalmatia contains several sculptures of the same date and style. In particular there is a doorhead at Cattaro erected by Andreasci Saracenis early in the 9th century which shows the same contrast in the execution of figure and ornament. As Cattaro

Cividale

Barbarous figure sculpture

Dalmatian examples

---

[1] Paul. Diac. IV. 6.

Cattaro

was then under the rule of the Eastern Empire[1] this indicates a remarkable uniformity of the decorative art in different kingdoms so remote as Lombardy and Southern Dalmatia. Similar carved slabs are found in Northern Dalmatia, a favourite device being to arrange the interlacing strapwork so as to form compartments or panels, in each of which is a bird or a beast. In this they resemble the earlier ambones at Ravenna, in the Duomo and S. Giovanni, though there the borders do not interlace.

Bathos of art in 8th century

If the sculptured ornament of the 8th century be compared with that of the 4th, as shown for instance in the early Christian sarcophagi, one realises the abject condition into which the arts had sunk in Italy during the interval.

The gradual change to better things may be seen in the old Etruscan city of Tuscania, re-named Toscanella by Boniface VIII in ridicule or revenge for its rebellion in 1300[2].

Toscanella S. Pietro

The church of S. Pietro is dated by Sign. Rivoira[3], as regards the principal part of the fabric, in the reign of Luitprand (712—743), the greatest of the Lombard kings: and as it appears from a deed of sale, dated 739, that the Comacine Master Rodpert was then in the place, it may be that he was the original architect. The church is lofty, spacious and well proportioned. The architecture is of various dates. The plan is basilican (Plate LV), with a single apse at the west end. There are five round arches on columns next the entrance at the east end: then follows a pier with two half columns attached from which on each side an arch springs to the two massive piers at

---

[1] Charlemagne conquered Dalmatia but restored the maritime cities to the Emperor Nicephorus ob amicitiam et junctum cum eo foedus. Eginhart, *Vita Carol. Magn.*

[2] *Toscanella e i suoi monumenti.* A. Aureli.

[3] Rivoira, Vol. I. p. 148.

Plate I.V

S. PIETRO—TOSCANELLA

Phot. Alinari

Plate LVI

S. PIETRO—TOSCANELLA

the beginning of the presbytery. The two eastern bays have either been re-built, or added at a later date, but the rest of the church westward, including the apse, is of the early building. The capitals of the half columns and the presbytery are extremely rude, roughly chopped down from square to round on the top of the shaft in the coarsest and most artless way. For the next two columns on each side antique capitals have been used; two of them are Corinthian: one is of tolerably good work, but its fellow being only cut in tufa is naturally rough. The two others are of rather rude Ionic; and they all are surmounted by deep abaci almost amounting to pulvini and answering the same purpose. The arches are round and have two orders, perhaps the earliest instance of such a feature; and Messer Rodpert has hit on the disagreeable idea of setting forward at irregular intervals the voussoirs of the inner order to the plane of the outer, which has a bizarre and disturbing effect. The triumphal arch is treated in the same way. Another peculiarity is that the voussoirs of both orders increase in width as they rise,— a feature that reappears in Italian Gothic. The narrow windows are splayed equally inside and out, a feature which Sign. Rivoira refers to at Arliano near Lucca, and at Bagnacavallo, and which I found in the Church of S. Ambrogio at Nona in Dalmatia. The "plutei" or parapet slabs which enclose the choir are carved with the same interlacing patterns and rude figures as those mentioned above at Cividale. They have evidently been a good deal misplaced, and some are set wrongly. One among them bears the Griffin with waving tail that appears in Etruscan tombs at Corneto, here set wrong way up. One familiar subject is a pair of crosses under two arches: both cross and arch are enriched with a

<sub>Toscanella
S. Pietro</sub>

Toscanella guilloche or with flutings, and the arch has a rude kind of
S. Pietro crocketing round it. Two pyramidal leaves or trees
occupy the two spaces right and left of the stem of the
cross, and rosettes or other ornaments fill the two spaces
above the cross arm (Fig. 47). This device occurs not
only here at Toscanella, but with little variety in the
churches of SS. Apostoli and S. Sabina at Rome, at
Torcello and Pola[1]; another instance of the intercommunication of art and artists in early times and at great
distances. Both internally and externally the clerestory

S. SABINA·ROME   POLA.   TOSCANELLA.

Fig. 47.

walls are decorated with blank arches, of which a few are
pierced with narrow lights. The aisles have arcaded
cornices under the eaves, generally springing from little
corbels, but at every third or fourth arch carried down the
wall with a narrow pilaster strip like those in our English
Saxon churches of the 8th or 10th century, such as
Corhampton or Earl's Barton. In the clerestory the
pilaster strip occurs at every arch, to which it forms a

[1] *v.* Rivoira, I. Ch. 3; my *Dalmatia*, Vols. I. and III.; Brindley and
Weatherley, Plate 32.

CH. XIV] TUSCANY 219

column, and the spandrils are enriched by thin bricks set Toscanella
edgeways in a vandyked pattern, leaving hollow recesses S. Pietro
between them, which give considerable richness to the
surface by points of deep shadow (Fig. 48).

A similar use of these bricks is made in the apse,
where Messer Rodpert has achieved a more signal
success, for its treble line of arcaded cornice, the various

Fig. 48.

piercings which give it brilliancy, and the pilaster strips
which emphasize its height, aided by the great elevation
arising from its position on the slope of the hill, produce
a very noble and satisfactory effect (Plate LVI).

Below the presbytery and apse is a very fine crypt The crypt
sustained by 28 columns in three rows forming four aisles
running crossways of the church, to which the columns

Toscanella S. Pietro — supporting the apse add four more. A further crypt down six steps opens from this on the north side, and from it a flight of steps leads up to the North aisle of the church. There is another stair to the crypt in the South aisle. This crypt is evidently later than the original fabric, and dates probably from the 11th or 12th century to judge by the capitals, which are much more advanced than those of Messer Rodpert. The vault has transverse but not diagonal ribs, the arris of the groin being just pinched up. Some of the columns have bases and some none. One column is replaced by an oblong pier of white marble fluted, carrying a delicate Roman capital intended for a round shaft, and another shaft is spirally fluted.

Eastern addition — The two Eastern bays of the nave, next the entrance, date from the 12th century, and are either a re-building or an extension of the original building. The arches have the same projecting voussoirs in the lower order as the earlier bays, but here they are carved like consoles or corbels, and are less objectionable. The capitals of this part are some of them antiques and others Romanesque, carved for the building (Plate LV).

The façade — The front of the church is coeval with these bays but it has been a good deal altered (Plate LVII). The two side doors are Romanesque, but the central door with mosaic inlays of Cosmatesque work, and two two-light windows above seem to have been inserted in the 13th century, and the great rose window (Plate LVIII), with the semi-classic husks that form the outer spokes of the wheel, looks like a work of the early Renaissance set in an early framework.

The pavement — The church has its pavement of *opus Alexandrinum* complete, and the aisles are parted from the nave by a dwarf wall between the pillars, and a seat on the side

Plate LVII

S. PIETRO—TOSCANELLA

Plate LVIII

S. PIETRO—TOSCANELLA

Phot. Alinari

next the nave. The men probably sat in one aisle, the women in the other, and the central nave, like the *schola Cantorum* of S. Clemente, or S. Maria in Cosmedin would have been reserved for the clergy. There are two baldacchini of which one is dated 1093, and this Rivoira thinks would be the date of the crypt also.

<small>Toscanella S. Pietro</small>

S. Pietro stands alone on the deserted site of the citadel of the old Tuscan city. It was formerly the Cathedral, and adjoining the west front is still a building with interesting 12th century windows once the residence of the Bishop and canons. The fortress was destroyed by the French troops of Charles VIII, and in the 16th century the bishop moved his seat to a new cathedral in the town. The church has since remained abandoned and disused.

<small>The Canonica</small>

Another derelict church stands outside the walls, even more beautiful than S. Pietro. S. Maria Maggiore lies low down at the bottom of a deep valley, and in front of the façade is a gigantic campanile, now partly ruined, built, so the story goes, that the builders of the façade of S. Pietro should not see and imitate the front in progress at S. Maria. This church (Plate LIX) has not the antiquity or the variety of dates of S. Pietro, though here too, curiously enough, the two bays next the entrance seem to be later additions. Like the other church the apse is at the west and the entrance at the east end. The plan is basilican; five bays of round arches on columns lead up to the great piers at the entrance of the presbytery whence once sprang the triumphal arch which has been removed, though the side arches across the aisles remain. Beyond is a transept, which however does not outrun the aisles but rises above

<small>S. Maria Maggiore</small>

Toscanella
S. Maria
Maggiore

them. The east end has three apses, and the wall above the apse arch is covered with fine medieval paintings. The local guides date the nave in the 10th or 11th century. It looks to me more like 12th century work. The shafts are monocylindrical and carry Romanesque capitals of two tiers of leaves with miniature volutes, surmounted by a deep plain abacus ornamented with a diaper or cresting. Into some capitals figures are introduced, which are barbarous in the extreme. The soffit of the arches has a quatrefoil diaper with anything but an early look. On the second pair of detached columns the arch springs towards the entrance like those beyond, but suddenly changes into a plainer and later moulding, and the quatrefoils stop[1]. There is a change also in the cornice that runs above the arches. The respond on the end wall is a cluster of small shafts with bands and base very like early English work. These two bays cannot be older than the 13th century.

The splendid façade (Plate LX) also shows the work of at least two dates. The two side doors are Romanesque, and in the zigzags[2] of the left portal and the dogteeth of the right hand one, we find with surprise features familiar to the northern eye (Fig. 49). With a little change the left hand door in particular, might have been in Kent, and in the other is something very like the ball-flower of Gloucester or Leominster. The tympanum of this door does not belong to it, but seems to have been part of an earlier doorway. It is in the middle portal however that the most puzzling change has taken place; originally a Romanesque doorway of brown

[1] See nearest arch shown in the plate.
[2] The church of S. Pancrazio at Corneto also has a window with zigzags in the arch.

Plate LIX

S. MARIA MAGGIORE—TOSCANELLA

Phot. Alinari

Plate LX

S. MARIA MAGGIORE—TOSCANELLA

stone like the others, of which the jambs remain, it was altered evidently in the 13th century by the insertion of slender marble shafts, banded half way up, carrying an arch of three orders and a label, two of the orders being moulded and the rest carved. This again has a queer semi-English look, and reminds one of some doorways in Lincolnshire. Beyond the last jamb shaft is a spiral column of marble, standing in advance of the wall and

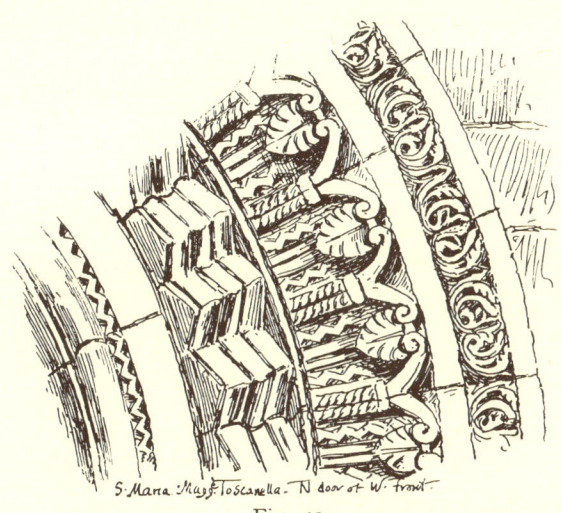

<small>Toscanella
S. Maria
Maggiore</small>

S. Maria Magg. Toscanella. N door of W. front.
Fig. 49.

resting on a small lion's back, a purely Italian feature. The tympanum, here too, seems out of place, as if it had belonged to a different doorhead. The figure of the Madonna is not in the middle, and the circle with the Lamb on one side does not balance the long oval or double circle on the other containing the Sacrifice of Isaac, and the story of Balaam.

Above, as at S. Pietro, is a graceful arcade of little arches or colonnettes, and in the wall over this, which is

Toscanella
S. Maria
Maggiore

Fig. 50.

square and not gabled, is a magnificent rose window, this *Toscanella S. Maria Maggiore* time a real wheel, with colonnettes for spokes, very far superior to that at S. Pietro.

Against the south presbytery pier stands a pulpit or ambo composed of pieces of 11th or 12th century work (Fig. 50), and in the north aisle is a fine early font.

Though deserted, these two remarkable churches are well cared for; and as they have been disused since the middle ages they have fortunately escaped the alterations and mutilations of Rococo and neo-classicism.

Toscanella has other points of interest. The church of S. Maria delle Rose has features of antiquity; the town walls, and gates, are very well preserved; and the Rivellino, or castle of the Priors, is worth a visit. There are some Etruscan tombs in the neighbouring valley, but I did not see them.

The beautiful city of VITERBO twelve miles away, *Viterbo* whence Toscanella can be reached most conveniently, has several early Romanesque churches. That of S. Sisto, with an apse that protrudes through the city wall, has capitals that break away from Roman example, and a strange clustered pillar spirally twisted. The Cathedral, though much modernized, has preserved its ancient Romanesque arcades, in which are capitals resembling Byzantine work, with eagles at the angles like those at Salonica, and quadruped sphinxes with a female head and a pair of wings.

The town is rich also in later work, and the town walls and gates are tolerably perfect.

In these buildings, and others that are coeval with *Promise of Lombard Romanesque* them, in spite of the rudeness of their execution and the coarseness of their figure sculpture, one cannot fail to see the seed of future excellence. It seemed necessary that

Promise of Lombard Romanesque the decline which set in with Constantine should reach a bathos before it was arrested, and gave way to the stirrings of a new life.

> Quando aliud ex alio reficit natura, nec ullam
> Rem gigni patitur nisi morte adjutam aliena[1].

Ancient tradition was dead or nearly so: technical skill was at the lowest possible ebb: for columns and capitals and such features as required dexterous workmanship, recourse was had to the spoils of ancient buildings: constructional problems were avoided, and the churches were mere walls with wooden roofs, vaults being beyond the builders' humble resources. But in the way these materials were put together, whether they were original or pilfered from old buildings, in the proportions adopted, and in the evident striving after beauty, we see that the artistic sense was alive, that it had in it all the promise of youth, and that it wanted nothing but practice, experience, and knowledge to develop a new and noble art.

Growth of papacy Among the influences that tended to sever the connexion of Italian art with the East must be included the growth of Papal power during the period of the Lombard kingdom. The unsettled state of the country, the struggle between Exarch and Lombard, the constant disturbance of the Lombard throne itself by rebellions, all favoured the advance of the Pope towards temporal power. The days were long past when Theodoric could summon a Pope to Ravenna and send him to Constantinople on a mission to secure liberty of worship for Arians, and on his return put him in prison for a traitor. Or when Pope Martin for anathematizing the Monothelites could be dragged to the Emperor's court at Constantinople and sent to die in the Chersonnese. Yet in the 7th century

[1] Lucretius, I. 264.

the Pope was still the obedient subject of the Eastern empire. His claim to precedence was disputed by the Patriarch of Constantinople. He was not even secure in his claim to ecclesiastical supremacy in Italy, for in 642 the Archbishops of Ravenna asserted and for a time maintained their independence of him[1].

But the weakness of the Exarchate, the existence of which was threatened by the Lombards, caused the Romans to rely on the Pontiff for the maintenance of order; and the character and virtues of Gregory I strengthened and confirmed the papal authority, and converted it almost into an independent sovereignty. The edict of the Emperor Leo the Isaurian in 726 forbidding the worship of images, and directing their destruction, gave the Popes the opportunity of putting themselves at the head of the image worshippers and of breaking finally with the Empire. *Growth of papal power* *Breach between East and West*

Having thus practically freed themselves from Constantinople a fresh danger presented itself in the Lombard kingdom. While in the position of subjects either to the Exarchate or the Lombards the Popes were no more than bishops of Rome, a position inconsistent with their pretensions to supremacy in Christendom. The Lombard kingdom was the object of their bitterest hatred, and the aid of the more distant Franks was invoked to destroy it. Desiderius the last Lombard king was conquered by Charlemagne in 774, and the Pope took possession of the Exarchate and thus first became a temporal sovereign. *Fall of Lombard kingdom*

---

[1] Agnellus laments the removal of the body of S. Andrew from Ravenna to Constantinople. Had it remained at Ravenna he says "nequaquam nos Romani Pontifices sic subjugassent." Justinian's argument was that as S. Peter was at old Rome his brother should be at new Rome. Agnellus, *Vita S. Maximiani*.

Decline of Byzantine influence on Italian art

This final separation of Italy from the Roman empire of the East had the effect of giving a more definitely national character to Italian architecture. In the 8th century it may be considered to have reached its bathos, and from that time it began to grow into something better. A superior technique may have been introduced by artists whose trade in Constantinople was ruined by the iconoclastic edicts, and who migrated in search of work to the country where iconoclasm was fiercely resisted. But though here and there the touch of a Greek hand may still be detected in details, the general style of the art henceforth shows little trace of Byzantine influence.

Admixture of races

Another thing that tended to give a new direction to Italian art may be found in the extensive introduction of foreign elements into the population. Under Theodoric and his successors large numbers of Goths settled in the peninsula. Two centuries of Lombard rule followed, and Paulus says that Alboin brought with him hosts of men of other nationalities, besides his own, who settled in villages well known in the 8th century[1]. The character of the race must have been largely affected by this infiltration of foreign blood, and in the fair hair and blue eyes that one sees especially in North Italy we may trace the mixture of northern races with the old Gallic or Latin stock.

---

[1] Unde usque hodie eorum in quibus habitant vicos, Gepidos, Bulgares, Sarmatas, Pannonios, Suavos, Noricos, vel aliis hujuscemodi nominibus appellamus. Paul. Diac., Lib. II. xxvi.

CHAPTER XV

VENICE

THE only people on the west of the Adriatic who still professed obedience to the Eastern empire in the 9th century were the Venetians, who wisely preferred a distant and nominal sovereign to an active one close at hand. When Pepin descended with his Franks to the rescue of the Pope, and summoned the Venetians to submit they replied that they chose rather to be the servants of the king of the Romans[1], and entrenched behind their marshes and lagunes they were able to defy the challenge. This detachment of Venice from the other Italian nationalities is reflected in her architecture, which from first to last has a character of its own distinct from that of the rest of Italy; and it is reflected no less in her policy, which till she acquired a territory in Lombardy was marked by a certain aloofness that placed her outside the great questions which agitated the neighbouring communes.

The islands of the lagunes from Grado to Chioggia had been the refuge of the inhabitants of Aquileja and other cities of Friuli and Venetia who were rendered homeless by the ravages of Goths, Huns, and Lombards. Here, to quote the famous letter of Cassiodorus, they squatted and nested like sea fowl. Each island had its

[1] ἡμεῖς δοῦλοι θέλομεν εἶναι τοῦ τῶν Ῥωμαίων βασιλέως.

The tribunes

The Doge

First church of S. Mark

tribune who met his brother tribunes in council, till about the end of the 7th century, their authority was superseded by the election of a Duke or Doge. At the beginning of the next century the seat of government was removed from Malamocco to the Rivus Altus, or Rialto, and the contiguous islands became consolidated into the city thenceforth called Venezia. Here Doge Giustiniano Participazio in 814 began to build the ducal palace and the church of S. Theodore near by, which served as the ducal chapel[1]. At the same time he built the church and convent of S. Zaccaria by the help of the Emperor Leo V, "the Armenian," who gave him money, and sent him "excellent masters in architecture." Of this Byzantine church unfortunately nothing remains. The probability is that it was basilican in form, as was also the church of S. Theodore, and that built by Doge Giovanni Participazio in 829, between S. Theodore and the ducal palace, to receive the body of S. Mark which was brought from Alexandria when that city was taken by the Moslem. This first church of S. Mark was burned during an insurrection in 976 in which Doge Pietro Candiano IV was killed. It was restored by the next Doge Pietro Orseolo I, but about the middle of the 11th century it was entirely re-built by Doge Domenico Contarini, and was finished and consecrated under Doge Vitale Falier in 1085.

If as most authorities suppose the old churches of S. Mark and S. Theodore, as well as that of S. Zaccaria, were basilican it would seem that Latin traditions were stronger at Venice in the 9th century than Greek. But the new S. Mark's is frankly Greek in plan and style, and is

---

[1] There is another opinion that the church of S. Theodore was built by Narses. De Verneilh., *L'Architecture Byzantine en France*, p. 121.

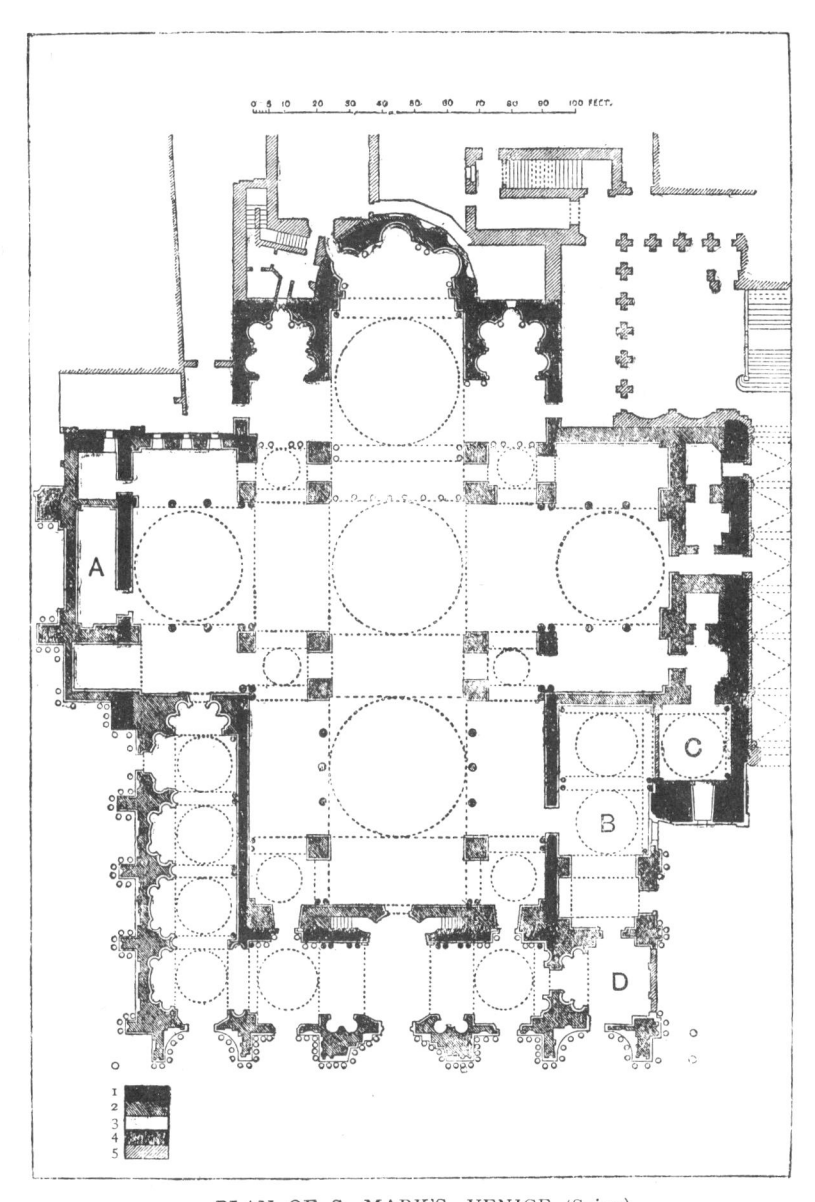

PLAN OF S. MARK'S, VENICE (Spiers)

1. Ancient work prior to 1063.
2. Domenico Contarini, 1063—1071.
3. Decorative (marble and mosaics), 1100—1350.
4. Work done about 1300.
5. Renaissance.

A. Chapel of S. Isidore.
B. Baptistery.
C. Treasury.
D. Chapel of S. Zeno.

Fig. 51.

Church of the Apostles Constantinople

a copy according to tradition of Justinian's vanished church of the Holy Apostles at Constantinople (*v. sup.* p. 109). Like it, S. Mark's is in plan a Greek cross (Fig. 51), with a slight prolongation of the western arm; and it has a central dome, surrounded by four others which unlike those at Constantinople are lighted by windows as well as the central one. The Church of the Apostles also seems to have had triforium galleries for the women, as the Greek usage was, which are wanting at S. Mark's, and the choir instead of being under the crossing is in the eastern arm. The new church occupies the site of the two old churches of S. Mark and S. Theodore, and from discoveries made during the recent restoration it would seem that the end wall of the North transept, between it and the chapel of S. Isidore, is the south wall of the church of S. Theodore, and that the north, west and south walls of the nave, and the three eastern apses, behind their later casings of marble, are those of the old S. Mark's. These limitations, it has been pointed out, account for the fact that the side domes are smaller than the central one[1].

New Church of S. Mark, Venice

The atrium or outer corridor that surrounds the nave on three sides was probably completed or nearly so by Doge Contarini who died in 1070[2]. His too must be the domes and the internal piers carrying them and so much of the outer walls as does not belong to the older churches. To imagine S. Mark's at this period of its

---

[1] *Architecture East and West.* R. Phené Spiers, pp. 131—132. Vasari's account confirms this. Ella fu sopra i medesimi fondamenti rifatta alla maniera Greca. *Proemio delle vite.*

[2] The atrium formerly bore the inscription:

    Anno milleno transacto, bisque triceno
    Desuper undecimo, fuit facta primo.

Verneilh. p. 123.

Plate LXI

Phot. Brogi

S. MARK'S—VENICE

Plate LXII

A. In North Front

B. In West Front

C. In Nave

D. In Nave

S. MARK'S—VENICE

life we must banish in imagination all the wealth of lovely marbles that now adorn it, and picture to ourselves a plain brick church, as plain externally as those at Ravenna; and instead of the great oriental looking domes of timber and lead which now surmount them the real brick domes of a depressed hemispherical form would be seen, pierced with windows of which the arched extrados would perhaps have been exposed like those of S. Theodore at Constantinople, S.S. Apostoli at Salonica and elsewhere in the East[1].

S. Mark's in 11th century

The decoration however was begun at once. Every ship that carried Venetian commerce throughout the Levant was charged to bring home columns and plaques of precious marbles. Sculptured capitals were imported from Constantinople[2], Greek artists were probably brought to Venice to work on the building, and the demolished churches of S. Mark and S. Isidore furnished materials for their successor. No building can compare with S. Mark's in the splendour and abundance of its marble decoration, either within or without (Plate LXI).

S. Mark's decoration

The capitals are of various kinds; some Corinthianizing with acanthus leaves, and now and then figures of animals at the corners instead of volutes; others of the convex type with surface carving, and some with leaves as if blown by the wind as at S. Demetrius at Thessalonica, and Ravenna. The true pulvino does not appear, but its place is taken by a strong upper abacus, which anticipates the Gothic upper abacus of the 12th and 13th centuries. It is enriched by an inlaid pattern incised and filled with black stopping (Plate LXII).

The capitals

In the balustrades of the galleries we find relics of

[1] Mr Spiers has made a conjectural restoration of the church at the end of the 11th century. *v.* his Fig. 58.
[2] The Thistle Capital, B. Pl. LXII, occurs also at S. Luke's monastery near Delphi, and at the mosque at Keirwan in Barbary, and in the Kibleh of Ibn Touloun at Cairo. Spiers, *East and West*, pp. 142, 143.

older structures; some probably from the Church of Participazio, some perhaps from the ruined cities of Aquileja, Altinum, Heraclea, and others that had been desolated by Attila. Indeed when we consider the utter disappearance of such a city as Aquileja, which is said to have had 600,000 inhabitants, it seems probable that Venice, which had no other quarry near, must be half built out of its ruins. These parapets at S. Mark's are carved in the Byzantine manner with knots and interlacing borders in flat relief upon slightly sunk grounds, and with chased lines on the bands. Except for a bird now and then animal form is not attempted, which perhaps is fortunate. We have seen that Byzantine sculptors avoided the figure either of animals or men almost as religiously as the Moslem, and that in the few cases when they attempted it their efforts were rarely successful.

An exception must be made in favour of some fine capitals at S. Mark's with figures of rams at the angles instead of volutes (Plate LXII *c*).

The completion of the decoration with marble linings and mosaic was slowly effected during the next 200 years; the present domes date from the 13th century, and it was not till the 14th century that the gables were crowned with those splendid riotous crockettings which offend the Purist, but deserve to be classed among the triumphs of decorative sculpture (Plate LXIII).

In S. Mark's we have on Italian soil a purely Byzantine church, that would be at home in Constantinople. It had no imitators, even in Venice, for the basilican type held its own in Italy and no more real domes were erected there till the time of Brunelleschi. But in the detail of sculptured ornament Greek taste survived at Venice till

Plate LXIII

S. MARK'S—VENICE

Plate LXIV

MURANO

a late period of the republic. There are several palaces on the Grand Canal with fronts of the 11th and 12th centuries, perhaps even later, which are thoroughly Byzantine in style. Those who like myself were fortunate enough to know the Fondaco dei Turchi before its lamentable restoration can realize from that, ruined though it was, what Venice must have been like in the days of the blind hero Dandolo. The churches of Torcello and Murano show Byzantine influence, both in plan and in detail; and on many a well head in the courts at Venice the Greek acanthus and Greek ornament can be traced to a comparatively late period, and have even deceived antiquaries[1]. One may perhaps, without being too fanciful, trace an oriental feeling in Venetian architecture from first to last: in the ogee arches of the windows and doors; in the strange Arabian-looking tester over the pulpit at Grado; in the picturesque decoration with inlaid plaques of the Palazzo Dario, built in the early days of the Renaissance. These are all features peculiar to Venice and the countries over which she ruled, and seem to show that she always looked east rather than west, as in the days when she professed her adherence to the king of the Romans at Byzantium.

Other Byzantine work at Venice

The Cathedral of TORCELLO on an island in the lagune, (Fig. 52) founded originally in the 7th century, was altered in 864, when the eastern apses and the tribune with the crypt below were built, and again in 1001–8 when the nave was reconstructed with the use of the old capitals and other materials. Close by is the interesting little church of S. FOSCA, said to have been once a basilican church, ending with three apses, and to have been re-modelled in 1008 to a Byzantine plan, and prepared

Torcello Cathedral

S. Fosca

---

[1] See Cattaneo.

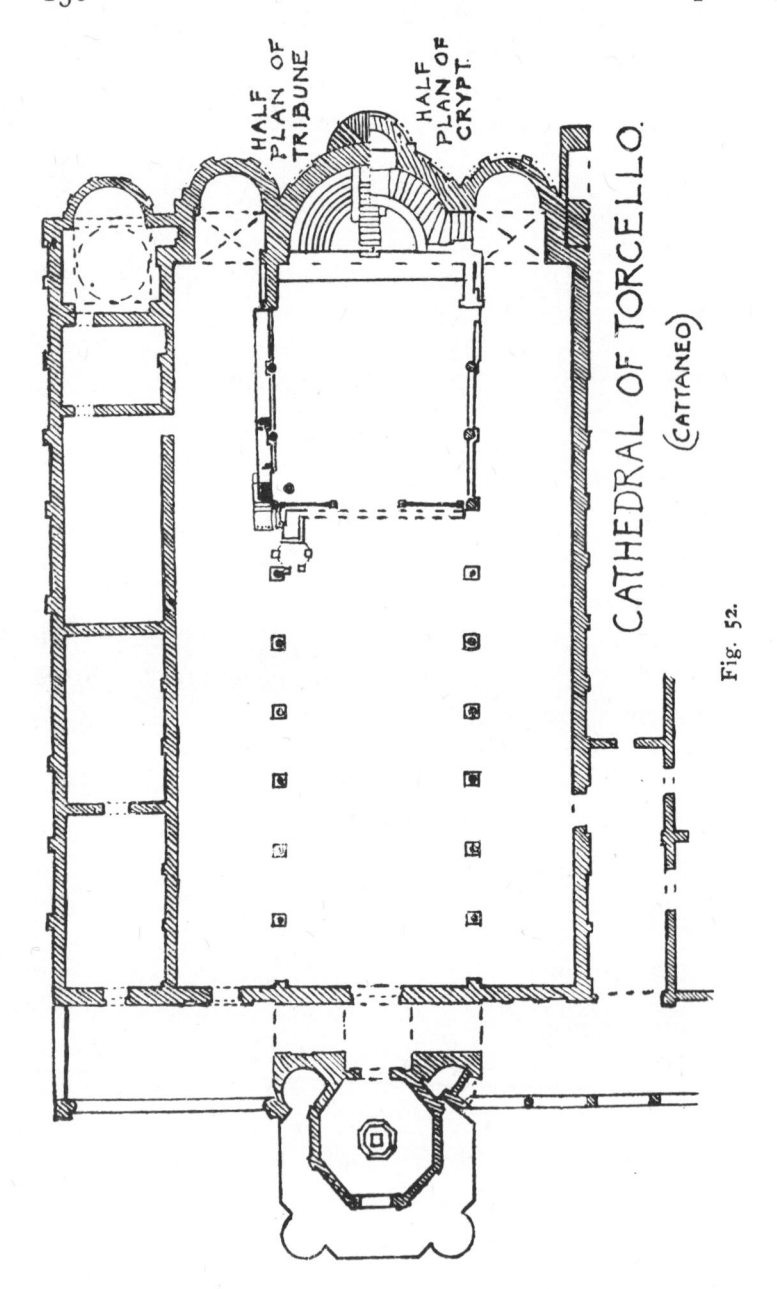

Fig. 52. CATHEDRAL OF TORCELLO. (CATTANEO)

HALF PLAN OF TRIBUNE

HALF PLAN OF CRYPT.

for a dome, which for want of sufficient skill the builders seem never to have accomplished. The central part is carried up as a drum, within which the dome would have been concealed as at S. Vitale, Ravenna, and S. George, Salonica, and it is covered by a pyramidal roof. Inside the whole weight of this and of so much of the dome as was finished is brought down upon the eight interior columns, a load which seems too much for them. There are no pendentives, which probably were beyond the art of the builders, but the square is brought to the necessary circle by a curious series of squinch arches in three tiers one above the other. Here, though we have a Greek inspiration, it is pretty clear there were no Greek builders: and had the dome ever been finished it would probably have fallen. S. Fosca Torcello

In this and in the somewhat later church on the island of MURANO which is said to have been re-modelled after the great earthquake of 1117 (Plate LXIV) is a singular decoration on the outside of the apse by triangular sunk panels. Those at S. Fosca are filled with ornament in stucco, but at Murano where there are two rows of them, the lower row has marble panels with incised ornament. They remind one in a humble way of the decorated triangular panels of the Persian palace at Mashita[1] which dates from the 7th century, but it can hardly be imagined that there is any connexion between them.

In all these churches there are fine specimens of Byzantine parapets (plutei) like those at S. Mark's, and as a rule dating from buildings older than those now existing.

---

[1] Illustrated in Fergusson's *Hist. of Archit.* I. pp. 403—404, Ed. 1893.

The Byzantine dentil

One feature that runs through all Venetian architecture down to the Renaissance, and which is found at S. Sophia, Constantinople, is the double dentil border formed by alternately bevelling off, to right and left, the edges of a narrow marble fillet (Fig. 53).

Byzantine marble linings

The Byzantine and Venetian mode of lining the walls has called down the animadversion of Mr Street. The whole is done with thin plates of marble. The soffits of arches are lined with these in short lengths so as to get round the curve, and their edges project enough to take the upright plates on the face of the wall. These edges are generally worked with the characteristic Venetian dentil just described. On the back of the brick arch to the soffit of which this lining is applied is another dentil border, which projects enough to take the large slabs of marble which clothe the surface of the brick wall and are fixed mainly by metal cramps. The space between the two dentil courses, representing the voussoirs of an arch, is covered with small plates of marble following the curve.

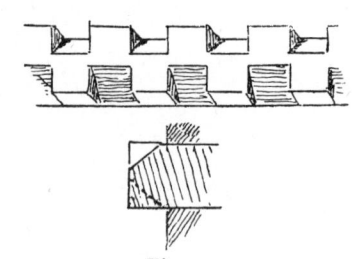

Fig. 53.

Mr Street says "the whole system was exceedingly weak, and this can nowhere be better seen than in the Fondaco dei Turchi, where almost the whole of the marble facing and beautiful medallions in which it was once so rich have peeled off, and left nothing but the plain and melancholy substratum of brick[1]." There is no doubt some justice in this, and the alternative method

---

[1] *Brick and Marble Architecture* by G. E. Street, R.A.

preferred by Mr Street, of building the marble in solid blocks as at the Broletto of Como, is certainly more substantial. But it fails to give the effect at which the Byzantine architects aimed, of displaying to advantage the varied colouring of the material. This can only be seen in large unbroken surfaces, and they made the most of them by splitting the slabs and opening and reversing them to get a sort of pattern in colour[1] as at S. Vitale, and on the walls of S. Mark's, or by using them in large sheets of self-colour as on the piers of the same church. It is obvious that this effect is not to be had on the system of the Como Broletto, which can at the most only achieve bands and stripes of colour. Nor is the Byzantine plan so wanting in durability. The Fondaco dei Turchi, it is true, had fallen into neglect under Austrian rule when I first remember seeing it, but there are other Byzantine palaces in Venice where this form of construction has stood very well, and there is plenty of it at S. Mark's. It is remarkable that at the Fondaco dei Turchi the linings of the arch soffits which one might have thought the weakest constructional part remained firm, while the wall linings had for the most part fallen off.

The Lombard use of marble

The architecture of Venice and Venetia stands, as has been said, somewhat by itself, apart from that of the rest of Italy.

Venetian architecture Byzantine

In the period with which we are now concerned it is distinctly Byzantine rather than Romanesque. Like Justinian's churches at Constantinople S. Mark's not only has its domes, which at first would have been visible externally like those of S. Sophia and SS. Sergius and

[1] Qui (marmorarii) eximie divisa conjungant et venis colludentibus illigata naturalem faciem laudabiliter mentiantur. Cassiodorus, *Var.* 1—6.

Character of Venetian architecture

Bacchus, but also vaults over the whole of the aisles and exterior atrium, while the rest of Italy at that time had not got beyond wooden roofs. In the skilful use of marble for decoration, and the splendid sculpture of her capitals, Venice was unsurpassed in the peninsula during the 11th and 12th centuries, and was no doubt indebted largely on their account to the Eastern capital. But it is perhaps in the construction of S. Mark's that she so far outstripped her neighbours. S. Vitale at Ravenna it is true has a dome, but it too was built during Byzantine supremacy and it is raised on an octagon without pendentives. But the domes of S. Mark's are true domes on spherical pendentives; the great arches or barrel vaults from which they spring are admirably planned to counter-thrust one another, and they are well abutted on the outside. The whole system of construction is simple and scientific, and has stood the test of nine centuries without failure.

S. Mark's not imitated in Italy

S. Mark's, however, had no followers in Italy, for the fantastic church of S. Antonio at Padua can hardly be said to resemble it, and the only imitation that exists must be looked for far away in the south of France.

Greatness of Venice commercial

The rise of Venetian greatness and prosperity was due to her commercial enterprize. An enormous sum must have been spent on her buildings during these three centuries, which however she could well afford. And it was not wrung from an oppressed and overtaxed people like that spent on the buildings of Justinian, but was the willing offering of a free and patriotic community. At the end of the 10th century Venice had made her maritime position secure, and acquired the over-lordship of the coast cities of Istria and Dalmatia. In 998 the great Doge Pietro Orseolo II had crushed the Slavs of the Narenta who disputed the command of the Adriatic, and Venice thenceforward to the end of her history remained mistress of that sea. Her ships traded with all parts of the Mediterranean, and she had the trade of the Levant in her hands. The coast cities of Dalmatia had sworn allegiance to Pietro Orseolo in 998, and though Venice had to contest their possession with Hungary after the 12th century, Zara the most valuable of them was seldom out of her hands for any length of time. At the end of the 10th century a colony of Venetians was established at Limoges on the line of traffic from the Gulf of Lyons through western France as far as Great Britain[1], and to this commercial intercourse is to be attributed the Byzantine influence that shows itself in the domed churches of Périgueux and Angoulême. The establishment of her commercial greatness synchronizes exactly with the re-building of S. Mark's on a splendid scale, and gave facilities for carrying it out. The Venetian marine was in touch with Constantinople, whence not only artists, but wrought sculptures in capital and parapet could be brought, and the ships came home laden with precious marbles from many a desolate temple, and many a town ruined by barbarian inroad, and deserted.

In an Italian city the founding of the great church or the public palace was commonly the mark of its achievement of municipal greatness, and S. Mark's may be regarded as setting the seal upon the arrival of Venice at the position of an European power.

[1] De Verneilh., p. 130, &c.

CHAPTER XVI

PISA, FLORENCE AND LUCCA

VENICE was not the only maritime commonwealth of Italy that by means of commerce rose to wealth and greatness. Genoa and Pisa in the 10th century had also become commercial powers, and the former was destined in after ages to bring Venice herself to her knees. Pisa, unlike Venice, was an old Roman town and a place of some consequence during the Empire. At the beginning of the 10th century the Pisans were already a maritime power, and in 1006 they began their great cathedral. But after repeated successes against the Saracens, from whom they conquered the island of Sardinia in 1025, and whose fleet they destroyed off Palermo in 1063, capturing six great vessels of the enemy laden with merchandize, they determined to devote part of their spoils to the adornment of their cathedral, and to build it in a more splendid manner than that they first intended. It was, as Vasari says, "no small matter at that time to set their hands to the bulk of a church of this kind of five naves, and almost all of marble inside and out." The architect was Boschetto, or Busketus, a Greek of Dulichium, a man of rare skill in that age, who was buried in his cathedral with three epitaphs over him.

<small>Pisa Cathedral</small>

<small>Busketus, architect</small>

It has been remarked that this church, to the adornment of which the spoils of the infidel were devoted, is a building in advance of its age; and it certainly is somewhat of an architectural prodigy, for it shows a perfectly

Plate LXV

Phot. Alinari

THE CATHEDRAL—PISA

Plate LXVI

THE CATHEDRAL—PISA

Phot. Brogi

CH. XVI] PISA 243

developed style, not approached by any other work of its time. The steps by which its perfection was reached are missing, for if there were any that led up to it they are unknown to us. S. Miniato at Florence, the only church of the date worthy to compare with it, is in a quite different style.

The duomo of Pisa

Though the architect is reported to be Greek, Latin tradition dictated a basilican rather than the domical plan

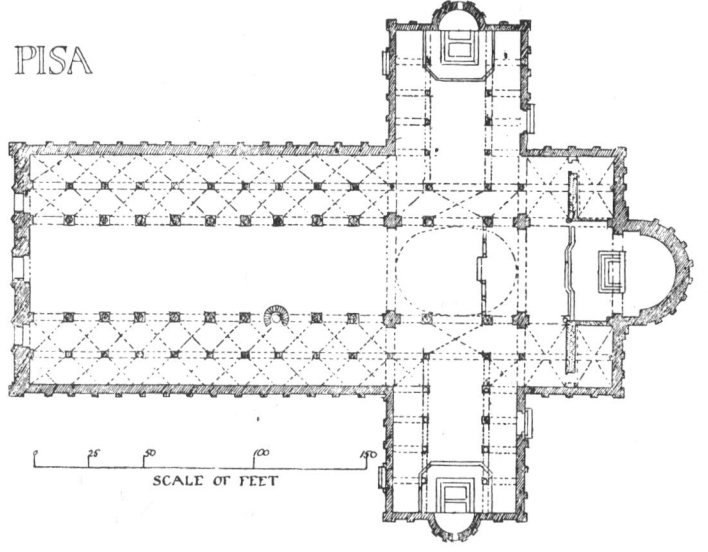

Fig. 54.

which would naturally have suggested itself to him. The church is a Latin cross (Fig. 54) with deep transepts, almost like a northern cathedral, and the transepts have aisles on both sides of them like those at Winchester[1]. The aisles are vaulted, but the nave has a wooden ceiling.

[1] It has been suggested that in the original plan the four arms of the cross were equal, and that the western part of the nave and the façade, from a point where the wall deviates from a straight line, is an extension of the 13th century. *v.* Rivoira, II. p. 596. Signor Supino (*Italia artistica*) sees no reason for this idea.

The Cathedral

Over the crossing of nave and transepts is a dome, in plan an elongated octagon, a mere covering in of the central space, not as in the Greek churches supplying the motive of the design. The 68 columns of the nave are said to be antiques,—Greek and Roman,—spoils of war (Plate LXV). The capitals are classic, some of them Corinthian others Composite: they have no pulvino on them, but a plain square slab, a veritable abacus. There is a triforium, banded in white and dark marble, a treatment which is carried up into the clerestory, the end walls and the dome. The outside of the church is more remarkable than the inside (Plate LXVI). It has three stages corresponding to the three of the interior. The lower which represents the main arcade is decorated with lofty blank arcading, in the head of which are squares set diamond-wise and filled with mosaic of marble. Above that, except round the apse and in the west front, the wall is ornamented with flat pilasters carrying the eaves of the triforium roof. Here too are diamond panels of mosaic in the head of each compartment. But in the apse and the west front these pilasters are exchanged for arcaded galleries with passages behind the columns, of which there are four tiers in the front and two round the apse.

Varied arrangement of colonnades

There is much to study in this western façade, which combines apparent symmetry with actual variety. Ruskin in his *Seven Lamps*, dwells on this: on the interest given by the slight inequalities in width of the seven ground floor arches; on the narrowing of the intervals in the wedge-shaped ends of the third storey so that the columns are not over those below, but have six intervals to their five; on the change in the fourth storey which has a column in the middle, and eight openings over nine in the third; on the narrowing of the eight openings in the top storey of all, leaving room for an angelic figure at each end; and above all on the variety in the height of the several storeys, and their subordination to the great arcade of the ground storey. All these varieties, though they do not challenge the eye, have an insensible influence and make a lively and satisfactory impression that perfect regularity would never effect.

The Cathedral

The spoils of Palermo did not suffice to finish so great a work, which came to a standstill in 1095, and was completed with the help of a subsidy from the Emperor at Constantinople. Pisa like Venice and Amalfi seems to have maintained relations with the Eastern Empire even after the fall of the Exarchate. But it would appear that in Italy even in the 11th century Constantinople was still regarded as the centre of art. Desiderius, Abbot of Monte Cassino, when re-building his abbey in 1065, sent to Constantinople to engage artists, whence came the sculptor Oelintus, the architect Aldo, and the painter Baleus, who carved and built and painted *per castella et eremos*[1].

The cathedral of Pisa, which was consecrated in 1118, by Pope Gelasius II, had a great influence on the progress of Italian architecture. Vasari says it aroused in all Italy and especially in Tuscany the spirit for many and fine undertakings. The men of Pistoja followed suit with their Church of S. Paolo, those of Lucca with S. Martin's, the designs, says Vasari, being given by pupils of Boschetto, for there were, he says, no other architects at that time in Tuscany[2]. But these other buildings are so much later

Influence of Pisan Cathedral

---

[1] *History of Monte Cassino*, cited De Verneilh., p. 127.
[2] Col disegno, non essendo all' hora altri architetti in Toscana, di certi discepoli di Boschetto. Vasari, *Proemio delle Vite*.

246   FLORENCE   [CH. XVI

than the time of Busketus that their architects could not have been actually his pupils.

S. Miniato, Florence

The church of S. MINIATO AL MONTE, on the hill opposite Florence, is slightly older than the Duomo of Pisa, having been begun in 1013. It is basilican in plan (Fig. 55); the columns seem to be antiques, and the capitals are often misfits, too small for the shafts. The

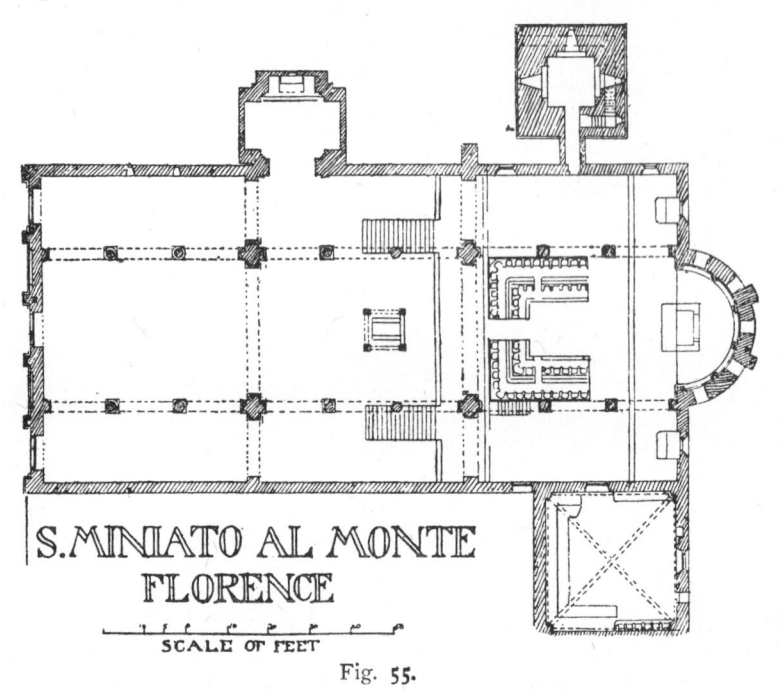

S. MINIATO AL MONTE
FLORENCE
SCALE OF FEET

Fig. 55.

nine bays are divided into groups of three by large piers which carry semi-circular arches across the nave. These are counterthrust by arches across the aisles. Here we

The crypt

find an early example of the spacious crypt, open to the nave, occasioning a great elevation of the choir above, which became fashionable in Italy, at Verona, Modena and elsewhere, and was formed at S. Lorenzo in Rome in

Plate LXVII

S. MINIATO AL MONTE—FLORENCE

Phot. Brogi

the 13th century. The crypt or lower church was the *confessio*, where the body or relic of the saint was laid, just as had been the case with the older crypts which were not thrown open to the church like this.

<small>S. Miniato al Monte</small>

The floor of the crypt being only four feet below that of the nave, the choir is very high and is reached on each side by a considerable flight of steps (Plate LXVII). The enclosure and ambo are of marble inlaid with a variety of figures, with a beautiful effect, showing a more advanced style than the primitive architecture of the nave and crypt. The walls over the nave arches are faced with white marble divided into patterns by simple bands of dark marble, probably a subsequent device, and the same decoration is employed on the west front which is said to have been re-built in the 14th century. The same style of decoration with bands of dark marble dividing a surface of white into figures and compartments occurs in the façade of the Badia of FIESOLE, and in the BAPTISTERY AT FLORENCE, Dante's "mio bel San Giovanni" (Fig. 56).

<small>The raised choir</small>

The history of this latter building has been a matter of controversy. It used to be said that behind its clothing of marble were the walls of a temple of Mars. Another theory is that it was built by Queen Theodelinda. Cattaneo considers the interior and most of the exterior architecture to date from the second half of the 11th century, and that the bare walls cannot be referred to the 6th century and Queen Theodelinda, as the construction of a domed building with so great a diameter was beyond the humble skill of that date. Fergusson again considers that the whole design of the building has been altered, and that the ancient columns of granite now placed against the wall once stood out on the floor and carried an architrave and an upper range of columns like those in Constantine's

<small>Baptistery, Florence</small>

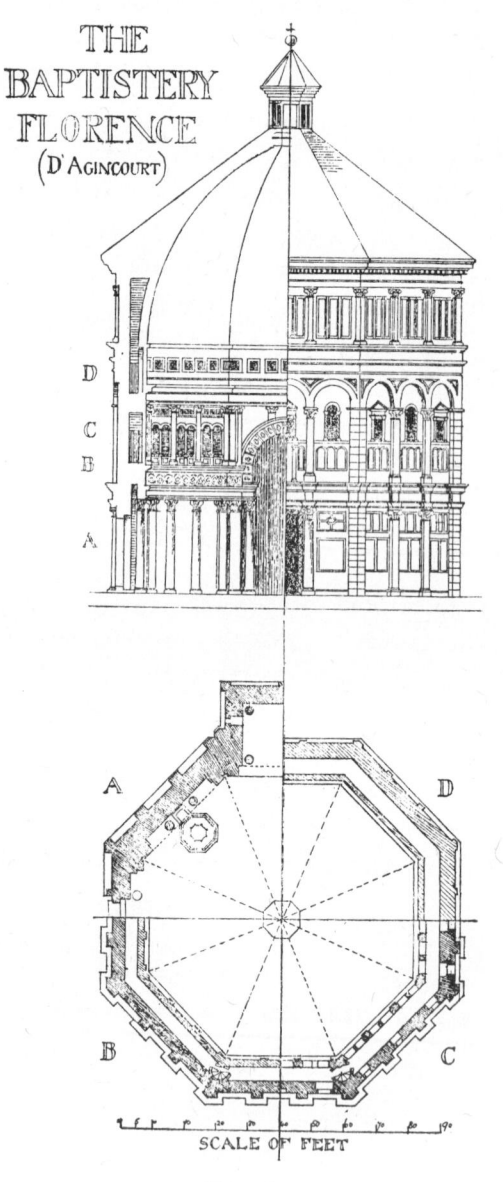

Fig. 56.

baptistery at the Lateran, with a wooden roof, or else a small dome like the church of S. Costanza at Rome. This would have got over Cattaneo's difficulty, but the building shows no sign of so radical a change as its present condition would have occasioned. The exterior seems to have been decorated by Arnolfo del Cambio in the 13th century, who cut out the plain stonework that was mixed with the marble facing, and substituted dark marble from Prato[1] in bands like those at S. Miniato.

<small>The Baptistery</small>

This baptistery (Fig. 56), once the Cathedral of Florence, is octagonal, with classic shafts and capitals supporting an upper storey of columns with three two-light openings between them in each face, and a gallery behind them. The details are for the date singularly classical. Five of the capitals are tolerably correct Corinthian: the leaves are rather coarsely raffled, and the piping stops square at the level of the lower tier. The volutes are cut through, and the abacus is thin, classic fashion. They are probably antique. Two of the others are Composite, with an ovolo on the edge of the bell, and the third has the same feature, but above it is a scroll which is quite foreign to classic use, and resembles some 12th century Romanesque work in France and Italy.

<small>Classical details</small>

On the west side a square choir is projected with a barrel vault which has a "bonnet" on each side over a window. Like the dome itself this vault is covered with mosaic, which is carried round the edges of the arch in the Byzantine manner.

Some of the columns are of marble, one of them fluted,

---

[1] * * * ed incrostar poi di marmi neri di Prato tutte le otto facciate di fuori di detto S. Giovanni, levandone i macigni, che prima erano fra que' marmi antichi. Vasari, *Vita d' Arnolfo*. Vasari calls him Arnolfo di Lapo; which is now considered incorrect. His parents were Cambio and Perfetta.

<small>Florence, the Baptistery</small>

and the rest are of granite, all evidently the spoils of ancient buildings. The columns of each stage carry regular entablatures with architrave frieze and cornice, which must have been made for the place, not taken like the columns from some ancient building; and this touch of classicism is surprising, to whichever of the above-mentioned dates the design may be referred.

<small>Pisan architecture elsewhere</small>

The style of these buildings belongs to Florence, and differs widely from that which made such a brilliant beginning at Pisa. This latter, as Vasari says, set the fashion for many other buildings in that part of Italy, a fashion which lasted through the 12th and 13th centuries. We find it in other churches at Pisa, notably at S. Paolo a Ripa d' Arno and S. Pietro in Grado: at S. Michele at Lucca as late as 1288, where the architect has run riot in all sorts of fantastic inlays on the spandrils of the arcading: in the façade of the Cathedral of Lucca, in 1204; in the arcaded façade and long galleried flank of the Duomo of Zara in Dalmatia consecrated in 1285; and in the church of S. Grisogono (1175) in the same city. The

<small>The arcaded gallery</small>

arcaded gallery was a very general feature round the apse even when absent elsewhere. The semi-dome of the apse was never exposed in Romanesque architecture, but the wall was carried up as a drum and covered with a roof of timber and tile, and this wall having but little weight to carry could safely be pierced by these open arcades. In some cases the outside of the dome may be seen through the arches but generally there is a back wall to the gallery. Now and then, as in two churches at Lucca and the baptistery at Parma, the colonnettes carry a straight lintel instead of the usual arches. We find the same apsidal gallery in Lombardy, at S. Fedele in Como, at the cathedrals of Parma and Modena, at S. MARIA

Plate LXVIII

BERGAMO

Plate LXIX

THE CATHEDRAL—LUCCA

CH. XVI] PISAN INFLUENCE 251

MAGGIORE IN BERGAMO (Plate LXVIII), and at SS. Giovanni e Paolo in Rome (Plate LI, p. 200). The fashion crossed the Alps and became a feature of German Romanesque. The cathedrals of Speyer, Mainz and Worms have galleried apses of the Lombard type, and at Cologne the churches of Great S. Martin, the Apostles, S. Gereon, and S. Maria in Capitolio. In England, where apses were not long in fashion, this feature does

S. Maria Maggiore, Bergamo

Fig. 57.

not appear, nor do I know of an instance of it in France. In Italy it lingered long. The fine apse of the Duomo of LUCCA (Plate LXIX) has the tall Pisan arcading below, and above it one of these galleries dated as late as the 14th century, but so exactly in the style of a century or a century and a half earlier, that the date seems incredible till one examines the carving of the capitals (Fig. 57), which resemble some of 1323 in the Capella della Spina at Pisa. There can however be no doubt about the

Lucca Cathedral

The Cathedral date, for it is recorded that 14 braccia of land were acquired in 1308 for extending the church eastward and building a new tribune[1]: and a tablet in the wall below the east window gives the dates of the beginning and completion of the work, and the names of the *operarii* or directors of it.

```
+·HOC·OPUS·INCEPTUM·FUIT·TEMPORE·S·MAC
THEI·CAMPARERII·OPERARII·OPE·SCĒ·CRUCIS·
·AD·M·CCC·UIII·ET·MORTUUS·Ē·D̄C̄S·OPARI
·AD·M·CCCXX·LOCO·EIU·SUCCESSIT·SER·
·BONAUENTURA·ROLENTDI·QUO·MO·IPM
OPUS·REASSUMSIT·AB·HIC·SUPRA·+·
```
LUCCA.

Another inscription in Lombardic lettering of the 13th century records the foundation of this Cathedral in the time of Alexander II (1061—1073), Anselmo Badagio who had been bishop of Lucca, the Pope who presented the consecrated banner to William of Normandy when he was about to invade England. There is however nothing left of that building, and the body of the church is in fully developed Italian Gothic, of which style it is one of the best examples. But the west front with its stately portico is still Romanesque, though only built in the 13th century. It consists of three large arches *The inlaid façade* opening into a portico or narthex of the whole width of the church, one arch being cramped by the tower and therefore smaller than the others. Above are three tiers of arcading, Pisan fashion, but enriched with inlays of black and white (Plate LXX) in spandril and column, some of the latter being also carved. The whole has an effect

---

[1] Ridolfi, *Guida di Lucca.*

Plate LXX

THE CATHEDRAL—LUCCA. West front

somewhat bizarre, but entirely delightful. On projecting *The Cathedral*
brackets in the lower storey is S. Martin, the patron of
the church, on horseback, dividing his cloak with a
beggar. These figures are perhaps a later addition, for
they seem too advanced in style for the date of the
façade, which is given by an inscription on a scroll held
by a little figure worked on the right hand colonnette of
the lowest tier of arcading;

```
MILL·CC
IIII .
CONDI-
DITELE
CTI·APUL
CRA^S DET
GUIDECTI
```
LUCCA

The figure itself no doubt represents the architect *The architect Guidetto*
Guidetto himself, whose "right hand (dextra) wrought
these so lovely shafts." He wears a tall pointed cap,
perhaps a hood; his hair is long and rests on his
shoulders, and his tunic reaches to the knee; evidently
he was a layman.

The columns of the three lower arches are magnificently carved with scroll-work (Fig. 58), typical of the
period, and no doubt wrought by the same dexterous

The Cathedral hand. The inner wall of the portico was finished a little later and an inscription gives the names of the *operarii*, Belenatus and Aldibrandus, with the date 1233.

✠ HOP'CĒPFIER ABELENATO ET ALOBRAD. OPRS. AO.MECXXX.III.
LUCCA

The pleasant city of Lucca, set between mountain ranges, and girdled by delightful rampart-walks under shady groves, abounds in arcaded fronts of Pisan Romanesque though there is only one other decorated with inlay, **S. Michele** that of S. MICHELE in the principal piazza[1] (Plate LXXI). This rises so high above the church behind as to amount to an architectural fraud. The arcaded façade of the fine **S. Pietro** church of S. PIETRO SOMALDI also offends in this way **S. Maria Bianca** though not so badly (Plate LXXII). S. MARIA BIANCA or Foris Portam, has another arcaded front finished above in brick. The apse of this church has a colonnaded gallery outside carrying lintels instead of arches, and so **S. Frediano** has the apse of the fine church of S. FREDIANO. The latter church was re-built and enlarged between 1112 and 1147, and has the apse at the west and the entrance at the east end. The façade is plain below, and the upper part instead of the Lucchese galleries has a splendid mosaic filling the gable. It is a fine basilica 12 bays long with cylindrical columns and Corinthianizing capitals. The inside of all these Lucchese churches is very similar; plain arcades, the arches cut square through the wall without mouldings, simple columns mostly no doubt

---

[1] This front has been entirely re-built. When I first saw it in 1864 it was half pulled down. Ridolfi regrets that so little of the old work was used again.

Plate LXXI

Phot. Brogi

S. MICHELE – LUCCA

Plate LXXII

S. PIETRO SOMALDI—LUCCA

Phot. Alinari

CH. XVI] LUCCA 255

antique, with Romanesque capitals, apses with a semi- Church interiors
dome, and the upper walls bare with small clerestory

LUCCA.
Fig. 58.

windows high up. Some of them have transepts like
S. Maria Bianca, and S. Giovanni, and the latter adjoins S. Giovanni
an ancient baptistery with a square ribbed dome that has

superseded an older covering of which the pilasters remain in the lower part of the walls. Many of them, like the Duomo, S. Michele, and S. Maria Bianca, have the tall Pisan blank arcading in the lower storey, and the doorways have commonly a fine sculptured lintel of unusual depth, surmounted by a lunette within a semicircular arch. The finest of these lintels is that in the little church of S. GIUSTO (Plate LXXIII), the scroll ornament of which resembles goldsmiths' work, and reminds one of the great *châsse* at Aix-la-Chapelle which was made by order of Frederick II in 1220[1]. In the capitals of the jamb pilasters it is curious to notice the prominence given to the Corinthian caulicoli, which are promoted to be the principal features. The same insistence on the caulicolus may be observed in the portico of the Duomo. At S. Giusto the Byzantine raffling of the acanthus leaves is remarkable.

S. Giusto

One peculiarity of the arcaded fronts here and at Pisa is that in most cases they finish in the upper stages with a column in the centre instead of an arch. It is so in the Cathedral and S. Michele in Borgo at Pisa, and in the Duomo, S. Maria Bianca, and S. Pietro Somaldi at Lucca. On the contrary at S. Paolo a ripa d' Arno in Pisa, and S. Giusto in Lucca and the Cathedral of Pistoja there is an arch in the centre, which to an architect's eye is more satisfactory.

Peculiarity in arcading

So much were the Pisans attached to their arcaded façades that they continued them long after Romanesque times, and the churches of S. Michele in Borgo and S. Caterina have arcaded galleries with pointed arches and trefoil cusping.

Late examples of arcaded fronts

---

[1] Illustrated in the *Mélanges d'Archéologie*, vol. I. Paris, 1847.

Plate LXXIII

Phot. Alinari

S. GIUSTO—LUCCA

Plate LXXIV

SCROLL ON THE BAPTISTERY PORTAL—PISA

The Pisan arcaded front does not appear in Lombardy, but there is something like it at Ancona at the church of S. Maria which is dated in 1210, where however it is not pierced for a gallery; and it crossed the Adriatic to Zara, when the façade of the Duomo is covered with blank arcading, and the north side has a practicable gallery behind columns and arches. When these arcaded fronts were entirely occupied by colonnaded galleries, as at S. Martin's in Lucca (Plate LXX), great western windows had to be given up, and only very small and comparatively unimportant windows could be had at the back of the passages. At the Cathedral of Zara, however, where the arcading of the front is not sunk for galleries like that of the north side of the church, but only applied to the surface, the design is interrupted at two levels by large rose windows[1]. This of course would have been impossible at Lucca or Pisa.

The arcaded front

The towers of Lucca belong rather to the Lombard type, than that which has been described at Rome. They are panelled between projecting styles at the angles, and divided into stages by a string course with a row of little arcadings on corbels which project as much as the angle styles, and connect them together. Within these panels are windows grouped in pairs or in threes with mid-wall shafts, the number of openings increasing from the lower storeys to the upper. At S. Frediano the panelling begins at the level of the aisle, and there are two storeys of windows in each panel. At the Cathedral, S. Pietro, and S. Michele (Plates LXXI, LXXII) the panelling begins higher up, and the panels coincide with the storeys. The campanile of S. Michele is the finest in Lucca, and has the peculiarity of being oblong instead of

Lucchese towers

[1] Illustrated in my *Dalmatia*, etc., vol. I.

J. A.   17

Lucchese towers

square. The forked battlements with which those of the Duomo and S. Frediano finish are ungraceful and disfiguring.

Campanile of Pisa begun 1173

The great CAMPANILE of the Cathedral of PISA is unlike any other (Plate LXVI). Here the Pisans have indulged to the full their passion for arcading, with a magnificent result. At the same time, strange as it may seem, I think the effect owes something to the accident of the tower leaning out of the perpendicular. Had it been upright I am not sure that all those arcades in contiguity to the multitudinous arcading of the Duomo would have pleased so well; there would have been too much of them; whereas the inclination gives them a fresh aspect.

Baptistery, Pisa

The BAPTISTERY OF PISA was begun in 1153, the architect being Diotisalvi[1]. It consists of a circular central domed area surrounded by a circular aisle, from which it is divided by a circular arcade. This consists of four piers with two columns between each pair, carrying twelve arches. Above the aisle is a second storey with twelve arches carried by plain rebated piers. The lower aisle is cross-vaulted with transverse ribs from capital to wall, and slender diagonal ribs of marble, sometimes cabled, which must be later than the original building. The upper storey has an annular vault, interrupted by cross arches carrying walls from each pier. The main walls are banded with Verde di Prato like the Duomo.

The four piers below have Romanesque capitals of a very classic character, and the other capitals are either

---

[1] MCLIII mense aūg. fundata fuit haec ecclesia: Deotisalvi magister huius operis. He was also architect of the Church and Campanile of S. Sepolcro in Pisa, which bears this inscription—huius operis fabricator Deus te salvet nominatur. Supino, *Italia Artistica*, No. 16.

fair imitations of Corinthian, or composed of figures of men and animals. *The Baptistery*

Externally the walls of the baptistery are of the original design up to the second storey. The lower stage has the tall blank arches of Pisan design like the basement of the Duomo. Above is a row of smaller arches now surmounted by pediments and crocketting of 14th century Gothic, which are continued in an upper storey reaching the dome.

The classic feeling of the interior sculpture shows itself again in that of the columns flanking the portals. In particular that of the doorway facing east has a magnificent sweep of foliage that could not have been surpassed in the best period of Roman art, and which is surprising at this date (Plate LXXIV). But in Italy the classic feeling never died out, and though Niccola Pisano's exquisite pulpit of 1260 in this baptistery is a Gothic work it has the Roman egg and dart moulding on the abacus of the central column, and the panels are filled with reliefs based on ancient example which paved the way for the Renaissance of Donatello and Brunelleschi. *Classic feeling in details*

Of Diotisalvi, the architect of the Pisan Baptistery, we hear again at Lucca, where an inscription on the wall claims him as the architect of S. Cristoforo. Ridolfi[1] believes him to be the original architect of S. Michele in that city, though the inlaid façade was probably by Guidetto the architect and sculptor of the cathedral front. *Diotisalvi*

---

[1] *Guida di Lucca*, p. 76.

CHAPTER XVII

LOMBARDY

Lombardy under the Franks

LOMBARDY was the cradle of communal liberty. On the fall of the Lombard kingdom in 774 the Lombard dukes were replaced by Frank counts: but a rival power existed side by side with them in the bishop, who finally dispossessed the counts within the city, leaving them for a time supreme over the outside territory, or *contado* (comitatus) and the *contadini* who peopled it[1]. Finally the bishops effaced the counts entirely there too, but had themselves to give way to the rising power of the Communes. Under the degenerate successors of Charlemagne the Empire had been forgotten in Italy and a short-lived kingdom was set up by Berengar. His overthrow by the Emperor Otho I in 962 who was crowned king of Italy, established finally that dependence of the country on the Empire which was never again denied during the middle ages. The 11th and 12th centuries were the period of the rise of the Communes to power and independence both of count, bishop, and nobles. In 1107 we hear of Consuls[2], and the cities appear as free republics; and in 1183, by the peace of Constance, the Empire was finally forced to recognize them as a privileged order of the Italian kingdom.

Otho, Emperor

Rise of the Communes

---

[1] *The Lombard Communes*, by W. F. Butler, p. 43.
[2] *Ibid.* p. 78.

CH. XVII] THE LOMBARD COMMUNES

The towns, after gaining individual freedom, had no coherence among themselves, and were involved in incessant wars with one another, the protagonists being always Pavia and Milan, round whom the other cities, Ghibelline or Guelf, grouped themselves in uncertain and variable alliance.

This period of turmoil and strife was not as might be supposed inimical to the progress of the arts. The independence of the towns and their local self-government aroused a passionate feeling of patriotism and emulation which impelled the citizen to adorn his city with buildings better and more beautiful than those of its neighbours and rivals. Disaster only provoked him to greater effort. Lodi was destroyed by Milan about 1104, Como was dismantled and pillaged by Milan in 1127, and in 1160 Milan itself was destroyed by Frederick Barbarossa with the aid of Pavia, Cremona and Novara, and also of Lodi and Como who thus revenged themselves on their old enemy. At the end of six days it is said not a fiftieth part of the city remained standing. But from all these disasters the Communes recovered themselves unbroken, and re-built their old homes with increased splendour; and Milan rose from her ashes to take the lead in the Lombard league and achieve the final victory of 1183.

Local patriotism

One venerable building in particular escaped destruction at the time of Barbarossa's triumph (Fig. 59).

S. Ambrogio

The church of S. AMBROGIO at Milan in its present state dates chiefly from the latter half of the 11th century. The old church built by S. Ambrose in the 4th century was re-built at the end of the 8th century (789—824) when Benedictine monks were installed there; but of that re-building only the eastern apses and their prolongation

S. Ambrogio

towards the nave now remain, together with the older of the two towers. Under Archbishop Angilbertus (824—859) the nave and aisles were again re-built and also the façade; but under Archbishop Guido (1046—1071) the building was converted from a columnar basilica into a vaulted church, and this must have involved an almost entire reconstruction.

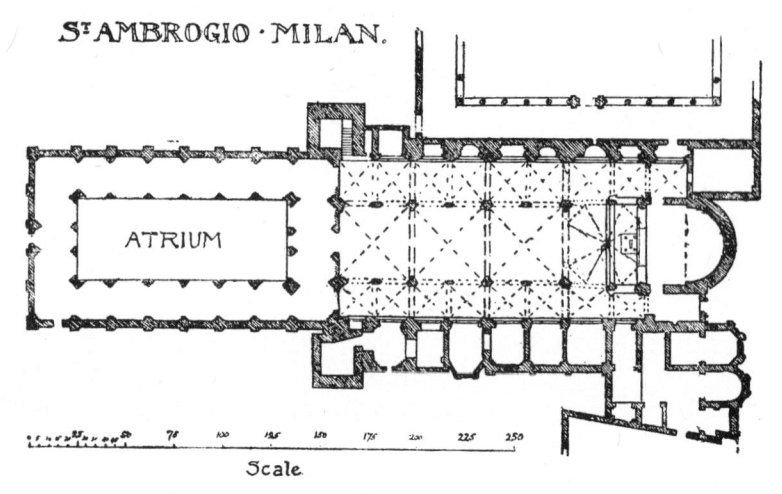

Fig. 59.

Archbishop Anspertus had built an atrium, as his epitaph declares:

QVOT SACRAS AEDES QVANTO SVDORE REFECIT
ATRIA VICINAS STRUXIT ET ANTE FORES

The Atrium

which apparently means that he built the atrium in front of the neighbouring doors of the church. But the style of the existing atrium (Plate LXXV) is inconsistent with the date of Anspertus who died in 882, and it was re-built probably late in the 11th century. Finally the northern campanile, that of the Canons, was erected between 1128

Plate LXXV

S. AMBROGIO—MILAN. The Atrium

Plate LXXVI

S. AMBROGIO—MILAN

and 1144[1]. The church has been a good deal meddled with by modern restorers, but it remains perhaps the earliest example of a completely vaulted church in Italy.

S. Ambrogio

The Eastern apse has the side walls prolonged to form a bay in advance of the nave, cross vaulted in the aisles, barrel vaulted in the choir, the object being to give more space for the monks who were established there in the 8th century, and for whom we suppose the rebuilding of this part took place. The body of the church consists of four square bays in the nave and eight in each aisle, the nave bays being articulated by massive clustered piers, with lesser piers between them corresponding to the bays in the aisles (Plate LXXVI). Over the aisles is a spacious triforium with two arches in each bay of the nave over the two of the arcade below, and it is vaulted. A single wide roof covers both nave and aisles so that there is no clerestory. The three western bays of the nave are cross-vaulted with transverse ribs of stone and diagonal ribs of brick, a very early instance of the diagonal rib if the dates are correct and the accuracy of the restoration may be trusted.

The apses

The nave

The bay next the east is raised by squinch arches of the kind M. Choisy calls a "tromp" into a low octagon which is pierced with windows, and lights admirably the ciborium and altar below. The rest of the church depends for light on windows in the side walls, which are rather small, and on the great west window, which is partly shaded by

[1] In dating S. Ambrogio I follow Rivoira with whom Cattaneo agrees more nearly than is usual between archaeologists. His dates are:
    The central apse, choir and monk's tower, 789—824.
    Lateral apses, 824—859.
    Nave, aisles, narthex and atrium, 11th century.
    Canon's tower, 1128—1144.
Lasteyrie however (p. 260) produces evidence that the church was rebuilt by Archbishop Anselmo di Pusterla, who built the Canon's tower 1128—1144. Biscaro dates the re-building 1098—1145.

an external loggia constructed over the eastern walk of the atrium, a very unusual feature (Plate LXXV).

This central lantern tower is surrounded outside by an open arcade carrying a pyramidal roof, and the back of the dome is visible through the arcading.

The details of the construction show a very great advance towards the logical expression of the later Gothic. There are clustered piers in which each member corresponds to the arch or rib it has to carry: there are recessed or subordinated orders with corresponding breaks in the piers that bear them: the system of rib and panel vaulting is thoroughly developed in the nave, though in the aisles the diagonal rib does not appear; all of these being features which must have been novel at the time they were made, if the date has been correctly ascertained.

The pulpit which stands against one of the main piers bears the name of the donor Guglielmus de Pomo, but unfortunately no date. Its style however speaks of the 12th century, the sculpture being more advanced than that of the church. It rests on an early Christian sarcophagus, which one would like to believe really that of the great Stilicho, and on eight marble columns, some round, and others octagonal, with capitals of foliage or birds or other animals. The arches are enriched with scrolls or interlaced knots; figures of animals, men, and angels fill the spandrils, and a cornice of running foliage intertwined with little beasts surrounds it at the level of its floor. The upper part is comparatively plain.

The sculpture both in atrium and nave shows scarcely any memory of classic art (Figs. 59, 60, 61). The capitals are rudely shaped with little distinction between bell and abacus, and singularly little projection, some of

CH. XVII] MILAN 265

them being no more than a splayed face decorated with S. Ambrogio
surface carving. Many of them are composed of animals—
rams, bears, and eagles—and the jambs and lintel of the
doorway are carved with interlacing patterns.

Fig. 59^A.

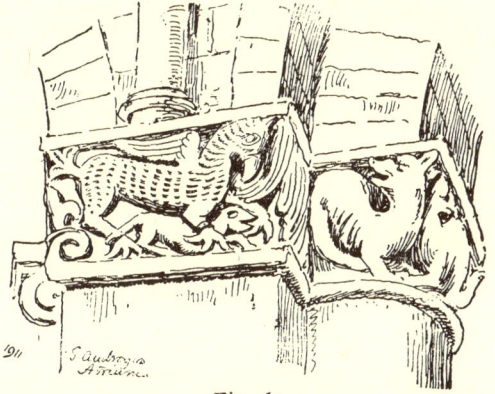

Fig. 60.

In the great western door we have slightly expressed Subordination
the recessing and subordination of orders, but in the of orders
portals of S. Michele and S. Pietro in Cielo d' Oro at PAVIA
the system is thoroughly developed. At S. MICHELE S. Michele,
(Plate LXXVII) there are no less than seven orders Pavia

17—5

S. Michele, Pavia regularly retired within one another, and four at S. Pietro. At S. Michele they consist of three round mouldings or rolls, between four square orders; at the other church all are square, and in both churches every order is carved with interlacing ornament and scroll-work, which is continued down the jambs. The section of jamb and arch is practically the same, and the capitals have so slight a projection and so little modelling as to amount to little more than an ornamental band at the springing.

Fig. 61.

Arcaded galleries The Pisan arcaded front does not appear in Lombardy, but arcaded galleries in another form are a common feature in North Italian churches, as at Parma in the Cathedral, and in S. Michele and S. Pietro in Cielo d' Oro at Pavia, where they run up the gables in a series of steps: and the baptistery at Parma is covered inside and out with colonnaded galleries having however straight lintels instead of arches. The arcaded galleries at the interest-

S. MICHELE—PAVIA

ing church of S. Andrea Vercelli are arranged Pisan fashion and do not ramp with the gables.

The wide pedimental gable end at S. Ambrogio is low-pitched, covering both nave and aisles, and is partly concealed by the abutting atrium, which disguises what would otherwise have been an awkward proportion. A similar wide pedimental façade at the two churches in Pavia which have been mentioned has a very bare, unsatisfactory appearance, only partly relieved by the practicable gallery that ramps with the gable, and the small windows which are the only other features except the doorways. One cannot but feel how very far in point of grace and comeliness this North Lombard work is behind the Pisan Romanesque of half a century or more before. Even Venice must yield in point of date to the rival Republic, for the splendid marble walls and colonnaded galleries of Busketus are contemporary with the re-building of S. Mark's in plain brickwork, as yet unclothed with its marble facing, and unadorned with its wealth of marble shafts. *Wide pedimental fronts* *Pavia* *Rudeness of Lombard work*

The older of the two towers of S. Ambrogio which dates from the 8th and 9th century is very plain and featureless, and probably incomplete. The other, built in the 12th century (Plate LXXV, *v. sup.* p. 262) is a good example of the Lombard brick campanile with the wide styles or flat piers at the angles joined at each stage by arcaded cornices which divide the wall into panels. Unlike the Lucchese towers of S. Frediano and the rest there are no windows but little slits till the top storey is reached, where there are three wide lights on each side surmounted by a brick dentil cornice and a low pyramidal roof. From between the windows narrow rounded strips or pilasters of bricks and marble run down, dividing the panels into three. *The Lombard campanile* *S. Ambrogio campanile*

Parma campanile

S. Satiro and S. Sepolcro, Milan

This type prevails through Lombardy. The great campanile of Parma cathedral, which is much later and has the little arcaded cornices cusped with trefoils, is divided vertically in the same way by narrow pilaster strips. The tower of S. SATIRO at Milan (Plate LXXVIII) is another good example, and the church of S. Sepolcro has a pair of towers one of which however has only been completed within the last few years.

Dalmatian campaniles

The campaniles of Dalmatia partake somewhat of the Lombard character. That of S. Maria at Zara has the angle pilasters and the panels of those we have been describing, with grouped lights and midwall shafts. So have some of the towers on the island of Arbe, though the finest of them, that of the cathedral, has no vertical pilasters or divisions, but is articulated more in the Roman fashion. It has also a stone spire like two of its fellows, and like the towers of Spalato and Traü; a feature foreign to the Lombard type[1]. This may have come from the Hungarian connexion: the church of Jak in Hungary has a pair of towers with spires, though they are panelled in the Lombard fashion[2]. The great campanile of Spalato stands alone, and seems to have no relations across the Adriatic.

S. Babila, Milan

The ancient church of S. Babila at Milan is ceiled with a barrel vault divided by transverse arches at each bay, and an octagonal dome on "tromps," which is enclosed like that at S. Ambrogio in a tower pierced with arcadings through which the back of the dome is seen. The colonnettes are of marble and have cushion capitals. The apse outside has been much restored: it is plain and

---

[1] My *Dalmatia, the Quarnero, and Istria*, Plates VIII, XX, XXIII, LVII.
[2] *Ibid.* Plate XXV.

S. SATIRO—MILAN

Plate LXXIX

BORGO S. DONNINO

has a very simple arcaded storey under the eaves, of brick arches on square piers of brickwork, through which the back of the apse semi-dome can be seen. There are similar arcaded apses of the simplest kind at S. Eustorgio, and S. Vincenzo in Prato. *S. Babila, Milan*

The cushion capital at S. Babila, S. Abbondio in Como, and elsewhere in North Italy, introduces us to a type we have not hitherto met with in our review of Italian Romanesque. It is a northern feature, and from Lombardy it spread across the Alps to Germany, France, and through Normandy to our own country. The simpler work of Lombardy is so closely followed by the Romanesque churches on the Rhine, that one is almost tempted to reverse the order and suspect a German hand in such buildings as the Duomo of Modena and the fine church of BORGO SAN DONNINO. *The cushion capital*

The latter building seems to date from the 12th century with several subsequent alterations. The nave is vaulted in double bays, that is to say one in the nave for two in the aisle. The nave arcade is simple, with two square orders resting on cushion capitals, and the triforium has four blank arches under an including one, the colonnettes having simple capitals *à crochet* (Fig. 62). All this is very unlike anything we have been considering in Rome or Tuscany. The nave vault is domical, quadripartite with wide flat transverse arches, and diagonal and wall ribs. Two small lights, round-arched, form the clerestory in each bay. The apse in the inside has three lights below a range of colonnettes carrying converging ribs. Outside (Plate LXXIX) it has the Pisan arcaded gallery, which was adopted by the Lombards, surmounting a lofty blank arcade, which is also a Pisan feature; but the apse being round and not very *Borgo San Donnino*

Fig. 62.

large the semi-circular arches are disagreeably distorted. The capitals here are very simply foliated. The choir is raised by 12 steps above a crypt with columns and capitals of the 13th century. The aisles are cross-vaulted. *Borgo S. Donnino*

The west front has traces of a 12th century design with Romanesque pilasters carrying Corinthian capitals, and many old bits of sculpture are built in. Three projecting porches however were added in the following century, which have altered the character of the façade. Although they hardly fall within our period I cannot but notice the two magnificent lions of white marble which flank the central doorway and carry the columns of the porch: they have no rivals in North Italy (Plate LXXX).

These lions guarding the portals, and bearing up the porches are not peculiar to Lombardy. I remember two at one of the churches in Rome, I think SS. Giov. e Paolo, and there are two at S. Maria Toscanella, but these are only half lions and very small. Those of Lombardy are much more important: they are whole lions and on a grand scale. At Parma recumbent lions guard both central and side doors of the façade. At Modena a pair sit up on their haunches at the main porches; there are others at the side doorway, and some with cross-legged figures squatting on their backs sustain the choir floor above the crypt. They are to be found at Verona, Ferrara, Piacenza and Bergamo. In Dalmatia, they carry the columns at the north door of Sebenico Cathedral; at Traü there is a pair which may challenge comparison with those of S. Donnino, but they carry nothing, and stand out on brackets; while at Curzola they are raised on projecting consoles high above the *The lion portals*

The lion portals — springing of the arch. They are to be found even in France, for at S. Gilles a pair of lions carry the base of a column, which they turn and bite; and at S. Porchaire in Poitiers though there are no figures of lions as in Italy, the doorway is not left unguarded, for there are two strange beasts (Vol. II, Fig. 85) in the capital which the sculptor considerately tells us are LEONES. In the interior of churches they carry the columns of pulpits, as in the Baptistery of Pisa, and at the churches of S. Giovanni and S. Bartolommeo at Pistoja; and a lion guards the Paschal candelabrum at S. Maria in Cosmedin at Rome. But though they occur in various places, and are used in various ways beyond the bounds of Lombardy, the great guardian lions at the portals are certainly one of the characteristics of Lombard architecture.

Exterior galleries — The Pisan exterior galleries are also common in Lombardy round the apse though not in the façade. At Parma they occur round the apses of both choir and transept. S. Maria Maggiore at Bergamo has one (Plate LXVIII, p. 250) and so has S. FEDELE at Como (Plate LXXXI). There is one round the apse of S. Michele, Pavia, but it is divided into bays by pilasters that run up from below. *Modena* — This is a new development of the feature. At Modena there is one treated somewhat in the same way, with the difference that three lights are grouped under an including arch, between the dividing pilasters. The same idea is carried out throughout the building outside and also inside, where the three-light triforium openings have mid-wall shafts with springers on them projecting fore and aft to carry the thick wall above. The whole church has rather a German look, though of course it must be remembered that Lombard architecture is the parent style, and German the daughter. Mr Porter con-

Plate LXXX

BORGO S. DONNINO

Plate LXXXI

S. FEDELE—COMO

siders that Modena was an important centre of the Lombard School, whence the development of the style was influenced very widely[1]. Lombard sculpture

We shall not find in works of the Lombard school the delicacy and refinement of Tuscany. Sculpture plays a less important part, and conventional ornament takes the place of a freer style of design. For the splendid scroll-work of Diotisalvi at Pisa we have the interlacing patterns of S. Ambrogio, and for the fine foliaged capitals of Lucca and Viterbo the cushion capitals of Borgo San Donnino and the roughly splayed capitals of the nave of S. Zenone at Verona. The wide spread Romanesque façades of Pavia and Parma crowned by a single flat-pitched gable are ungraceful, and will not bear comparison with the fronts of Lucca, Pisa and Pistoja, though in the next century they were relieved by the projecting porches, sometimes two storeys in height, carried on lion-borne columns, which form so very characteristic a feature of North Italian churches. Lombard façades

But the Lombard was a strong virile style, and was better suited perhaps than the more refined work of central Italy to influence the infant arts of the less civilised transalpine nations. It influenced especially Norman Romanesque, which indeed may claim descent from it through William of Volpiano and the School of Burgundy, as will be seen by and by. The same influence was brought into our country by the Normans, and it will be remembered that the two first Archbishops of Canterbury after the conquest were Lombards, Lanfranc of Pavia, and Anslem of Aosta. Characteristics of the Lombard style

[1] Mr Porter's recently published *Lombard Architecture*, Yale University Press, contains an exhaustive study of the style down to the end of the 12th century, with copious illustrations of no fewer than 200 churches.

South Italy and Sicily

The south of Italy remained much longer under the Byzantine Exarchate than the north, and this influenced its architecture. There are domed churches at Molfetta and Trani, and the cathedral of Canosa has no less than five domes. They do not appear however to be exposed on the exterior, but are concealed within drums and covered with pyramidal roofs. Fresh influences were imported by Saracenic and Norman invaders and settlers which may be traced especially in Sicily, whence the Normans expelled the Saracens in 1090. Their great cathedrals of Cefalù, Palermo and Monreale, however, were not begun till the middle and end of the 12th century, when the pointed style had been developed, and they therefore scarcely come within the limits of our period. Descriptions and illustrations of them will be found in the subsequent volumes of this series[1].

[1] v. *Gothic Architecture in France, England, and Italy*, Vol. II.

Printed in U.S.A. by
NOBLE OFFSET PRINTERS, INC.
NEW YORK, N.Y. 10003

NA 370 .J3 1975

pt.1
390375

Jackson

Byzantine and Romanesque architecture.